Gramsci
and the
Italian State

Gramsci and the Italian State

Richard Bellamy
and Darrow Schecter

Manchester University Press
Manchester and New York
Distributed exclusively in the USA and Canada by St. Martin's Press

Copyright © Richard Bellamy and Darrow Schecter 1993

Published by Manchester University Press
Oxford Road, Manchester M13 9PL, UK
and Room 400, 175 Fifth Avenue, New York, NY 10010, USA

Distributed exclusively in the USA and Canada
by St. Martin's Press, Inc., 175 Fifth Avenue, New York
NY 10010, USA

British Library Cataloguing-in-Publication Data
A catalogue record for this book is available from the British
Library

Library of Congress Cataloging-in-Publication Data applied for

ISBN 0 7190 3342–X *hardback*

Photoset in Linotron Sabon
by Northern Phototypesetting Co. Ltd, Bolton

Printed in Great Britain
by Bookcraft (Bath) Limited

Contents

Biographical outline[1]

1891
Born in Ales, Sardinia on 22 January. Fourth of seven children.

1897–1900
His father, a minor public official, accused of administrative irregularities. Father is imprisoned on 8 August 1898 and tried and convicted on 27 October 1900.

1903–5
Having finished elementary school, G. obliged to work in the local tax office because of the family's straitened circumstances. Father released from prison 3 January 1904.

1905–8
Finally able to start secondary school at a village 15 kilometres from home, where he stays with a peasant family. Encouraged by his elder brother Gennaro, he starts to read the socialist press.

1908–11
Moves to Cagliari to complete his schooling. Lives with Gennaro, now a trade union official and PSI (Italian Socialist Party) activist, and has first contacts with socialist movement. Also becomes involved in Sardinian nationalism and in 1910 publishes his first article in *L'Unione sarda*.

1911–12
Wins scholarship to University of Turin, where he specialises in linguistics. Inspired by the pioneering socio-linguist Matteo Bartoli to study Sard dialect. Meets Angelo Tasca and Palmiro Togliatti, also students there, and

[1] This outline draws on Sergio Caprioglio's 'Cronologia della Vita di Antonio Gramsci' in A. Gramsci, *Lettere dal carcere*, ed. S. Caprioglio and E. Fubini, Turin: Einaudi, 1965, pp. xxi–xlvi.

becomes involved in local socialist politics. Passes first exams with high marks.

1913–14
Attends a variety of courses, but ill health hinders his academic progress. Nevertheless, successfully takes a number of exams in 1914. Avid reader of Giuseppe Prezzolini's *La Voce* and Gaetano Salvemini's *L'Unità*. Becomes involved in PSI activity in Turin and starts writing for socialist press, entering the debate on Italian intervention in the war – which he favoured – in an article on 'Active and operative neutrality'.

1915–16
A crisis in his health and increasing political involvements lead him to break off his studies without graduating. Joins the Turin editorial committee of the Socialist daily *Avanti!*, to which he contributes a column on the theatre and culture generally in the 'Sotto la Mole' section from 1916, and writes regularly for the local weekly *Il Grido del popolo* ('The People's Cry').

1917
Edits a volume of essays entitled *La Città futura* ('The Future City') for the Piedmontese Socialist Youth Federation, stressing the importance of integrating social, economic and political activity within a distinctive pro-letarian culture. Founds the 'Club of Moral Life' to promote this end. Assumes the management of *Il Grido del popolo* and broadens the range of its articles, including a special issue on free trade. Particularly engaged in observing events in Russia, publishing his article 'The revolution against *Capital*' in *Avanti!* in December.

1918–19
Accused of 'voluntarism' and engages in debate with Claudio Treves in an article on 'Critical Criticism'. Police associate him with the revolutionary wing of the PSI. *Il Grido del popolo* becomes absorbed into the Turin section of *Avanti!*, and in 1919 G., Tasca, Togliatti and Umberto Terracini decide to start up *L'Ordine nuovo* as 'a weekly review of socialist culture'. However, with G.'s article on 'Workers' democracy' in June, the focus of the journal switches to the internal factory commissions as 'centres of proletarian life' and future 'organs of proletarian power'. G. also translates a series of documents on parallel developments in Russia, France, England and else-where. November–December, Factory Council movement develops in Turin.

1920
13–24 April general strike in Turin involving over 200,000 workers, but without the support of PSI or CGL (the socialist trade union organisation) it

soon fails. The experience leads G. to call for the reform of the Socialist Party and in July breaks with Tasca over the function and autonomy of the Factory Councils *vis-à-vis* the unions. In a report on the Turin council movement sent to the Communist International (Comintern), G. advocates 'factory communist groups' as the base of a future Communist Party. The Second Congress of the Comintern sets conditions (the '21 Points') for membership and the PSI is invited to expel its reformists. Lenin praises Gramsci's motion calling 'For a renewal of the Socialist Party' against the objections of the Italian delegation. In September the 'occupation of the factories' occurs, involving 500,000 workers in northern industrial cities. However, the CGL votes against the occupation taking a revolutionary turn and the movement collapses. G. advocates acceptance of the 21 Points and participates in November at PSI congress in Imola, where the communist fraction is formed. The Turin edition of *Avanti!* assumes the masthead of *L'Ordine nuovo*, which is transformed into a daily under G.'s direction.

1921
G. and others found the Institute of Proletarian Culture, affiliated to the Soviet *Proletkult*. At the Seventeenth Congress of the PSI held in Livorno the communist fraction secedes and on 21 January creates the Communist Party of Italy (PCd'I). General Secretary is Amadeo Bordiga, G. a member of the Central Committee. However, in December the Comintern launches its 'united front' policy for collaboration between communists and socialists at both Party and union level. Policy opposed by PCd'I.

1922
At Second Congress of PCd'I 'Rome Theses' criticising the 'united front' passed by large majority. G. designated PCd'I representative to Comintern and departs for the Soviet Union, not returning to Italy for two years. Taken ill in Moscow and spends several months in a sanatorium, where he meets his future wife Julia Schucht. On 28 October Mussolini seizes power with the 'March on Rome'. Trotsky later recalled that G. alone in seeing the seriousness of the Fascist threat, which he begins to analyse in a series of articles. Fourth Congress of Comintern deals with the 'Italian question' and recommends the fusion of PCd'I and PSI. Majority of PCd'I against this resolution but accept it out of discipline. However, the fusion never takes place. Gennaro is badly beaten up by Fascists.

1923
In February, the Italian police arrest a number of the executive committee of the PCd'I. Bordiga sends an appeal to Party comrades from prison criticising the Comintern's decisions. Originally accepted by Togliatti and others, Gramsci refuses to sign it and speaks against Bordiga's line at Moscow. A new executive is chosen for the PCd'I by the Comintern and Bordiga resigns

from the Central Committee. In a letter, G. communicates to the new
executive committee the Comintern's decision to publish a new workers'
newspaper with the collaboration of the Third International. G. proposes
the name *L'Unità*, and for the first time develops his thesis of the need for an
alliance between the northern proletariat and the southern peasants. Police
arrest the new committee in September and hold them for three months.
However, in October the trial against Bordiga and other Party leaders
collapses. In November the Comintern transfers G. to Vienna to maintain
links between PCd'I and other European communist parties.

1924
Publication begins of *L'Unità* and a new fortnightly series of *L'Ordine
nuovo*. Writing from Vienna, G. outlines to Togliatti and Terracini the need
to create a new Party leadership around the positions of the Comintern. In
April he is elected a deputy, and protected by parliamentary immunity
returns to Italy in May. He joins the executive of the PCd'I, becoming
General Secretary in August. In a number of articles he starts to elaborate his
conception of the Party's role in the present crisis and begins its structural
reorganisation on the basis of cells. Following Matteotti's assassination by
the Fascists on 10 June, G. participates in the meetings of the parliamentary
opposition. However, he conducts a campaign against the passivity and
legalism of the Aventine successionists, who restrict their activity to a refusal
to take part in Parliament. G., in contrast, advocates a general strike and an
appeal to the masses. In October he proposes the constitution of an Opposition Parliament, but this is rejected and the PCd'I decides to break ranks and
return to Parliament when sessions start in November. His first child, Delio,
is born in Moscow and his marriage to Julia is registered.

1925
Returns to Moscow in March for meeting of Comintern Executive and sees
Delio for the first time. Back in Italy, speaks in May against Fascist legislation aimed at outlawing secret societies, rightly suspecting it of sinister
motives. Sets in train the 'bolshevisation' of the Party desired by the
Comintern and negotiates the dissolution of an internal grouping of leftist
elements gathered around Bordiga. Joined by wife and baby in Rome, where
they live with his sister-in-law Tatiana Schucht.

1926
Third Congress of the PCd'I held at Lyons in January. The new leadership
wins overwhelming support with 90.8 per cent of the vote compared to 9.2
per cent for Bordiga's faction. Prepares with Togliatti the 'Lyons Theses'
outlining the general political situation in Italy. Julia, expecting another
child, returns to Moscow where Giuliano is born. G. only ever sees him in
photographs. On 14 October, G. sends a letter on behalf of the political

office of the PCd'I to the Central Committee of the Soviet Communist Party expressing disquiet at the factional disputes between Stalin and Bukharin on the one side and Trotsky, Zinoviev and Kamenev on the other. In Moscow, Togliatti holds on to the letter, regarding it as imprudent, but conveys its contents to Bukharin. In November the Fascist regime passes exceptional measures taking away parliamentary immunity. G., together with other Communist deputies, is arrested, and on the 18th under laws pertaining to public security, is sentenced to five years in police custody. He is sent along with other political detainees to the island of Ustica in the South, where he shares a house with Bordiga and other comrades. Together with them, he organises a school, with Bordiga directing the scientific courses and G. those on history and literature. To help him study in prison his friend Piero Sraffa, the Marxist economist based in Cambridge, opens an unlimited account on his behalf at a bookshop in Milan.

1927

G. is brought to Milan to be tried before a special military tribunal concerned with the defence of the State. The journey, via 'ordinary transit', takes nineteen days and causes serious damage to G.'s health. Obtains rights to read certain newspapers and a double entitlement to library books, allowing him to take out eight books a week. Thanks to Sraffa, he also receives books and journals from outside. Announces in a letter to Tatiana in March his plan of study and his desire to write something *für ewig* whilst in prison.

1928

On 28 May the trial against G. and other PCd'I leaders begins. The prosecutor says of G.: 'We must stop this brain from functioning for twenty years.' G. sentenced to 20 years, 4 months and 5 days of prison. As a result of a medical examination, G. sent to a special penitentiary at Turi, Bari. Initially in a cell with five other prisoners, his brother Carlo sets the procedures in motion for him to be on his own and have permission to write. In December he suffers a urinary problem which means that for three months he must either sit out the daily prison exercise period or be supported by a fellow-inmate.

1929

Starts work on the *Prison Notebooks* in February, telling Tatiana of his plan of study in March. In December she moves to Turi and remains there until July 1930. His sister-in-law is to be G.'s main contact with the outside world, and most of his letters are addressed to her. His wife, who remains in Moscow, suffers a breakdown and only corresponds sporadically.

1930

Towards the end of the year further Party members arrive in Turi. G., who has already started up political conversations with other comrades during the exercise period, initiates a series of discussions on particular themes, such as the intellectuals and the Party. In 1928–9 the Comintern abandoned the policy of a 'united front', pronounced the imminent demise of capitalism and identified social democracy as the ultimate reactionary force (the theory of 'social fascism'). The Italian Communist Party adheres to this line and foresees the collapse of the Fascist regime. Three members of executive who disagree with this new policy – Leonetti, Tresso and Ravazzoli – expelled from the Party. G. visited by Gennaro in June and informed of this development. According to his brother's later statement, G. opposes this move, but Gennaro hides this opposition from Togliatti for fear that G. might also be expelled. G. holds to the position he adopted after the Matteotti crisis and continues to advocate the need to work with other antifascist groups. Disputes with some of his comrades leads him to break off the discussions.

1931
On 3 August G. suffers the first serious breakdown in his health, probably a stroke.

1932
On 29 August G. confesses to Tatiana that his powers of resistance are beginning to fade. She presses for his examination by a doctor. Instead he is seen by the prison health officer. In November, as part of the general amnesty to celebrate ten years of the regime, G.'s sentence is reduced to 12 years 4 months. Sraffa presses for his conditional release, but G. refuses to plead for it himself. In December his mother dies, although G. not informed immediately.

1933
On 7 March G. suffers a second grave crisis and is in a feverish delirium for two weeks and has to be attended by a fellow-prisoner. He is visited by Prof. Arcangeli who certifies that 'Gramsci cannot survive long in present conditions: I consider it necessary for him to be transferred to a civil hospital or clinic, unless he can be granted conditional liberty.' Nevertheless, G. refuses to allow him to submit a plea for mercy to the authorities. However, Arcangeli's statement is published in *L'Humanité* and leads to an international campaign for his release. In December he is transferred to a clinic at Formia. Here he begins the process of rewriting and grouping together various of the notes into a series of 'special' notebooks on particular themes.

1934
G. asks to be transferred to a different clinic at Fiesole and in October submits a request for conditional release, which is granted.

1935

He suffers a further deterioration in June, and in August the authorities allow his transfer to a clinic in Rome. Exhausted and still under surveillance, he has ceased to work on the *Notebooks* but resumes correspondence with his wife and children.

1937

In April he is finally granted unconditional freedom but is too ill to move. On the 25th he suffers a cerebral haemorrhage and dies two days later. He is buried in the English cemetary in Rome, the only one to accept atheists.

Introduction

1991 marked the hundredth anniversary of Antonio Gramsci's birth on 22 January 1891. The fact that the previous three years witnessed the collapse of much he helped or wished to build inevitably dampened the celebrations of this event. For although many of his admirers have rightly wished to stress that his contribution lay in having attempted to map out a distinctive 'third road to socialism' in contrast to western social democracy on the one hand and the Soviet-dominated model of the Eastern bloc on the other, Gramsci's thought was inevitably shaped by the early experiences and ideals of a communist movement and system which now seem condemned by the very judgement of history in which he and his comrades had such faith. Even the Italian Communist Party (PCI), which he took part in founding and briefly led, has been forced decisively to abandon Marxist-Leninism and change its name and doctrine to the Party of the Democratic Left. For a long period boasting the largest membership of any Communist Party outside the Soviet bloc and constituting the main opposition party in Italy, its success was regularly associated with Gramsci's ideas for a western revolutionary strategy suited to advanced industrial democratic states. Many western Marxists outside Italy naturally looked to his works for inspiration, and almost all the secondary literature reflects this aim. Whatever their merits in the past, however, in the light of recent events such exercises no longer seem particularly relevant.

Why add another book to the voluminous literature on Gramsci, therefore? Almost inevitably, most earlier studies – both in Italian and in other languages – sought to employ the study of Gramsci as part of an ongoing debate concerning the nature and tasks of Marxism in the present. As a result, his writings were often manipulated to apply to concerns and ideas far removed from his original preoccupations. Whilst it is inevitable that a major thinker's theories will take on a life of their own in this way after his death, such creative developments by others as frequently detract from and diminish their significance, as contribute to their true value. For whilst Gramsci did theorise the nature of democratic struggles within western societies far more adequately than most other writers within the Marxist tradition, it must nevertheless be borne in mind that his ideas took shape in conditions that are fundamentally different to those that confronted western communist parties in the post-World War II period. We accordingly believe that the abiding interest of Gramsci can only be discovered by returning him to his historical context.

The purpose of this book is to examine an important aspect of his work that has been relatively neglected – namely the influence of the Italian political tradition and social and institutional structures on his thinking. Our aim has been deliberately to shift the emphasis away from Gramsci's contribution to and engagement with western Marxism, and to concentrate on how his arguments were shaped by the contemporary debate on the nature of the Italian State. We shall show that Gramsci's attraction to and interpretation of Marx's conception of a future self-governing society of producers stemmed from a more particular concern with the social as well as the political unification of Italy. In contrast to the majority of studies surveying his whole career, this project has involved giving as much attention to his early writings as to the *Prison Notebooks*. The result of this exercise is to make us Gramsci's contemporaries rather than the other way round. We would suggest that this historical approach reveals the true and enduring worth of his life and work.

In writing this book, we have incurred the usual debts and obligations. Richard Bellamy wishes to thank Martin Clark, Stephen Gundle, Richard Gunn, Giuliano Marini, Mario Piccinini, Franco Sbarberi and Danilo Zolo who have all been very generous not only with sharing their own ideas on this topic, but in providing articles and information hard to obtain in either Edinburgh or Oxford. Darrow Schecter thanks the British Academy for the award of a Post-Doctoral Fellowship and the British School at Rome for allowing him to stay there in the summer of 1991, when he was working on this study. He would also like to acknowledge the support of the Master and Fellows of University College, Oxford.

We are both grateful to the Warden and Fellows of Nuffield College, Oxford for continuing to allow us to use the college's computer and library facilities, and we wish to thank Elaine Herman once again for solving many of the mysteries of word processing. Stephen Gundle kindly read Chapter 3 and Walter Adamson and Joseph Femia the whole manuscript. We have benefited greatly from their comments and criticisms. We also wish to thank Celia Ashcroft and Richard Purslow at Manchester University Press for having been such patient and supportive editors. Needless to say, the usual caveats apply, with all remaining errors and weaknesses being the fault of the authors alone. Although this book has been conceived as far as possible jointly, we have divided the writing down the middle, with Darrow Schecter being responsible for Chapters 1–3 and Richard Bellamy Chapters 4–6. We are, however, jointly responsible for the whole work.

1

Political apprenticeship

Antonio Gramsci was born in Ales, Sardinia, on 22 January 1891. Though his political career would take him to Rome, Vienna and Moscow, his early experiences on the island had a permanent impact on the author of the *Prison Notebooks*. At the turn of the century the prevailing sentiment of most Italians was that Sardinia was a remote and relatively backward corner of the world. But Gramsci's recollections of his boyhood reveal that he loved the island's beautiful landscape, its culture, and the Sardinian language. His precociously developed sense of outrage against injustice was nurtured by his early experience of Sardinia's existence on the periphery of Italian political life. This led him to the conclusion that despite legal unification, Italy was far from being a politically or culturally unified nation. From a very early age the young Sard began to think about how the Italian State might be reconstructed on a truly popular foundation.[1]

His father, Francesco, was descended from Albanians who had come to Italy in 1821 during the war for independence with Greece. His mother's side traced its roots back to one of the many families of Spanish and Italian origin which settled in southern Italy or the islands, though Gramsci's mother, Giuseppina Marcias, was born and raised in Sardinia. Here she met the 21-year-old Francesco, who arrived from the continent in 1861 to take up a position at the local registry office. They married in 1883, and the year after Gramsci's older brother Gennaro was born. In 1891 Antonio was born in what could thus be considered a relatively comfortable family by Sardinian standards, given Francesco's stable employment. This situation changed dramatically on 9 August 1898, when Francesco was convicted of embezzlement, and sentenced to 5 years, 8 months and 22 days of imprisonment. The humiliation and financial hardship this caused was further aggravated for Antonio by the fact that he became a hunchback at the age of 4. Antonio's family attributed his condition to a fall from the hands of a maid, since in Sardinia it would have been considered very bad luck for a child to be naturally deformed. The spinal injuries and subsequent related problems from his condition contributed to a lifelong battle with chronic illness and generally bad health. Moreover, in the superstitious and fatalistic society of Sardinia at the turn of the century, Antonio became the object of fear and persecution. The local children kept the hunchback out of their games and threw stones at him.[2]

With her husband in gaol and lacking any source of stable income, Peppina Marcias took on the onerous responsibility of looking after all seven of the Gramsci children. The fact that she came from a lower social station than Francesco resulted in a less than warm welcome from his family, and she refused to look to them for help. She sold some of the family land, and took in a lodger in their already cramped quarters. In order to earn extra money Peppina made shirts, hats and other clothing. As a result of his father's incarceration Antonio was forced to leave the village school in Ales at the age of 11 to work as an office boy in the local registry for three years, until his parents managed to send him to a secondary school. From there he moved to a *liceo* in Cagliari, the capital of Sardinia, where he moved in with Gennaro, who had some money from his job as an accountant in a local steel factory. Gramsci's biographer Giuseppe Fiori describes Cagliari at this time as a small but lively town. There were three daily newspapers, *L'Unione sarda*, *Il Paese*, and the *Corriere dell'isola*, as well as several weekly reviews, such as the socialist *La Voce del popolo*. Music halls and theatres provided an extremely stimulating atmosphere for the young Antonio, who had spent the first eighteen years of his life in very small towns like Ghilarza and Santulussurgiu. By the time Gennaro returned from military service in Turin in 1911 he was an active member of the Italian Socialist Party (PSI), and had local contacts with PSI leaders in Cagliari. Antonio had the opportunity to meet some of these militants, and he read much of the socialist literature Gennaro brought home. Antonio started reading Marx out of 'intellectual curiosity', and enjoyed the political and literary debates in Giuseppe Prezzolini's Florentine journal *La Voce* – the most prominent review of politics and culture in Italy at this time.[3]

Despite this early initiation into socialist politics, however, in 1910–11 Antonio was more of a Sardinian nationalist than a socialist, as his cry that the Italians could be thrown 'in the sea' demonstrates. At this time 'Sardism' was represented by three main currents: radical separatism, socialist autonomy, and moderate anti-government sentiment harboured by those who were disappointed with the realities of Italian unification, but wished to remain part of Italy. Gramsci was part of the first current, choosing to write in *L'Unione sarda* rather than the socialist press. He was warmly supported by his professor of Italian, Raffa Garzia, and was inspired by the Sardinian politician Cocco Ortu. Sardism gradually matured into a national understanding of Italian political problems when Gramsci went to the University of Turin on a scholarship in 1911. Intellectual curiosity was transformed into lived experience: Gramsci's first real contact with a modern industrial proletariat guided all of his subsequent analyses concerning the need for the northern working class to unite with the peasantry of the South and the islands to achieve a more just social order.[4]

At the University of Turin he took courses in Italian, Latin, Greek, literature, linguistics, Romance languages, German, geography, modern history, the history of philosophy and theoretical philosophy. In his first years in Turin he was not active in socialist politics. He published articles in several scholarly journals in the field of linguistics, and his professor Matteo Bartoli hoped that Gramsci might take up a career as a linguist. Another professor who had an impact on Gramsci was Umberto Cosmo, whose lectures on Dante introduced students to the works of the great literary critic Francesco De Sanctis (1817–1883), and to the philosophies of Hegel and Benedetto Croce.[5] Croce, a Neapolitan philosopher born in 1866, was probably the most dominant political and cultural influence on the young Gramsci. In a series of books written from 1893 onwards, when he published *History Subsumed under the Concept of Art*, Croce developed a tremendous following amongst the younger generation of idealists, who welcomed his penetrating attacks on the positivist faith that the methods of the natural sciences could be applied to the study of society. He underscored the importance of intuitive imagination and understanding for the study of historical change and artistic creation. Croce criticised both Marx and Hegel, yet remained broadly within the Hegelian tradition stressing that history was the history of the human spirit. This had a great appeal to

young militants like Gramsci who were attracted to Marxism, but
who were repelled by the mechanical models of Marxism which
spread to Italy with the rise of positivism. James Joll notes that in
addition to the influence of Croce, the young Sard familiarised
himself with the works of the major intellectual figures of the day
who were widely read at the University of Turin. He studied the ideas
of Vilfredo Pareto and Gaetano Mosca on elites and democracy, and
read the French theorist of revolutionary syndicalism Georges Sorel,
whose *L'Avenir socialiste des syndicats* was translated into Italian in
1903. But Gramsci was most interested in the ideas of Sorel's
Réflexions sur la violence of 1908, which stressed that the working
class would have to make its own revolution without the help of
career politicians who would inevitably corrupt the moral purity of
the class struggle with debilitating compromises. This work inspired
Gramsci's lifelong belief that the working class would have to edu-
cate itself in its own political and educational institutions. It is also
clear that Gramsci already knew a good deal about Marx. Many of
Marx's works had been translated into Italian in Marx's lifetime,
and by the time of Gramsci's arrival in Turin Italian intellectuals
were well acquainted with Marx's ideas through discussions of the
works of Sorel, Croce and Pareto.[6]

When Gramsci returned to Sardinia for summer vacation in 1913,
the island was in the midst of an electoral campaign under a newly-
expanded franchise system which had greatly increased the number
of eligible voters. He quickly saw that in order for the local landowners to ensure the victory of their candidates, they would have to
solicit the aid of power brokers on the continent. Gramsci participated actively on behalf of the socialist candidates, signing a pro-
South anti-protectionist petition which was supported by socialists
on the mainland and reprinted in *La Voce*. Gramsci was deeply
impressed by the event, and on his return to Turin he joined the PSI.
In the winter and spring of 1915 Gramsci was deeply absorbed in his
fourth and final year in the Faculty of Letters, where he continued to
read Croce, Machiavelli, Dante, Hegel and De Sanctis. In addition he
was writing for the Turin socialist weekly *Il Grido del popolo*, where
he covered contemporary political events and also wrote reviews of
the works Pirandello and other dramatists. By this time Gramsci was
wondering if he should continue his university work or become a
full-time political journalist. When Italy declared war on Austria–
Hungary on 23 May 1915, he chose politics as a vocation.[7]

Though Gramsci was now fully in tune with the rhythms of life in the modern industrial city of Turin, his early writings reflect a continued passion for the plight of Sardinia and the Italian South or *Mezzogiorno*. His roots in Sardinia were deep, not only because of his experience of poverty and injustice, but because he also respected the indigenous cultural and linguistic traditions of the island. His initial interest in the Sard dialect was pursued during his university years in the Faculty of Letters. Moreover, following De Sanctis, Gramsci was keenly interested in the social and historical origins of language and the material basis of literature. In this context the situation of Sardinia was a constant reminder of the superficial nature of the *Risorgimento*, the Italian unification, and revealed the alarming extent to which the integration of the various regions of Italy was still to be accomplished. Indeed, from his earliest writings on the Italian South to his mature reflections in the *Quaderni*, a central theme in Gramsci's work is the failed nature of the *Risorgimento*, and the ensuing social and political conflicts it generated. The *Risorgimento* and the legacy of problems it bequeathed to future generations thus becomes the esential background for understanding Gramsci's development as a thinker and activist. Future chapters will be dedicated to an analysis of Gramsci's project to lead a truly popular *Risorgimento* which would restructure the Italian state and society along socialist lines, creating a political and ethical unity between the people and the State. Though he was a Marxist, it will be shown how the Italian context in which he was working shaped Gramsci's most important ideas on hegemony, the role of the intellectuals, and the war of position.[8]

The politics of militant idealism

The most important problem following unification was how to create a national political system out of Italy's various regions, each of which had its own traditions, dialect and political culture. Moderate liberalism and Mazzinian radicalism represented the dominant conceptions of how to organise political life. But despite the hopes of creating the necessary conditions for the functioning of a modern democracy, few Italians fully understood the rights and obligations of citizenship. This should not have been surprising, since only a small minority of Italians participated in the formation of the State. The political elite, comprised primarily of northern liberals which engineered the unification movement, was aware that the new State had no mass base and that the great majority of Italians were alienated from the political institutions of the country. But this was not a problem for most of these politicians, for whom the *Risorgimento* represented the establishment of the most appropriate political form for the defence of the State from the masses.[9]

From the outset the newly-unified nation had to contend with glaring inequalities between the educated classes and the large number of illiterate workers and peasants. In 1861, 75 per cent of the population could not read, and a mere 8 per cent spoke Italian rather than a local dialect. This problem was compounded by the vast disparities between life in the growing industrial centres of the North such as Turin, Genoa and Milan, on the one hand, and what has been described as the semi-feudal social structure of the impoverished *Mezzogiorno*, on the other. Under these conditions regional interests largely prevailed over national interests. Tradition, language and economic dependence ensured that the local population remained under the dominance of existing power brokers – especially in the South. Here large landowners or *latifundisti* controlled the lives of the peasants to the extent that any independent political action on their part was impossible, thus generating the famous *Questione meridionale* (the 'Southern question').[10]

Initially Italian parliamentary politics was dominated by two groups known simply as the 'Right' and the 'Left', though they did not have the organisational structures of modern political parties and tended to function as a broad ideological tendencies. Members of the Right were likely to come from northern aristocratic families who were the driving force behind Italian unification. The Right also enjoyed the support of some prominent southern philosophers such as De Sanctis, Bertrando and Silvio Spaventa, and later Croce, who helped spread German idealist philosophy to Italy and became the chief representatives of the Neapolitan Hegelian tradition. These thinkers believed that the ideal of nationality had to be realised in the institutions of the State, and that the task of patriotic intellectuals was to create an Italian political culture rooted in the Italian language and the traditions of the people. This project required more than the classical liberal conception of the State which is seen as originating in the social contract and designed to promote individual self-interest. Rather, the these thinkers argued that the State was based on the 'common substance' of a nation that united all citizens

above their particular interests. While De Sanctis was chiefly concerned with historical and cultural questions, the Spaventas argued
that the State was the realisation of liberty, not a set of authoritarian
institutions used to suppress conflicting interests. Because of the
fundamental unity transcending such interests, conflicts could be
harmonised in what Bertrando Spavanta called an 'organic whole'.
The Neapolitan Hegelians thus provided the philosophical
justification of Italian political and cultural unity. Their ideas were of
fundamental importance for Giovanni Gentile, an idealist philosopher who influenced Gramsci and who engaged in vociferous
debates with Croce on the possibility of creating such an Ethical
State in Italy, as we shall see in Chapter 6 below on the Italian State
tradition.[11]

The representatives of the Left were more likely to be lawyers than
landowners, controlling power at the local level through personal
ties. The Right favoured a strong central government and stressed
the need to reaffirm the new national unity, while members of the
Left sought to channel government money to their friends in the
municipalities and thereby to protect their local bases. Given the lack
of a national party structure and the clientalistic nature of regional
politics, it is not surprising that the ideals of the *Risorgimento* paled
before a much bleaker reality. In 1876 the parliamentary majority
supporting the Right collapsed, and subsequent governments came
and went in accordance with their ability to buy the support of the
various powerful factions around the country. The strategy of
trasformismo – winning the support of a former opponent through
bribery and corruption – became a common method for creating
governments comprised of highly unstable coalitions of interests.
The term became closely associated with the governing style of
Giovanni Giolitti, who headed four ministries between 1903 and
1921, and who effectively maintained power by playing off different
interests in his own favour.[12]

The discrpeancy between the ideals of Mazzini and the Neapolitan
Hegelians and the reality of post-unification politics was striking.
Many of the preconditions for liberal and democratic political institutions were absent. The politics of the new State seemed to be
primarily concerned with the protection of bourgeois sectional
interests rather than providing citizens with a civic education or
some sense of Italy's political future.[13] Whether of the Left or Right,
the younger critics of Italian politics during the Giolitti years dis-

played the profound influence of Mazzini's political idealism. In this fervour the generation of young intellectuals which included Gramsci and Piero Gobetti became dissatisfied with Croce's political ideas. They turned to more militant philosophers like Giovanni Gentile, who insisted that the *Risorgimento* had only begun the project of "making Italians". Gramsci's vision of the new order or *Ordine nuovo* demanded the establishment of a truly democratic State which fully involved the people in the participatory institutions of self-government. In order to see how Gramsci arrived at his conception of the *Ordine nuovo*, it is first necessary to look at the formative influence of the idealist philosophies of Croce and Gentile. Gramsci believed that he could borrow what was vital from the Italian idealist tradition to aid him in the project of making Italians within a Marxist framework.

In the tenth notebook of the *Quaderni: la filosofia di Benedetto Croce*, Gramsci maintains that by 1917 his most important intellectual influence was Croce's philosophy. At this point he was certainly more familiar with Croce than he was with Marx. But as he came to formulate his own interpretation of Marx, he increasingly saw his task as subjecting Croce to the same type of criticism that Marx deployed against Hegel. Both Hegel and Croce were important philosophers who correctly perceived that humanity is a constantly evolving creation of history rather than a timeless fact or an object of observation, as the positivists had supposed. But by positing the existence of ideal categories that remained separate from historical practice they had not gone far enough in rescuing philosophy from the ethereal realm of *Geist*, or spirit. For Gramsci this was typified by Croce's separation of theory and practice.[14] Gramsci argued that a truly practical, i.e. humanised idealist philosophy was necessary to go beyond the discovery of categories of the understanding capable of theoretically explaining the present. The present had to be transformed through a consciously constructed unity of theory and practice, that is through labour. Marx noted that even the most inexperienced worker was superior to the most efficient bee, since the worker had a conception that he or she sought to realise through practice: the product would enable him or her to refine the original conception. History, as the sum of such human endeavours, either validated or rejected our mental images of the world as they were tested in practice. Thus the world was known to humans through the sensuous activity of work; knowledge could not be attained without practical activity. Society, as a human creation, could be consciously transformed to satisfy human needs. This insight guided Gramsci's belief that humans could transform the world, know the world, and could collectively shape it in accordance with a rational design. His approach had obvious revolutionary implications in a country such as Italy where the Catholic Church and its doctrine of an immutable divine order continued to hold sway over the vast majority of workers and peasants.[15]

Croce and his followers reacted vehemently against the increasing predominance of positivism in university and intellectual circles, which he feared might usher in the reign of a kind of 'materialist metaphysics' that would only exacerbate the social consequences of the decline of traditional religion. Croce hoped that philosophy could act as the basis of a modern secular religion. However, he denied that Marxism, as a materialist philosophy, could solve the modern dilemma of providing an immanent philosophy of human existence.[16] His studies of historical materialism were directly inspired by the work of the Neapolitan philosopher Antonio Labriola, who had originally designated Marxism as a philosophy of praxis and a total and autonomous vision of reality. Croce initially believed that socialism could fulfil humanity's religious quest for meaning, and he admitted that his initial discussions with Labriola convinced him that Marxism was indeed the religion of the twentieth century.[17] However, in a series of debates towards the turn of the century which provoked the 'crisis of Marxism', Croce expressed grave doubts about the philosophical and normative status of Marxism. In an article in *La Voce* in 1911, he argued that by positing the primacy of matter, historical materialism had no explicit moral message, and as such it had no future as a philosophy of human existence. Croce insisted that Italy must break with all forms of positivism, including Marxism, to create its own system of beliefs that corresponded to Italian society and its moral requirements[18]. Gramsci's lifelong project was to refute Croce and demonstrate that socialism would replace religion as the guiding normative principle of the modern world. In this task he was more successful than Labriola in arguing that historical materialism could be rescued from positivist distortion when tempered by the appropriate framework suggested by German and Italian idealism.

But how could a synthesis of Marxism and idealism be fashioned? By the time of the outbreak of World War I, Croce's distinction between theory and practice appeared inadequate to the growing number of young intellectuals on the left attracted to 'militant idealism'. Such activists emerged from the First World War with ever-greater hopes of completing the task of making Italians. Many of them believed that this could be accomplished by instituting an aggressively participatory version of Hegelianism, which at this time was represented by Giovanni Gentile's philosophy of Actualism.[19] Gentile translated Marx's *Preface to a Contribution to a Critique of Political Economy* and *Theses on Feuerbach* into Italian for the first time. Gentile's reading of Marx led the young Sicilian to believe that Marx was an idealist for whom thought creates reality. Marx's dictum that philosophers have only interpreted the world while the point is to change it reinforced Vico's thesis that man only knows what he makes. In accordance with the third thesis on Feuerbach, the unity of thought and action had to be conceived in terms of revolutionary practice.[20] In two important works of 1916, the *The General Theory of the Spirit as Pure Act* and *The Foundations of the Philosophy of Law*, Gentile argued that to consider the individual and the universal separately is as meaningless as to separate subject and object. The real individual is the concrete synthesis of the particular and the universal. Political life is marked by conflicting individual interests and aspirations, but all individuals are united in the overall conflict as a single collectivity called society. Gentile thus posited the interpenetration of the individual and society as an ontological reality. Society is not a reality that exists between individuals or *inter homines*, but rather exists within them, or *in homine interiore* as the universal-individual. This implied the total identification of the individual with the State as the unity of the particular and the universal. Moreover, where the individual and the State form a single will, there is no valid distinction between force and law. Thus, for Gentile the individual achieves universality in the State, not in an authoritarian way, but as the very essence of self-realisation and genuine democracy. This was clearly an indictment of Italian political life under Giolitti and suggested that a new kind of State would be necessary to realise the aspirations of the *Risorgimento*. Gramsci shared many of Gentile's criticisms of Italian politics, and in an article in *Il Grido del popolo* in February 1918 entitled 'Socialism and Contemporary Philosophy' he praises Gentile as:

the Italian philosopher who has in the last few years produced the most in his field of philosophical thought. His philosophical system is the final development of German idealism which culminated with George Hegel, teacher of Karl Marx, and is the negation of all transcendentalism, marking the identification of philosophy and history, and the act with thought, in which the actual and the true are united in a dialectical progression which is never completed.[21]

Both Gramsci and Gentile saw the need to overcome the limited forms of poltical participation afforded by the parliamentary State, and strove to theorise new political forms in which participation was part of the people's daily life as producers. In the next chapter we will look at Gramsci's vision of the new order and his belief that the Factory Council represented a new expansive political form which replaced the sham democracy of *trasformismo* with a genuine workers' democracy.

In considering Gramsci's formative influences we must also take into account the problem of the Italian South. In this context it should be noted that Gramsci's analysis of the *Questione meridionale* owed much to his reading of Gaetano Salvemini's journal *L'Unità* during the years 1911–19. *L'Unità* was the focal point of debate about the *Mezzogiorno* at this time. While the rebirth of idealism in Italy shaped Gramsci's philosophical understanding of politics, Salvemini provided an important model of political journalism. Employing an accessible style and empirical methodology, Salvemini amassed a formidable body of data to show that Italian unity was only a chimera as long as the problems of illiteracy and corruption remained unsolved. Moreover, he demonstrated that the South would never become a fully integrated part of the country while it continued to be a source of cheap labour power and food for the industrial North.[22] Gramsci shared Salvemini's analysis, and advocated his candidature for a legislative seat vacated in Turin in June 1914 as a gesture of solidarity between northern industrial workers and southern peasants, whose interests had been split by an alliance between northern industrial capitalists and southern *latifundisti*. This bloc of forces guaranteed northern workers relatively high wages, since northern industrial products could compete on the international markets as long as labour and food from the South could be purchased at an artificially low price because of protectionist policies. These policies made it difficult to sell southern products abroad, thus perpetuating the state of dependence of the South on the North. Salvemini refused to run as a PSI candidate, insisting that by looking out exclusively for the interests of northern organised labour, the Party had ceased to be an effective opposition to the political forces backing Giolitti.[23]

It is interesting to note that in this stage of his development as a thinker, Gramsci the socialist supported free trade against protectionism. In September 1916, Gramsci maintains that if Giolitti was correct in saying that by pursuing a reformist strategy the PSI had 'put Marx in the attic', the Italian bourgeoisie had been equally unfaithful to its social and political patrimony by renouncing the liberal economic programme of Cavour. Cavour's programme was based on free trade, yet the Italian bourgeoisie, especially in the South, had proved itself incapable of fulfilling the tasks Cavour bequeathed to his post-unification successors.[24] Gramsci argues that the proletariat must finish the work initiated by Cavour, but that this could never be resolved within the parameters of the corrupt Italian parliamentary system. Gramsci thus criticises the Italian parliamentary State in terms of the ideal parliamentary State – often represented by England – and then demonstrates that national problems could only be solved in a new State framework. Ideally, free competition and the minimal State represent progressive elements of bourgeois society in its ascendancy. Such conditions were conspicuously absent in Italy with its highly centralised and interventionist State, which was hopelessly compromised in the politics of *trasformismo*. Hence in February 1918 Gramsci writes: 'We are persuaded that as long as there is a bourgeois regime, free trade is the best method, and the bourgeois State must be reduced to the minimum functions possible.'[25]

Evidence of the influence of Salvemini's polemic against protectionism during the 1916–18 period is demonstrated by Gramsci's sollecitation of articles by the liberal economists Edoardo Giretti and Luigi Einaudi in *Il Grido* and *Avanti*! which defend the superiority of free trade. Gramsci supported free trade not only in the interests of the *Mezzogiorno*, but also in the interests of consumers of industrial and agricultural products. In April 1917 Gramsci asserts that in Italy, unlike other industrial countries, the State is the chief enemy of the citizens and the cause of corruption in public life and economic stagnation.[26] In associating free trade and the minimalist State with ascendant capitalism, Gramsci begins to distinguish between the different relations between State and civil society in capitalist versus socialist societies. If the United States and England can maintain the separation between the State and civil society, it is because the entrepreneurial class in those countries is strong enough to manage production without State intervention. Individual rights, a free press, free association and other political liberties are more entrenched there than in Italy, where the entrepreneurial class and its technicians and managers 'have not yet lived'. The Italian bourgeoisie is a gathering of political intriguers rather than a disciplined class of producers, and is therefore ripe for replacement by an army of workers ready to carry production forward.[27]

Gramsci acknowledged the accuracy of Salvemini's criticisms of the PSI's inadequate response to the *Questione meridionale*. As an emigrant from Sardinia, Gramsci was only too aware of the pliability of the State to strong interests in the North. But if the PSI had made too many concessions to Giolitti's political strategy of absorbing the political power of labour with material concessions, what political strategy followed from Salvemini's *problemismo*? For Gramsci, Salvemini's crucial limitation was that he approached the problem of southern poverty as a moralist: by prescribing general, national reforms such as universal suffrage, he failed to provide a class analysis of State power. He was simply another critic of Italian politics who could not provide any indication of how to reconstruct the State on truly popular bases. Thus Salvemini's empirical studies had to be combined with Gentile's meditations on the State to overcome the degeneration of Italian politics; 'men of good will' would not suffice. By separating political culture from political and economic organisation, Salvemini failed to see that only a revolution could unite people and State.[28] Gramsci concluded that the problems of Italian politics – social fragmentation, the *Questione meridionale*, class exploitation – were impossible to separate. The entire social structure would have to be changed.[29] But what kind of political institutions could replace the existing State? What kind of strategy was appropriate to bring the masses into politics without letting them be placated by Giolitti's transformistic strategies? Gramsci's vision of the new order matured in response to the syndicalist challenge to the PSI leadership and the impact of the Russian Revolution. The syndicalists helped Gramsci sharpen his ideas about the fundamental importance of the *Questione meridionale* in any future Italian revolution, while the role of the Soviet, or workers' Council, in Russia suggested the possibility of new forms of State which were truly democratic. We will look at these two important influences in turn.

The Syndicalist challenge

The Italian Socialist Party formulated its vision of revolution in the statutes of the founding congress at Genoa in 1892. Anarchists of Bakuninist inspiration, militants of the sectarian Workers' Party which enjoyed success only in Lombardy, and Filippo Turati's evolutionist socialists comprised the three main factions. Despite opposition from the left of the Party, Turati's views initially prevailed. His brand of evolutionary socialism began to take shape around 1889 with the aid of Camillo Prampolini, Anna Kuliscioff and Leonida Bissolati, all of whom worked out of Milan. From his reading of Marx and Engels, Turati developed a positivist theory of evolutionary socialism based on the thesis that the economy was governed by objective laws which had to be respected and protected from voluntarist interventions.[30] Turati consulted with Engels at international socialist congresses in Brussels in 1891 and Zurich in 1893, and maintained a steady correspondence with him throughout the 1890s. The emerging strategy of the Italian labour movement which resulted from both these congresses and Turati's positivist interpretation of historical materialism aimed at the socialisation of the means of production and exchange. The PSI leadership, as the class conscious vanguard of the Italian proletariat, would be charged with organising the 'administration of things'. In the interim, the Party began to reform capitalism in the interests of the working class: important concessions in the field of social legislation were gained in the period 1892–1904, marked by the the rise of Giolitti to power.[31]

In 1906 the first national professional trade federations combined with the equivalent peasant organisations to form the Confederazione Generale del Lavoro (CGL). The CGL was reformist and opposed the general strike of 1904 led by the revolutionary syndicalist wing of the Party. The syndicalists rejected the positivism and evolutionism underpinning the PSI strategy during the period of Turati's leadership, and also rejected the conception of socialism as a series of reforms within existing institutional arrangements. This style of reformist politics became the hallmark of Second International socialism, and conformed to the official line of the orthodox German Social Democratic Party (SPD). For Turati, Marxism as a positivist science of the economy naturally accompanied political reformism; given that material conditions were steadily evolving towards the realisation of socialism, all that could be done in the meantime was to ameliorate the daily life of the working class by improving their standard of living. While the parliamentary Party safeguarded the broad political goals of the labour movement, the trade unions were occupied with daily questions of hours, wages and working conditions. This strategy seemed to correspond with the doctrine of scientific socialism, but when the inevitable result of the class struggle was called into question following the 'crisis of Marxism', the political strategy of gradual reformism was also discredited amongst revolutionaries. For the syndicalists it then became necessary to infuse socialism with new moral energy which would generate a militant class consciousness and reject the existing order in spite of any promise of better wages and improvements in working conditions.[32]

The founding statutes of the PSI at Genoa separated the Italian labour movement into its political and economic wings. In Italy the existence of Camere del Lavoro (Chambers of Labour) presented the PSI with the opportunity of combining political and economic activity. The Camere initially served as worker-controlled labour exchanges and information centres which complemented union activity. In places where union organisation lacked structure, the Camere could organise the labour force of an entire district in support of a particular group. They tended to be more radical than the unions, and often engineered local general strikes. The founding statutes of the PSI declared that the Camere were instruments of the trade union movement, however, creating a permanent division between the political and economic objectives of the workers' movement. As the Party struggled for political power, the Camere, following the guidelines established at their congress at Parma in 1893, pursued economic objectives concerning wage increases and improvements in working conditions. Later PSI congresses ratified this division of labour. The CGL claimed exclusive control over economic as opposed to political strikes, in accordance with the Stuttgart congress of the Second International in 1907. The Pact of Alliance between the PSI and the CGL in September 1918 reconfirmed this tendency.[33]

The Italian revolutionary syndicalists sought to bridge the separation between economic and political objectives. They rejected Turati's economic theories and the widespread belief that the most appropriate political strategy to be taken while economic laws unfolded was to secure reforms in the form of social legislation. In so

doing the syndicalists posed the question of the relationship between
socialism, democracy and revolution in very different terms than the
reformists within the PSI. The syndicalists also had a very different
idea of revolution than the Maximalists, who succeeded Turati's
faction and gained control of the PSI in 1912. Their faction was
headed at this time by Constantino Lazzari, Benito Mussolini and G.
M. Serrati. Though the Maximalists claimed to represent the left
wing of the Party, they did not depart from the economic determinism underlying Turati's Marxism. Serrati's statement that as
Marxists it was more important correctly to interpret the laws of
history than to make history showed that they too envisaged a
catastrophic collapse of capitalism in which economic forces moved
according to their own ineluctable patterns.[34]

However, despite differences in revolutionary and reformist
rhetoric, both Turati's and the Maximalist vision of revolution relied
on a terribly important premise, that is, that capitalism developed
according to laws which created the conditions for its inevitable
collapse as a social and economic system. In practice both reformists
and Maximalists were strong on revolutionary rhetoric, and weak
on concrete programmes of social transformation. Thus, revolutionary syndicalism posed the most serious alternative to the PSI
strategy prior to the *biennio rosso* of 1919–20.[35] Gramsci's initial
ideas on the *Questione meridionale*, the State, and the role of the
trade unions and the political Party in the Italian revolution were
formulated in response to syndicalist ideas. He was especially sympathetic to their analysis of the problems of the South. In an article in
Il Grido del popolo in 1916, Gramsci observes that apart from
Salvemini, the Neapolitan syndicalist Arturo Labriola had been
amongst the first to point out the fact that: 'the unification of Italy's
regions under one centralised State has had disastrous consequences
for the *Mezzogiorno*, and the shortsightedness of the government,
neglecting Cavour's economic programme, has only exacerbated the
state of affairs from whence derived the perennial and chronic
Southern Question.'[36]

Syndicalist ideas are of special significance, since Gramsci's
factory council theory, which we will examine in the next chapter,
was denounced as a syndicalist theory by Gramsci's opponents.
Gramsci was thus compelled to sharpen his own ideas and develop a
revolutionary strategy distinct from revolutionary syndicalism. As
the last section of this chapter will show, the Russian Revolution

gave Gramsci new ideas about the State which forced him to abandon syndicalism altogether. Prior to the Russian Revolution he had not worked out his own theory of the State with any clarity. He was greatly influenced by the syndicalist celebration of the role of the producers, on the one hand, and attracted to Gentilian ideas on overcoming Italy's social and political fragmentation in an ethically unified State, on the other. The role of the *Soviets*, or workers' Councils, in the Russian Revolution inspired Gramsci's ideas on the Italian revolution.

For the present an analysis of syndicalist ideas will serve as an important point of comparison for the discussion of Gramsci's ideas in the next chapter, since both Gramsci and the syndicalists were struggling with the problem of conceiving new forms of socialism that relied neither on the leading role of the political Party, nor on the nationalisation of the means of production by the State. Though Gramsci agreed with their assertion that the producers would have a critical role in any revolution in Italy, he had definite reservations about the leading role they assigned to the trade union. The Italian syndicalists attempted to incorporate Sorel's insistence that the working class be absolutely autonomous from all bourgeois State institutions with their own analysis of the Italian situation. Sorel postulated that a society of producers could absorb the functions of the State, thus rendering the State superfluous. His ideas were developed in Italy by Arturo Labriola, Enrico Leone, Sergio Panunzio, Paolo Orano and others who felt that Turati's reformism would eventually result in some form of State socialism that exploited the worker as badly as capitalism; State ownership could in no way be equated with worker control of industry. The syndicalist argument against the State applied Sorel's ideas to the specifically Italian problem of the *Mezzogiorno*. These militant theorists, many of southern Italian origin themselves, understood that it was the Italian State which solidified the bloc of northern industrialists and large southern landowning interests. This bloc of forces undermined popular aspirations for self-government and had to be overturned. Thus, while Gramsci later suggested that syndicalism was little more than a polemic for free trade, Italian revolutionary syndicalism in fact provided a theoretically sophisticated analysis of the most urgent problems facing the post-unification State.[37]

Arturo Labriola argued that the existence of social classes was the result of the separation of the State from civil society, such that the chimeric political equality of citizens masked more basic underlying inequalities in the factories and fields. As long as the material interests of the bourgeoisie were not affected by the demands of citizens because they could be expressed in a separate political sphere such as Parliament, the bourgeoisie would have no serious objections to parliamentary democracy as a form of State. In fact, the universal connotation of citizenship was an ideal means to deflect attention from the reality of the class struggle. The syndicalists analysed this phenomenon in an Italian context, and argued that the parliamentary State would have to be abolished if social classes were to be abolished. This was a direct refutation of the reformist line, since their strategy was to gain control of the parliamentary State. Once there were enough socialist deputies, the reformists believed that the existing State institutions could be directed toward the objective of establishing a socialist society. Given Giolitti's skill at quelling revolutionary demands with parliamentary concessions, Gramsci admits that the PSI had fallen right into his trap. Thus, revolutionary syndicalism had a salutary effect on the socialist movement. Gramsci writes that:

the Socialist Party became the instrument of Giolitti's political strategy. If one observes closely, in the decade 1900–1910 the most radical crises of the Socialist and workers' movement occur: the masses react spontaneously against the political strategy of the reformist leaders. Syndicalism is born, which is the instinctive, elementary, primitive but basically healthy expression of the workers against the alliance with the bourgeoisie and for an alliance with the peasantry, and especially with the Southern peasantry.[38]

Sorel's belief that the basis of a new society is contained within the working-class trade union was the basic inspiration behind syndicalist analyses of Italian politics. But with the formation of the CGL in 1906 and its formal separation from the PSI, Italian socialism was marked by a division of labour in which the PSI sought to defend the reformist demands of the CGL, such that a Party ostensibly committed to overthrowing the State actually relied on the existing State as its chief method of transforming society. Giolitti had thus effectively managed to prevent the emergence any 'State within a State' as an alternative source of legitimacy within the existing order. Northern organised labour and the southern peasantry were thus split into separate interest groups. While the PSI represented the demands of the industrial working class, the peasants of the South were poorly organised and underrepresented. A frequently heard 'common sense' explanation for this was that there were two Italies, one of which was simply more modern and efficient.[39]

For defenders of the South such as Salvemini and syndicalist critics of the PSI, the *Questione meridionale* was the most urgent problem of a united Italy. Italy would become a modern State in the full sense only when a new group of social forces set about the task of organising what Gramsci would in prison call the national-popular will.[40] Salvemini argued that the Italian situation required a federal system limiting the power of both powerful economic interests and the bureaucratic central State. He believed that a federal system could accommodate regional diversity within a national polity, and called for an agrarian democracy based on everyone's right to ownership reminescent of Rousseau.[41] Arturo Labriola denied the contemporary relevance of such an approach. He asserted that Proudhon had clearly demonstrated the incompatibility between socialism and the existence of the State. The State socialist approach to revolution, reformist or revolutionary, was also outdated: State ownership put the workers no closer to the means of production than they were under a system of private ownership. Labriola argued that State socialism would resemble a feudal social order in which everyone was assigned a place in the planning hierarchy. Far from abolishing classes, this would inevitably lead to the domination of the working class by 'socialist' intellectuals, as Sorel had feared. Proudhon saw the power of the State as equally menacing as the power of capital, and in this respect he was more prescient than Marx. Collective ownership demanded real shop-floor control by workers managing their own enterprises. In order to establish a society in which members are united by purely economic ties, Labriola and the syndicalists envisaged an important role for price, competition, and the market.[42]

Leone, Panunzio and Prezzolini argued that the material needs of all members of society could be satisfied once production was organised as a competition between worker-managed enterprises. The parliamentary State was superfluous to the extent that it did not directly contribute to production, and repressive to the extent that it protected the interests of private property even when these were impediments to the further advance of industry, i.e., in the case of the stagnant *latifundisti*. The central State could be replaced by a federation of communes which conferred with the unions on matters of co-ordinating production demands with local imperatives. Labriola argued that it was profoundly mistaken to conceive of socialism as an economic matter and democracy as a political matter: socialism and democracy converged when the producers had access to power through participatory institutions like the commune and trade union. The reality of the Giolitti years was that the bourgeoisie ruled by keeping the masses out of the State, removed from the running of the economy, and ignorant of the institutions of local government.[43]

By 1917–18 Gramsci agreed with much of this. His support of free trade revealed the influence of the Salveminian and syndicalist critique of the parasite State. He was also in agreement with the productivist argument against parliamentary democracy and capitalism. Gramsci was especially in favour of the idea that it was only through participatory institutions that the proletariat could transform all of society into a unified moral organism. But if the parasite State which the PSI hankered after was to be abolished, Gramsci saw the task of constructing a new moral order as fundamentally that of constructing a new kind of State which had never been seen in history. The possibility of creating such a State in Italy became real as a result of the Russian Revolution.[44]

The impact of the Russian Revolution

All orthodox positivist and evolutionist Marxist theories were defied in Russia in 1917 when revolution set a largely agrarian and feudal society on the path toward rapid industrialisation and socialism. The defenders of historical materialism as a science of social development had always maintained that all societies, with minor variations, arrived at socialism after an unavoidable period of bourgeois government. The most advanced bourgeois capitalist countries such as England and Germany showed the less developed countries the inevitable direction of their future development. As we have seen, this conception was also widely held amongst Italian socialists who had equated Marxism with positivist science. But the Russian Revolution proved, with more clarity than any theory could, that with the proper forms of political organisation and indomitable will, men and women could take history into their own hands and shape institutions in accordance with their needs. The revolution confirmed Gramsci's suspicion of the equation of Marxism with positivism. In the now famous article 'The revolution against *Capital*' of

November 1917, Gramsci writes that the revolution is

the revolution against Karl Marx's *Capital*. In Russia Marx's *Capital* was more the book of the bourgeoisie than it was the book of the proletariat. It was the critical demonstration of the inevitable necessity for Russia to develop a bourgeois class, undergo an era of capitalism, and establish a western-style civilisation before the proletariat could even think of its redemption, its class demands, and its revolution. The facts have overrun ideologies. The facts have shattered the critical schemes within which Russian history was supposed to unfold in accordance with the canons of historical materialism . .. [The Bolsheviks] are living Marxist thought, that which will never die, which is the continuation of German and Italian idealist thought, which in Marx had become contaminated with positivist and naturalist encrustations.[45]

The 'revolution against *Capital*' heralded the importance of Leninism as the theory and practice of socialist revolution, and the arrival of a new form of self-government, the workers' and soldiers' Council, or Soviet. It was now the Soviet, not the bourgeois democracies of England and Germany, which showed the world its future form of State. The Soviet first appeared in Russia in the 1905 Revolution as a democratically elected workers' and soldiers' Council which organised grassroots opposition to the Czarist regime. But the idea of such an alternative to the parliamentary State dated from the Paris Commune of March and April 1871, when the people of Paris refused to hand the city over to the Prussian army after France's defeat in the Franco-Prussian War. In their analyses of the new revolutionary upheavals in Germany in 1848–50 and the tyrannical rule of Louis Bonaparte in France, Marx and Engels concluded that the emancipated society they envisaged could not be achieved through the institutions of the modern State. Marx argued that a real revolution in Europe would destroy the existing bureaucratic and military apparatus of the State, not transfer that oppressive machinery to a new set of rulers. In their preface to the 1872 German edition of the *Communist Manifesto*, Marx and Engels noted that the 1848 version needed important qualification as a result of the Paris events: the existing parliamentary State could not be seized and utilised for socialist purposes.[46]

In stark contrast to the Bonapartist State, the Paris Commune abolished the repressive aspects of government and democratised what Marx considered the legitimate functions of government. From the moment a representative no longer enjoyed the support of the people whose interests he or she was supposed to defend, the repre-

sentative was recalled. The mechanism of recall on demand enabled
the people of Paris to substitute the 'armed people' for the standing
army. The same popular vigilance was used to control the judiciary
and administration. Government was no longer divided into
executive and legislative functions; these functions were performed
by the same people entrusted with an immediately revocable mandate. All officials were thus elected, responsible and revocable. Marx
concluded that the Commune was to be the political form of even the
smallest country village, it was 'the poltical form at last discovered to
work out the economic emancipation of labour'. He saw in the Paris
Commune the political solution to the economic problem of class: by
binding political issues and class issues in one institution, the Commune guaranteed the 'self-government of the producers'.[47]

The triumphant Bolshevik leaders claimed that their revolution
drew upon and extended the lessons of the Paris Commune and the
Russian Revolution of 1905. Reporting to the seventh Bolshevik
Congress of March 1918, Lenin maintained that the Bolsheviks were
standing on the shoulders of the Paris Commune.[48] Lenin's *The State
and Revolution*, written in the months directly preceding the
November Revolution of 1917, provided an analysis of Marx's
Commune writings in order to demonstrate that the existing ready-
made State machine had to be replaced by a federation of workers',
soldiers' and peasants' Councils. During the years 1917–21 Gramsci
insisted that Lenin was the theorist of Council communism, not the
theorist of the vanguard Party. Gramsci believed that what was truly
revolutionary about the Russian situation was that a new form of
State based on the Council was emerging. Political parties and trade
unions had existed for some time under capitalism and had played an
important role in defending workers' interests within the capitalist
system. But by setting up a system of 'dual power' alongside the
established organs of government and economy, the Councils posed
a direct challenge to bourgeois authority in both the factory and
State, preparing the workers to take over when the balance of forces
was propitious. This marked a decisive advance over the defensive
capacities of the traditional institutions of the labour movement.[49]

Gramsci insisted on the the anti-Jacobin character of the Russian
Revolution. He derided Jacobinism as a 'purely bourgeois phenomenon', since it was a movement designed to replace one ruling class
with another, not the transfer of power to the people. Thus for
Gramsci the *Risorgimento* was a kind of non-violent Jacobin

Revolution, which in prison he describes as a passive revolution.[50] There was a fundamental difference between the French and Russian Revolutions: while the former was a bourgeois revolution liberating man as citizen, the latter was a liberation of the individual as producer, i.e., in terms of a more universal activity than restricted participation in the institutions of the democratic parliamentary State. Thus, the Russian Revolution was the harbinger of a new universal morality, rooted in the 'conscience of everyone'. Civil society was transformed from the realm of 'property rights, utility and Bentham' into a moral sphere regulated by custom, so that there was no longer any tension between liberty and law. Since order and discipline existed in the mass of the people in the form of social organisation, it did not have to be imposed by an authoritarian State estranged from their daily lives. The Revolution substituted a society based on individualism, competition, and the separation between civil and poltical spheres, on the one hand, with a society based on the unity of politics, production and culture, on the other. For Gramsci bourgeois society was undisciplined and atomistic; communist society brings market anarchy under the control of the community of associated producers.[51]

The Soviet was the basic unit of the new workers' State and socialist community. Like the Paris Commune, it was a fundamentally new political institution in the history of relations between governors and governed. By incorporating the principle of socialist democracy, the Soviet eliminated private interests and gave expression to the interests of the entire working population: popular sovereignty became a reality, while in the past it was only the owners of the means of production that were sovereign.[52] Writing in a quasi-mystical tone reminiscent of Sorel, Gramsci hailed the Soviet as the institution through which the chaos of competing individuals in bourgeois society was reduced to a single social will and a single spiritual authority.[53]

Thus, the urgent task of all Italian revolutionaries was to promote and develop forms of workers' democracy to prepare the working class for the day when it would manage the political and economic affairs of society in institutions similar to the Paris Commune and Russian Soviet. Moreover, an immense cultural, philosophical and artistic revolution would also be necessary to free the proletariat of bourgeois ideas. Gramsci understood, however, that existing political, economic and cultural institutions were not adequate to this task. The trade union schools, the Popular University and other educational institutions promoted workers' interests as subordinate members of bourgeois society, but did little to promote the development of a revolutionary class consciousness capable of conceiving new forms of social relations. This moral and intellectual reform was the hallmark of all revolutionay periods. The example of the Enlightenment period preceding the French Revolution was a case in point. In fact, 'the same phenomenon is repeating itself today with socialism. By way of the critique of capitalist civilisation the class consciousness of the proletariat is in the process of formation, where critique means culture, not spontaneous or natural evolution.'[54]

The Russians had understoood this, and set about constucting the bases of a communist producers' culture with its own canons of beauty and excellence. During the years 1917–21 half a million Russians joined the association Proletarskaja (proletarian art) or *Proletkult*, as it was called, to attend to the specifically cultural aspects of the revolution. The leadership of the group was formed in 1913 around the secretary of *Pravda*, Sergei Malysev, with whom Gorky and other writers committed to revolution published a first series dedicated to the cultivation of proletarian aesthetics for a new society. In the years immediately after, clubs, schools, and worker educational associations sprung up in the major urban centres of the country. Following the October Revolution, Anatoly Lunacharsky, the People's Commissariat for Enlightenment, insisted that the *Proletkult* movement be given generous State support as a vital part of the transition to communism. By February 1919 the first Proletarian School of Journalism was founded In Moscow, along with the Proletarian University of Moscow.[55]

Gramsci had followed these developments in Russia and was convinced that the Italian proletariat needed its own cultural and educational institutions to prepare the masses for revolution. His stress on the importance of the cultural bases of the revolution is evident in the project *La Città futura* in February 1917. In this publication of the Piedmont youth section of the PSI, Gramsci combined his own attacks on positivism with a selection of writings on the importance of culture and education. Included were 'What is culture?' by Salvemini, Croce's 'Religion' and 'What is life?' by the Gentilian Armando Carlini. In these efforts Gramsci was reacting against the prevailing views at the National Congress of young Socialists in September 1912, which, he argued, continued to impede a correct understanding of the relation between theory and practice in the socialist movement. At this Congress Angelo Tasca of Turin put forth what Gramsci considered an excessively abstract view of culture which was distant from the realities of working life. The Neapolitan militant Amadeo Bordiga declared that he had never read a page of Croce, and that culture was a bourgeois luxury that the working class could do without. Gramsci believed that the revolution certainly turned on the decisive moment of seizing power, but was concerned to emphasise that the revolution was also *in homine interiore*, compelling each individual to be the master of himself or herself as a precondition for changing the external world. The general tenor of the writings in *La Città futura* exhorted individual sacrifice as the basis of real liberty. Morality consisted in eschewing indifference and recognising that living meant being unequivocally partisan. Gentile's ideas on the identity of thought and activity, knowledge and action, and teacher and student pervade the pages of *La Città futura*.[56]

The moral fervour of Gramsci's cultural messianism is also evident in two other projects of this period, his proposal in December 1917 for an Associazione di Cultura as the third organ of the labour movement next to the PSI and CGL, and the Club di Vita Morale. He argued that the Italian Popular University imparted a vague spiritual humanism which had to be supplanted with a militant communist education emanating from the realities of the class struggle. The proposal was opposed by reformists and Maximalists alike as 'intellectualistic' and extremist. Notwithstanding such opposition, Gramsci insisted on the similarity of his proposals in 1917–18 in Italy with those of *Proletkult*. Gramsci's letter to the Gentilian Giuseppe Lombardo Radice in March 1918 and the articles of his colleagues Attilio Carena and Andrea Viglongo in *Il Grido del popolo* attest to the distance separating Gramsci and his supporters from the main currents in the PSI. His southern background, training in linguistics, and especially his study of idealist philosophy gave him a far different conception of socialism than the leaders of the trade unions or the career politicians. For Gramsci, socialism was something fundamentally different from the project of rectifying the ills of bourgeois society with palliative measures. He was aiming at the creation of a new *civiltà*, a new proletarian civilisation which he called for in his proposal for the Associazione di Cultura, writing that: 'Socialism is an integral vision of life with its own philosophy, mysticism and morality.'[57]

These initiatives were combined with the founding of the Club di Vita Morale, a discussion group in which various topics in political and moral philosophy were examined. Gramsci presided over the discussions, which he hoped would generate analytical rigour in formulating concepts which formed part of the socialist idea of culture. But in general these efforts were designed with the idea that workers must develop both the technical and the philosophical capacities to become completely independent of bourgeois institutions and to discard what was outdated in working class culture. The notion of culture as the ability to amass facts in order to have an advantage over one's fellows was rejected in favour of a conception which promoted each individual's ability to take part in a discussion, form an opinion, be criticised, and revise opinions as the basis for collective decision-making. Once the Club had to disband, as the mobilization for World War I demanded the service of a large number of its members, Gramsci continued educational work of this kind with workers in Turin. It should be added that at this stage in his development Gramsci tended to have a highly moralistic notion of culture. Members of the Club were made to comply with demanding criteria of self-criticism. Moreover, Gramsci had not yet adequately separated his concern that all workers become familiar with the best of bourgeois culture from the imperative to found a new producers' culture. This led to contradictory statements affirming the necessity of art for art's sake in some instances, and the need to find distinctly proletarian art forms in others.[58]

During World War I Gramsci's journalistic responsabilities increased as many of his socialist colleagues had been sent to the front. If the PSI enjoyed the merit of denying suport for the war (unlike most other European socialist parties), it had little to offer apart from playing the role of a spectator to the great event. While the position of 'absolute neutrality' had been tenable in the early stages of the conflict as a position of intransigent opposition, it was imperative that the proletariat adopt a position of active resistance. Hence Gramsci advocated 'active and operative neutrality', which drew further charges decrying his idealism and interventionism from the mainstream PSI leadership. He began to see that a day might soon come when it would be necesary to break with the Party. Nonetheless he rejoiced in the fact that the war created the requisite conditions for the emergence of a collective will in Russia. The great merit of the Bolsheviks was to have given order and discipline to these collective spiritual energies in a new form of State realising a new form of democracy. The War had produced a similar rejection of the old order in Italy, and the same bases of a new collective will were present. The Italian bourgeois revolution had failed, while the Bolsheviks had proved that historical stages in the evolution of capitalist societies could be skipped. Given the right institutions, sufficient discipline and cultural preparation, the proletariat could establish its own dictatorship without waiting for Italy to become a mature capitalist country. While Gramsci had previously believed that the revolutionary political Party could be the source of dual power in opposition to the democratic parliamentary State, by 1919 events in Russia convinced him that it was necessary to dinstinguish the workers' Council as the basis of the State, on the one hand, from the party as the political elite or vanguard, on the other. In May 1919, Gramsci began to search for the Italian equivalent of the Russian Soviet. He believed that he had found it in the Factory Councils in the factories of Turin. An examination of the Factory Council movement in Chapter 2 provides an understanding of Gramsci's designation of the Council as the Italian Soviet and the germ cell of the future producers' society.

2

The *biennio rosso*, 1919–1920

The atmosphere in Turin towards the end of the First World War was extremely tense, and was marked by several large-scale uprisings against the government such as the great insurrection for 'peace and bread' which broke out on 21 August 1917. The post-war period was equally turbulent and difficult for the government. The national economy was devastated, and the hopes raised by the Italian victory were quickly dispelled. Many Italians, especially veterans, felt that they had not been treated as victors in the post-war settlements. Moreover, there was the widespread perception on both the political Left and Right that a return to the old order was not possible. It was in this climate of upheaval that Angelo Tasca, Palmiro Togliatti, Umberto Terracini and Gramsci founded *L'Ordine nuovo* in May 1919, as an attempt to give expression to the desire of these young intellectuals to unite political militancy with the equally important cultural side of the socialist revolution. In this sense *L'Ordine nuovo* was a continuation of previous projects such as *La Città futura* and the Club di Vita Morale, and was directly inspired by similar experiments, such as Lunacharsky's *Proletkult* movement in Russia. Thus, in addition to covering the most important political events of the day, the journal was dedicated to the ideal of publishing a wide range of contributions constructing a new socialist humanity. A typical issue was likely to include one or more of the following: selections of Marx's writings on the Paris Commune; an article on John Reed's experiences in Soviet Russia; Sylvia Pankhurst's observations on the women's movement in England; Henri Barbusse on the relevance of Beethoven's music for international peace and solidarity, etc. As Mario Montagnana observed, *L'Ordine nuovo* was to be for the new generation of socialist militants what *La Voce* had previously been for enlightened members of the Italian bourgeoisie.[1]

The *Ordine nuovo* experiment figures as an extremely important event in the history of modern Italy. Its principal members would go on to found the Communist Party of Italy (PCd'I) in January 1921, and it is in the pages of this Turin weekly that Gramsci develops his theory of socialist democracy based on the *Consigli di fabbrica*, or Factory Councils. Gramsci's Factory Council theory represents the culmination of the early phase of his development as a political thinker and militant. It is here that he integrates his ideas on the failures of the PSI with an Italian solution to Marx's riddle of finding a truly democratic form of State, or as Marx put it with regard to the Paris Commune, 'the political form at last discovered to work out the economic emancipation of labour'. Many of the problems Gramsci takes up in prison concerning the role of the Party versus workers' institutions were first encountered during the Council movement of 1919–20. Gramsci's vision of Italy as a network of workers' and peasants' Councils was his first sustained attempt to show how the Italian State might be reconstructed on a radically democratic basis. This preliminary sketch of the new Italian State prefigures his prison writings, in which he incorporates his ideas on the successes and failures of the Council movement into his mature vision of socialism. Indeed, it is his conception of the Council State that marks Gramsci's entry into the ongoing dialogue on the Italian State which is examined in detail in Chapter 6. A brief look at the origins of the Factory Council movement will enable us to examine Gramsci's initial vision of the workers' State.[2]

The Internal Commissions

In the period from the turn of the century until World War I, large concentrations of workers came from all over Italy to the urban centres of the North. These demographic shifts created a series of new problems in industrial relations. The less shortsighted industrialists began to realise that the influx of semi- and unskilled labour from the South gave them the opportunity to reassert their power in the factory with greater flexibility than they could under the traditional trade union structure. The possibility of achieving this flexibility was suggested by the experiences of the war, in which *ad hoc* commissions operated on the shop floor to resolve wage and related disputes. These so called Internal Commissions (*Commissioni*

Interne, or CI) often were comprised of representatives of both labour and management, and received a certain measure of trade union support. During the wartime effort to maintain high levels of production, they were formed to deal with problems as they arose, and dissolved again once their task was completed. Their jurisdiction was initially limited to disciplinary measures, while the unions retained control of questions concerning wages and hours.[3] In October 1906 the first CI was set up following a collective contract between the Federation of Italian Metal Workers (FIOM) and the Turin automobile firm, Itala. It was decided that the CI was to be in session for three years, and that all disputes concerning contracts between FIOM and the firm would be resolved by an agreement between representatives of Itala and the CI. Irresolvable disagreements between the Internal Commission and management would be handled by an arbitration committee comprised of FIOM leaders and the Executive Council of Itala. However, this was intended only as a last resort, and it was emphasised that the CI should deal with the majority of problems as they arose.[4]

The Commissions achieved recognition by the management in most Turin factories by the summer of 1918. Management recognition became an important matter of principle in factories where they had not yet been established. In November 1918 at the National Congress of FIOM in Rome, the question of the establishment and spread of the CI was a central issue. The future of the CI caused a great deal of debate amongst the leading factions of the Italian labour movement: syndicalists feared possible accommodation to reformist plans for their domestication, since the FIOM leadership saw them as a means of consolidating union power on the shop floor. Gramsci and *L'Ordine nuovo* insisted that since they could surmount trade union distinctions, the CI could potentially overcome the limited demands of trade union reformism; thus it was imperative to maintain the strictest possible separation between Commission and union functions. This meant that the percentage of unionised and non-unionised workers comprising the Commissions became a highly charged matter. Many workers who had been in FIOM for some time were very wary of the unskilled southern workers without factory experience who would be able to vote for the CI.[5]

In any case it became increasingly clear that the the growing importance of the Internal Commissions was a direct challenge to the hegemony of the trade union bureaucracy. The new institutions negotiated on central issues such as wages and hours, substituting their authority for what had always been the domain of the union. The Commissions were also responsible for the Special Committees of Agitation, which were charged with resolving matters of general disagreement with management. As we shall see, Gramsci argues that the Factory Council, as an emanation from the existing Internal Commission, embodied the principle of proletarian unity. It was therefore superior to the trade union, which separated workers on the basis of craft distinctions, thus perpetuating divisions in the working class based on wage and skill differentials. The Council tended to break with existing power relations by asserting that there was only one class in the factory, the proletarian class, which had no need of the bourgeoisie or its managers to organise production. Before moving to an analysis of Gramsci's specific arguments in favour of the Councils, it is necessary to look at his views on the limitations of the unions and the party. These criticisms of the traditional institutions of the socialist movement provide a clear understanding of how he conceived of the Council as the basis of a new kind of State in 1919–20.

Councils and the unions

As we saw in the last chapter, Gramsci's early development was marked by his assimilation of syndicalist ideas both in Cagliari and later in Turin. Although Gramsci had distanced himself from syndicalism on the issue of the State, many syndicalists regarded *L'Ordine nuovo* as an important ally in the struggle against trade union reformism, and approved of the idea of shop floor power emanating directly from the representatives of the working class. Given that both Council communists and syndicalists regarded CGL–PSI reformism as the major obstacle to the Italian revolution, Gramsci had to distinguish his Factory Council theory from what to many seemed like a syndicalist position. By 1919, FIOM leaders could see that control of the CI would enhance their ability to control left-wing elements in the factory pressing for radical action. In fact, FIOM support for the Internal Commissions probably resulted from an awareness that the union was losing ground to revolutionaries whose support had increased due to the pain and suffering experienced during the war.[6] The battle between reformists and revolutionaries in post-World War I Italy thus turned around the future development of the CI. Echoing the ideas of the Dutch Marxist Anton Pannekoek, Gramsci maintained that the traditional vehicles of working-class struggle were no longer the primary agents of the socialist revolution, since they originated as defensive institutions during the period of bourgeois ascendancy. The age of monopoly capitalism, world war and imperialism signalled the end of the old order and its institutions. Indeed, this was the crucial lesson to be drawn from the leading role of the Soviet in the Russian Revolution. The old State institutions were no longer in step with the level of expansion attained by the productive forces, while the traditional forms of struggle could not generate new 'State institutions':

The traditional institutions of the movement have become incapable of containing the flowering of revolutionary activity. Their very structure is inadequate to the task of disciplining the forces which now dominate the conscious historical process. They are not dead. Born in response to free competition, they must continue to exist until the suppression of every residue of competition, classes and parties, and the fusion of national proletarian dictatorships is realised in the Communist International. But next to these institutions must rise and develop institutions of a new kind – State institutions – which will substitute the private and public institutions of the democratic parliamentary State.[7]

Gramsci distinguishes his position from either a syndicalist or anarchist conception by affirming the absolute necessity of the State, and differs from the reformists on the grounds that the new State must break with all old forms, as the Russians and Communards had done.[8] Bourgeois society celebrates its universality because citizenship is the right of every individual, regardless of any class differences which might separate them. For Gramsci, however, this is precisely why bourgeois claims to universality are merely ideological screens behind which the reality of the class struggle is omnipresent. When organising opposition to capitalism through the trade union or political Party, the worker remains within the parameters of a society that has different criteria of equality for different spheres of action. But what is universal about the fact that one can possess equality of citizenship, and yet be subject to class oppression as a worker? As long as the division of society into public and private spheres was accepted as 'natural', this contradiction would undermine any claims to universality bourgeois apologists might offer.[9]

Gramsci's workers' democracy eliminates the contradiction

between political equality and economic inequality, since in the new order, membership in the State is based on class. There can be no political equality divorced from production, since production becomes the basis of the State. Distinctions of merit and status are no longer linked to the type of craft practised or the level of skill possessed, but to the contribution that each worker makes to the goal of increased production. Thus the revolution does not eliminate the State; on the contrary, it gives the masses direct access to the State via its constituent organ – the Factory Council. Syndicalists and anarchists had failed to understand that the State was the 'protagonist of history'. In their attempt to conceive of a stateless society, 'the syndicalists worked outside of reality, and hence their politics were fundamentally mistaken'.[10] The PSI made many mistakes and was objectively limited in what it could achieve by working within the bourgeois State, but the experiences of the masses under liberal democracy could not be transcended until the liberal experience had been assimilated and criticised. In this sense PSI politics, however mistaken at times, were superior to syndicalist and anarchist politics.

Gramsci developed his critique of syndicalism and his own early views on the State in a series of articles in October and November 1919. Here he elaborates the notion of a workers' democracy as public and non-contractual; the realm of contractually-based private institutions is absorbed within the ambit of the State. He declares that the 'Workers' Democracy' article of 21 June 1919 transformed *L'Ordine nuovo* from a journal of abstract culture which could have been published in virtually any Italian city, into the theoretical organ of the Turin Factory Council movement. However, it was only as the Factory Council movement itself began to gain momentum in the autumn of 1919 that Gramsci was able to give his initial pronouncements greater clarity. Theory and practice were closely intertwined as Gramsci's ideas evolved rapidly in conjunction with developments in the factories that sparked further reflection.[11]

In the *Ordine nuovo* article 'Unions and Councils' of 11 October, Gramsci argues that the Factory Council 'is the model of the proletarian State'. The essential role of the trade union, by contrast, is to defend the interests of the worker within a competitive market economy.[12] He amplifies these remarks in 'Syndicalism and the Councils' of 8 November. Syndicalist theory offered no alternative to the tendency of the unions to separate workers on the basis of either the tool they used in their craft, or according to the natural resource to be transformed in the production process. In either case the integrity of the craft was preserved at the expense of class unity. However effective the general strike might be in spontaneously galvanising large numbers of workers, syndicalism offered no way of overcoming these divisions within the working class. The Factory Council, by contrast, prepared workers for the collaborative task of organising production even before the revolution. The post-revolutionary situation would be effectively controlled by workers who had acquired the requisite proletarian discipline while still under bourgeois property relations. This framework pointed the way out of the simplistic 'reform versus revolution' framework which created numerous strategic and theoretical impasses for the labour movement.[13]

Gramsci was not for the abolition of the unions; he believed they would be necessary for the future organisation of production. Once all power had been vested in workers' Councils, the unions would contribute a great deal to the transition to a planned economy, as the Russian example showed.[14] But he was scathing in his contempt for the trade union bureaucracy and its tendency to bridle the revolutionary movement. Gramsci would not quickly forget how his proposals for an Associazione di Cultura were met with great hostility by the trade union leadership, which feared that opening up the minds of the workers to the world of ideas and culture would signify a loss in their authority. He objected, too, that technical experience and dedication to work had never been criteria for electing leaders of the CGL or USI (Unione Sindacale Italiana, the revolutionary syndicalists' union), who relied instead on their demagogic qualities to maintain their positions of power. Gramsci decried the formation of a hierarchical 'caste' of union functionaries who separated themselves from the mass of the workers. Such privileged officials were the labour equivalent of the 'cavalier of industry' who had become a 'dead branch' in production, merely clinging to prerogatives they had managed to usurp from the workers on the shop floor. Given that many of its top officials had an important stake in retaining the present industrial system which gave them their jobs, it was little wonder that the union was bureaucratic and reformist. The position of the trade union bureaucracy to its membership was analogous to the relation between the executive and legislature of the capitalist State: the bureaucracy usurped and dominated the rightful source of authority. This had the obvious consequence of discouraging workers from revolutionary activity.[15]

Just as syndicalism lacked a theory of the State and any new contribution to industrial organisation, so too the anarchists failed to see that every ruling class establishes its dictatorship through the State, not outside of or against the State. Gramsci's view of anarchism depended on the context of the argument. On the one hand, anarchism was the product of political immaturity, or as he puts it, it is the conception of every oppressed class that sees the root of its problems in the State. On the other hand, anarchism had a positive connotation when it signified the absolute freedom of a dominant class once it gained control of the means of production. No conflict between liberty and authority is possible in this case. Gramsci was aware that the proletariat's instinctive sense of rebellion would initially be directed toward the State, especially when it was still in the hands of the bourgeoisie. That was why it was imperative for the working classes to overcome its anti-Statist prejudices by building its own State from the ground. The Council was ideally suited to this task. Meanwhile, Gramsci hoped that the concrete experience in the Councils would convince anarchist workers of the necessity of securing the proletarian dictatorship, and the vital role of the political Party in this mission.[16]

But if the new State is founded on producers' institutions, where does that leave the class conscious vanguard? If the workers' State cannot be based on the traditional institutions of the workers' movement, what is the role of the Party? In the *Ordine nuovo* article 'Message to the anarchists' written during the General Strike of April 1920 in Turin, Gramsci alludes to the necessity of a major role for the vanguard. Yet he retained some important reservations about the Party, which, as we shall see, are intrinsic to his defence of the Councils.

Councils and the party

In Chapter 1 it was seen how Gramsci extolled the virtues of the Soviet in almost messianic terms which recalled Sorel's concept of myth. For Gramsci, the Soviet represented more than a Russian experience. It heralded a new producers' *civiltà* with its own 'mysticism and morality'. Gramsci's writings on Council democracy from May 1919 to April 1920 continually reiterate the belief that the socialist revolution was above all a producers' revolution, not the

substitution of one set of elites for another. This position linked him
with other anti-Bolshevik theorists such as Pannekoek and Rosa
Luxemburg. Long after the appearance of Lenin's *The State and
Revolution*, Gramsci continued to follow Sorel in associating parties
with bourgeois parliaments which separated the masses from the
machinery of government. The Paris Commune proved that in
revolutionary circumstances the masses could create their own forms
of government, and the Russian Revolution reinforced Gramsci's
belief that a caste of professional politicians could no longer represent the revolutionary energy of the working class. In marked contrast to the Jacobin Revolution, the advent of the Soviets in the
Russian Revolution had completely changed the relationship
between governers and governed. As *L'Ordine nuovo* prepared for
its first issue, Gramsci wrote: 'The essential fact of the Russian
Revolution is the establishment of a new type of State: the Council
State . . . Everything else is contingent.'[17]

By the time of the Bologna Congress of the PSI in October 1919 it
was clear that the majority of the Party felt that the time of useful
reforms had passed. This meant that the future of the existing
institutions of the labour movement was uncertain. Giolitti had
successfully managed to integrate the forces of Italian socialism
within the ambit of the parliamentary democratic State during the
period of Turati's leadership. But the imperative to follow the
Bolshevik example and smash the State raised the question of what
kind of State should be put in its place. Gramsci, of course, envisaged
a federation of workers' and peasants' Councils. His views on
revolutionary and reformist trade unionism were clear from his
pronouncements on the necessity of every society to discipline itself
in the institutions of the State, and on the belief that the trade union
could not fulfil this function. But if the Russian Revolution marked
the triumph of the Soviet, one could not deny that it was also the
triumph of the Bolsheviks. He thus had to attempt theoretically to
square this apparent contradiction.

Once Gramsci had decided that the foundations of the Council
State were organic and bore no relation to a social contract that the
worker could annul at any time, the Party could be the 'maximum
agent' of the revolution and new order; but its importance was still
surpassed by the Council, at least up until to Turin general strike of
April 1920. This distinction between the agents of the revolution and
the fundamental unit of the State remained firm for Gramsci. It was

here that he differed from the Maximalist leader G. M. Serrati, who
continued a difficult effort to hold the disparate factions of the PSI
together in the name of proletarian unity. Serrati still believed that
the Party was the most vital element of the Italian revolution as long
as it remained at least verbally committed to revolution. Amadeo
Bordiga, leader of the Abstentionist wing of the Party, differed from
both Gramsci and Serrati by arguing that the Party had to be purged
of all reformists, including long-standing leaders such as Turati. For
Bordiga the Communist Party was necessarily the primary actor in
the revolution and would be the central authority of the new State.
The establishment of producers' institutions could only come after
the seizure of power, and in any case they would be subordinate to
the decisions of the Party; any other strategy was inevitably
reformist. The debate between *L'Ordine nuovo* and Bordiga's *Il
Soviet* group based in Naples was of the utmost importance, since
their respective members would form the future nucleus of the PCd'I.
This was especially true once it became clear that Serrati would not
be able to hold the Party together, and PSI militants looked to Turin
and Naples for leadership.[18] By the time the Council movement
began losing momentum in the spring and summer of 1920, there
was no longer any doubt in Gramsci's mind that the PSI as it was then
constituted was not a revolutionary force for the radical transformation of Italy. He complained that the Socialist Party was like a
libertarian society which members could join voluntarily and quit
again when this suited them. Because membership was based on a
contract that could be annulled at any time, the Party had its origins
in the social contract rather than any organic conception. This had
been Gramsci's view for some time. In the *Ordine nuovo* article, 'The
conquest of the State' of July 1919, he affirms that the producers'
State cannot 'incarnate itself' in the institutions of the parliamentary
State. Political parties and trade unions are essentially structured to
promote the competition of particular interests in civil society. Substituting Serrati or even Bordiga for Giolitti in an effort to transform
Italy in a socialist direction was futile.[19]

By the summer of 1920 Gramsci saw that a drastic reform of the
PSI was urgent, though he continued to equate Leninism with Soviet
democracy rather than vanguardism. The State had to be based on
the activity of the masses in order for it to be a truly popular State
which broke with every elitist tradition of the *Risorgimento*.
Gramsci had already clearly stated his position in 'The problem of

power' of November 1919. Here he underscores the fact that all of
the revolutionary fervour in the world cannot save the Party from the
fact that it operates on a terrain which is distant from the factories
and fields:

The workers' and peasants' vanguard have intuited these necessities
immanent in the present economic situation, in the catastrophic equilibrium
of the forces and relations of production. And they have done all that they
could do in a democratic society, that is, a society that is politically configured. They have designated the Socialist Party as the force which represents their ideas and the programme they want realised as their natural
political hierarchy, and they have indicated to the Party the way to power,
which is constituted not on a Parliament elected through universal suffrage,
of exploited as well as exploiters, but is constituted as a system of workers'
and peasants' Councils. The Councils incarnate political as well as economic
power, and are thus instruments both for the expulsion of the capitalists
from the production process as well as for the suppression of the bourgeoisie
as the dominant class.[20]

For Gramsci, capitalist society affirms the equality of citizens but
admits economic exploitation; such a society is 'politically configured'. Equality in this society is limited to formal political criteria.
Since individuals have interests as producers in addition to their
interests as citizens and members of different communities, the institutions of a 'politically configured' society must be replaced with
social institutions capable of establishing democracy as the key
criterion in all spheres of social action – not just a dismembered
political realm. The logic of his argument calls for the complete
democratisation and accountability of power wherever it is exercised
in civil society and the State.

However, Gramsci follows Marx on the Commune in concentrating all of his attention on the problem of finding the political
institution appropriate for the emancipation of labour. The labour
process which evolved in accordance with the hegemony of private
accumulation is not analysed. Rather, it is assumed that eliminating
the inequalities in civil society stemming from private ownership of
the means of production can be achieved by centralizing the means of
production in the hands of the State. Like Marx in *The Civil War in
France*, Gramsci thought the key to the emancipation of labour was
to be found in a the creation of a new form of State with all of the
characteristics Marx ascribed to the Commune – workmen's wages
for all, recall on demand of all representatives, abolition of the
standing army and its replacement with a popular militia, and

perhaps most importantly, fusion of legislative and executive functions. The Factory Council captured this fusion in exemplary
fashion: the Council decided on production matters, and then members set about carrying out their own decisions. Political power was
no longer alienated to unaccountable bodies distant from the site of
production; everyone was a producer and a legislator at the same
time. But the ability of individual Councils to enjoy such a high level
of participatory democracy was necessarily predicated on their
having a definite sphere of autonomy from the State. If the State set
production targets and allocated resources, shop-floor decisions
would simply be ratifications of decisions that had been taken in the
higher-level central Councils, not in individual workplaces. Similarly, for local political Soviets to have any real power, they too
would need autonomy from the State. Thus, while Marx and
Gramsci seemed to be calling for radical democratisation and
decentralisation, their views on abolishing market anarchy with
central planning negated the efficacy of the participatory institutions
they hoped would replace the oppressive bureaucracy of the parliamentary State. In prison, Gramsci continued to search for a model
capable of restoring political power to a non-exploitative civil
society without thereby absorbing the civil sphere within an ethical
State. In Chapters 4, 5 and 6 we will see to what extent he was
successful in this project.[21]

It is fair to say that during the *biennio rosso* Gramsci seems to view
all social conflict as essentially class conflict. He theorises as if the
class structure of Turin was representative of Italy as a whole, when
clearly it was not. Thus the crisis of bourgeois society is above all a
production crisis, rather than a legitimation crisis in the wider sense.
Gramsci is completely dedicated to founding a producers' State,
rather than a pluralist State safeguarding individual interests in
terms of ethnicity, gender, religion, local identities, etc. Again, we
can see the problem that in attempting to overcome the contradictions of a 'politically figured society', he reasons that the sphere
of inequality could be absorbed by harmonising insitutions like the
Councils. What Gramsci does not see at this point is that even if the
civil sphere could somehow be harmonised within a different kind of
State, one would still have to count on having to adjudicate between
workers with different ideas on the best methods of production,
between political leaders with conflicting visions of how society
should be organised, between administrators and political leaders,

and between conservatives and innovators in general. As we shall see, Gramsci does not develop any theory of how non-economic conflicts will be resolved in the new State. Political problems are reduced to economic ones:

The revolutionary institutions (the political Party and the professional trade union) are born in the sphere of political liberty, in the sphere of bourgeois democracy, as an affirmation and development of liberty and democracy in general, in a sphere in which the obtaining political relation is that between citizen and citizen: the revolutionary process is realised in the sphere of production, in the factory, where the obtaining relation is that between oppressor and oppressed, exploiter and exploited, where there is no liberty or democracy for the worker.[22]

Gramsci highlights the contradiction between the political equality of citizens and the inequality obtaining between capitalists and workers by calling for the abolition of the realm of citizens. Rather than seeking a political system which will defend workers' interests with the same vigour that it protects the interests of citizens, in 1919–20 Gramsci seeks to collapse the distinction between worker and citizen in the figure of the producer. Echoing syndicalist themes, the production crisis calls for the abolition of the parasitic bourgeois State and its substitution with a producers' State. In the article 'Two revolutions' of July 1920, written shortly before the September factory occupations, Gramsci asserts that every form of political power can only be the legal expression of real economic power, and that this fundamental canon of historical materialism sums up the entire complex of theses that the advocates of the Council movement had been defending since May 1919. Gramsci goes as far as saying that the Italian revolution will be communist only 'to the extent that it liberates the proletarian and communist forces of production' which had been maturing in the womb of bourgeois society, and were now fettered by bourgeois legal forms. The revolution will involve all of Italy's oppressed classes that had been destroyed by the imperialist war. While a vanguard Party could hasten the overthrow of the existing institutional order by channelling popular frustration against the capitalist regime, in order for this overthrow to evolve in a communist direction the appropriate producers' institutions for managing the crisis had to be in place. In the meantime all possible measures to prepare the masses had to be taken. In a pointed criticism of Bordiga, Gramsci insists that by abstaining from elections the Party would only alienate itself from the masses. Such vanguard tactics were appropriate for 'a collection of doctrinaires and little Machiavelli's', not for a Party preparing the masses for self-government.[23]

Into the late summer and autumn 1920 Gramsci maintained his basic position on the primacy of the Councils. But several important events required him to rethink the role of the Party. We must now look at how he attempted to reconcile his belief in the leading role of the Councils with his growing appreciation of the importance of the Party.

Towards a workers' democracy

Tensions between Party and Council functions were already fore-shadowed at the theoretical level by the 'Workers' democracy' article of June 1919, which contains several ambiguities. First, Gramsci makes no mention as yet of Factory Councils, focusing instead on revolutionising the Internal Commissions: 'Today the Internal Commissions limit the power of the capitalist in the factory and settle matters pertaining to workshop arbitration and discipline. Developed and enriched, tomorrow they must function as the organs of proletarian power capable of substituting the capitalist in all his present useful functions of direction and administration.'[24] Second, Gramsci suggests that the elected delegates in the workplace should also be members of district committees which would represent workers of all trades based in local factories. With the Russian experience in mind, Gramsci was aiming at the creation of Soviet style workers' Councils. However, as the theory itself became bogged down in polemics with Party leaders and trade unionists, his emphasis on Soviets would fade from later writings, adding weight to the charge that he was advocating some form of industrial unionism which had more in common with Daniel De Leon's syndicalism than with Leninism. In subsequent articles Gramsci argues that Soviets must be constituted in co-ordination with local factory delegates. He thus departed from the Russian model in so far as purely political Soviets based on urban districts were no longer the basic unit of the State.[25] The Party and the unions would continue to exist and would be relied upon to perform vital co-ordinating functions, but 'will not be immediately identified with the proletarian State'.[26] The Party is the champion of revolutionary doctrine and the leader of *Proletkult* and other such initiatives. As such it is comprised of a political elite which is forged on the basis of years of collective experiences and cannot have a mass base.[27] Since the Socialist Party and the unions 'cannot absorb all of the working class', they will not be identified with the proletarian State. The basis of the State is not based on the individual choice to join or not to join, as in the case of the unions and Party. The Party had to be a vanguard with limited numbers. The high proportion of non-unionised workers in the CI was immediate evidence of the fact that the unions failed to secure the participation of all workers in the nascent indust-rial democracy.[28]

Following the 'Workers' democracy' article, it was imperative to select a method for choosing factory representatives. Two principles were insisted upon by the *Ordine nuovo* group: the Internal Com-missions should be elected by a council of Workshop Commissars, each representing the workers of a particular department in the factory, rather than by union members on the shop floor; in addition, all workers in the factory, whether union members or not, were to be eligible to vote for a Commissar. Subsequent meetings discussed the possibility of different methods of election, but these two proposals remained as an integral part of the *L'Ordine nuovo* position. Gramsci's proposal of giving the Internal Commission an indepen-dent electoral base from the union underlined the impossibility of confusing Council and union functions.[29] Two days after 'Workers' democracy', Gramsci developed his ideas more fully in a series of meetings of the Turin section of the PSI. Several days later the Turin editor of *Avanti!*, Ottavio Pastore, called for a meeting of all the Internal Commissions from the different industries in the city to discuss the revolutionary transition to a communist planned economy and to give *L'Ordine nuovo* ideas wider exposure. Though the journal had been transformed from an organ of 'abstract culture' to the champion of the CI and Factory Councils, it remained to explain how the Councils could be transformed into the basis of a new State. During the summer of 1919 Gramsci was attending as many as four meetings in an afternoon in an effort to clarify the *Ordine nuovo* ideal.[30]

By October the main contours of the Factory Council theory were coming into focus. In 'Unions and Councils' of 11 October, Gramsci stresses that the Factory Council would unite all of the working class above any distinctions based on trade and level of skill. At this point he is insisting on the theoretical distinction between Council and union so that there could be no mistaking the new institutions as simply agents for discrediting the trade union bureaucracy:

The factory Council is the model of the proletarian State . . . The Council is the most appropriate organ for the mutual education of workers and the development of the new social spirit that the proletariat has succeeded in drawing from the vibrant and fertile experience of collective labour. The solidarity which in the trade union was directed against capitalism, in suffering and sacrifice, becomes something positive and permanent in the Council. This solidarity is incarnated even in the most trivial moments of industrial production. It is captured in the joyous realisation of forming part of an organic whole, a homogeneous and compact system of productive labour which disinterestedly produces social wealth, affirms its sovereignty, and realises its power and ability to create history.[31]

Gramsci's producers' State would combine the radically demo-cratic measure of instant recall that Marx praised in the Paris Com-mune, on the one hand, with a planned economy based on a hier-archy of producers' councils, on the other: every factory is sub-divided into departments and each department or workshop is divided into crews with different skills, each of which perform a different part of the labour process. The workers in each crew elect one of their members as a delegate, entrusting that person with an authoritative, though immediately revocable mandate. The assembly of delegates from the entire factory forms a Factory Council. The Factory Council then elects an Executive Committee from its own ranks (sometimes called the Internal Commission), which in turn designates a Political Secretary. The deliberative body of Political Secretaries of the various Executive Committees of the different factories in a city forms the Central Committee of Factory Councils. This assembly in turn elects from its ranks an Urban Commissariat for drawing up production plans, the approval or rejection of projects and proposals of single firms and even single workers, the general orientation of the labour process, and the organisation of cultural activities for worker education.[32]

According to Gramsci, a society organised on these principles would bring about the *democratic dictatorship* of the working class. The means of production are no longer privately owned, thus there are no longer any exploiting classes. *All* producers participate in the State, regardless of whether they are inserted at a higher or lower level of the Council pyramid. By combining productive-technical functions with the political activity of voting in the Councils, Gramsci believed he had found the formula for a truly popular State.

At the same time, the Council structure would solve the production crisis of bourgeois society and allow the forces of production to expand to the fullest under the new socialist relations of production. But given that the necessities of industrial production would determine the development of the new State, it seems obvious that politics would be reduced to the technical requirements of increasing productivity to ever-greater levels. In this context it should be noted that Gramsci, like Lenin, had no objections to Taylorism and other forms of industrial organisation associated with capitalism, provided that they were harnessed in support of the workers' State. Indeed, even in prison Gramsci referred back to the *Ordine nuovo* project as advocating a form of Taylorism which was acceptable to the workers. Unlike Marx, Gramsci never developed a theory of alienated labour. Residual elements of this productivism will also appear in the *Quaderni*, as we shall see.[33]

Thus Gramsci formulated the Factory Council blueprint as if production was the single most important activity in an individual's life. While the economic Council structure culminates in an apex where the top planning decisions are made, there is no equivalent political hierarchy of authority. The Council leads the transition to a planned socialist economic system, yet there is no participatory political institution such as the Commune or Soviet leading the transition to a democratic political system.[34] Indeed, Gramsci explicitly states that political Soviets will only flourish after a network of Councils has already been established.[35] The reductionist view of the political inherent in Gramsci's scheme was pointed out by Tasca and Bordiga. They argued that despite the novelty of the Councils, Gramsci's theory was more syndicalist than Marxist.[36]

Defining the respective tasks of Council and union had to be faced in view of the forthcoming annual general meeting of the Turin branch of FIOM. On 22 October a meeting of the representatives of the Internal Commissions of seventeen factories was held. It was resolved that Council activity should be co-ordinated with FIOM activity by suggesting a list of candidates which needed to be approved by all the Commissars for the new Executive Committee of the Turin branch of FIOM. It was hoped that this would contribute to spreading the opposition to FIOM shown by many of Turin's highly skilled metal workers. There was a comprehensive discussion of the programme drawn up by the Committee of Study, as well as other general problems concerning relations with the unions in a meeting of the Workshop Commissars the night before the election at FIOM. This programme, entitled 'The Programme of the Workshop Commissars', stipulated that union members who were also active in Council decisions would continue to accept union authority on industrial conflicts, but *only* when the union's directives had been approved by the elected delegates in the factories.[37] The 'Programme' was unanimously approved by the Workshop Commissars. Needless to say it was rejected by FIOM officials who perceived that electing the Executive of the union from the shop floor would drastically reduce their current prerogatives. The resolution adopted by the Committee of Study and laid down in the 'Programme', however inimical to the interests of the trade union bureaucracy, also broke with Gramsci's plea to keep the Council untainted with the name of the union. In fact, both Workshop Commissars and FIOM officials bargained over alternative plans to link Council and union functions. It was soon apparent that *L'Ordine nuovo* ideas were successful in Turin largely because they seemed to coincide with the widespread opposition to local union reformists, rather than as an expression of any deep agreement with the details of Gramsci's Council theory. While Gramsci sought to formulate an original theory demonstrating the revolutionary properties of the Councils and their role as the 'model of the proletarian State', the disparate conglomeration of syndicalists, anarchists and Council communists supporting the Factory Councils were often simply heaped together as opponents of trade union reformism.[38]

Moreover, the 'Programme' is marked by several ambiguities that reveal problems with Gramsci's attempt to theorise an independent role for the Councils. It called for the subordination of the unions to Council directives, yet urged all workers to join the CGL. While on the one hand insisting that the two institutions were distinct, the Councils were supposed to elect the executive of local union branches. Other issues needed clarification, such as the question of the role of non-unionised workers in elections for Workshop Commissars. Was it fair to allow them to participate in factory elections on an equal basis with experienced foremen? How would shop-floor Councils address the needs of the unemployed? The peasantry? Gramsci's opponents asked why and how would the Councils function differently from the traditional Internal Commissions. Syndicalist and anarchist revolutionaries feared that they would be domesticated within the same legal framework in which the former CI functioned. Gramsci specifies that 'the most delicate and important task of the Commissar' is to always be the faithful interpreter of the sentiments of the workers on the shop floor. But if the Councils were intended as more than a vehicle for shaking up the union bureaucracy, it was not clear why a streamlined and responsive union was incapable of performing the same tasks. The 'Programme' asserts that the Councils 'incarnate the power of the organised working class in the workplace, in direct opposition to the authority of management'; moreover, a workers' democracy cannot be based on individual citizens, but only on organic groups of producers' organisations.[39] Still, this did not refute Bordiga's objection that the Councils would function rather like the factory-based arbitration bodies which were already widespread throughout the industrial North of the country.

In fact, Bordiga demanded to know what was revolutionary about following the call for Commissars to oversee the exact application of work contracts, resolve controversies between work crews and management, settle disputes between workers and supervisors, and maintain order on the job. Union officials could have performed the various tasks assigned to the Workshop Commissars, such as obtaining information about the amount of capital spent in their particular departments, studying production methods, and ascertaining how a greater yield from current capital investment might be secured. In a more polemical vein, Bordiga and other critics demanded to know what was revolutionary about helping the bourgeoisie balance its accounts and helping it manage the crisis of capitalism. The demand requiring Commissars to prevent capital flight from the factories where they were employed was potentially radical, though they had no effective means of doing this while capital was still privately owned.[40]

The *Ordine nuovo* group realised that without the support of the left wing of the Party, the Council movement would not be able to withstand the opposition of reformists in the Party and their allies in the trade unions. Gramsci had never been in doubt that these groups would oppose him, yet he believed that if the post-war crisis reached revolutionary proportions, the PSI would expel its reformists, assume the role of a Bolshevik Party, and seize upon the chance to give its political action a mass base via the Councils. But the Party's left wing was still committed to a vanguard strategy and suspicious of a revolutionary strategy based on radical industrial democracy. By March 1920, Serrati regarded the Councils as a dangerous innovation likely to provoke local uprisings the Party would not be able to control, thus the Councils would have to be disciplined by both the Party and the trade unions. The PSI leadership put forward a number of alternative proposals to the *L'Ordine nuovo* vision which rested on some combination of union or Party control of the Councils. The PSI was especially wary of syndicalist support for the new institutions, and it was feared that the Councils would be the vehicle of syndicalist attacks on PSI and CGL reformism. In the face of syndicalist and anarchist militancy, the Maximalist wing of the Party felt compelled to support trade union leaders in the battle for control of the shop floor. Into the spring of 1920, militant workers had to defend their new institutions against employer attacks without the support of any national political or union organisation. *L'Ordine nuovo* failed to revolutionise the PSI. Though support was strong in Turin, the Council movement could not hope to conquer the State without a strong base in Milan, Genoa and elsewhere. If the situation in Turin was already somewhat exceptional given the class structure of the rest of Italy (especially the South), the failure of the general strike of Piedmont in April 1920 reinforced the image of an isolated northern working class. But Gramsci had not yet given up hope, and affirmed that the presence of the Councils indicated the enduring influence of the Turin journal.[41]

However, the isolation of the Council movement could only be painful for those like Gramsci who had hoped that the Italian revolution was close at hand. The glaring incapacity of the Party became a salient target of *L'Ordine nuovo* invective. In January 1920 Gramsci called for a 'renewal' of the PSI; for all its numerous faults, he still insisted that the Party could be reformed. These faults became more intolerable with the failure of the April strike action, however, which found the militant metal workers in Piedmont isolated, and *L'Ordine nuovo* discredited at the national level. This is reflected in the fact that after the April events in Piedmont, the Council theory coming out of Turin faded in importance in national debates.[42] Gramsci was forced to react to these events, and as a conequence he wrote two articles giving testimony to a shift in his thinking on the role of the Party in the revolution. These are entitled 'For a renewal of the Socialist Party' (May 1920) and 'The Communist groups' (July 1920). The first, once again calling for the Party's 'renewal', declares that the Bologna Congress in effect had done nothing to transform the Party into a revolutionary force. The Party continued to work within the narrow confines of a politically configured society, while reformists and adventurers continued to sap its strength. Worse still, the Party had not gone beyond electioneering to become an organ of political education. In reality, the PSI had become part of the general confusion and decay that followed the war, and proved itself incapable of rising above the chaos to lead the masses towards the new order. In order to do so, the Party had to be purged of its reformist elements at once.[43]

The possibility of setting up 'communist groups' in the factory is suggested for the first time in the article, 'For a renewal of the Socialist Party'. Gramsci argued that small groups of communist militants could infiltrate the factories, and while working alongside shop-floor workers, disseminate the theory and strategy of the Party. The call for the establishment of such groups marked a break with Gramsci's previous insistence on the necessity to keep the Councils separate from other working-class institutions. The success of the revolution still depended primarily on the establishment and spread of the Councils, but the vanguard was now designated as 'the fundamental and indispensable pre-condition for attempting any Soviet experiment'. This shift was at once a departure from the articles of the fall and winter of 1919 and an important concession to Bordiga. Gramsci accounted for the isolation of the Councils by cautioning that until the masses had reached political maturity, the Councils might temporarily fall into the hands of either syndicalists or reformists. This problem would be overcome, it was hoped, when the educative experience of collectively taking charge of the production process would convince the masses that supporting the proletarian vanguard was the most appropriate way to hasten the revolution. Gramsci was responding to an obvious Italian reality, i.e., that working-class allegiances continued to be fragmented on such problems as allegiance to the Vatican, the *Questione meridionale*, and reform versus revolution. The Council theory was based on the premise that artificial divisions between workers disappear through the collaborative effort demanded by Council practice. Despite the singularity of Turin, Gramsci remained convinced that the proletarian class was a united producers' class comprised of individuals skilled in different trades, but who nevertheless had an identical class interest regardless of their other affiliations in civil society. When the Councils could not unify the Italian working class, Gramsci attempted to regain the theoretical offensive by asserting that the inexorable forward motion of the productive forces was creating the material bases for class unity where ideological unity was still lacking; he lambasts the syndicalists and other groups for retarding this process.

However, as the Council movement stagnated, he was forced to reconsider the premise underlying the entire Council theory: perhaps the vanguard Party would have to recompose the divisions within the working class if Factory Councils could not perform this vital function. When the Bolsheviks were faced with a similar dilemma, Lenin decided to renounce the programme he called for in *The State and Revolution*. Soviets without Bolsheviks were not favourable to the revolution, regardless of whether the Soviet was the model institution of the proletarian State. By the time Gramsci wrote 'The Communist groups' he was unwilling to endorse Bordiga's vanguardism. Increasingly dissatisfied with the PSI, though fearful that the Council movement might not sustain its momentum, he saw no immediate path for the Italian revolution. He had invested a great deal of effort in attempting to show that his conception sketched the proper relation between the vanguard activity of the Party and the spontaneous revolutionary action of the Councils. But as the *biennio* drew to a close, the precise formulation of this relation continued to elude him.[44]

Meanwhile plans for alternatives to the Turin version of Councils and Soviets faded from discussion when the Council movement appeared to be on the point of collapse. Angelo Tasca, Gramsci's co-editor at *L'Ordine nuovo*, had been formulating his own ideas independently of the group's nucleus since January. His ideas resembled those proposed by Schiavello at Milan in May, to the extent that both sought to link Council and union activity. Tasca directly challenged Gramsci in claiming that the Councils could act as an ideal force for the democratisation of the unions. He argued that it was logical to combine their functions since both aimed at preparing the working class for self-government. Tasca proposed the Councils as the impetus for the transformation of the craft unions into industrial unions.[45] His plan to co-ordinate Councils and unions gained him a sympathetic audience amongst the delegates to the Camera di Lavoro congress in May 1920. Gramsci reacted to the challenge by launching a fierce theoretical attack against Tasca's positions in the

pages of *L'Ordine nuovo*. However, this resulted in Gramsci's complete isolation on the editorial board, since by this time he had
differences with Terracini and Togliatti which prevented any concerted action amongst the leaders of the journal. The next several
issues of the journal were thus embroiled in polemics between
Gramsci and Tasca. Gramsci used the opportunity to restate his
position on the primacy of the Councils. This was a tragically
wasteful use of time, given that critical space in the pages of the
journal was being used to criticise proposals that had already been
approved by FIOM and the Camera di Lavoro. Rather than being at
the forefront of workers' shop-floor demands, the *Ordine nuovo*
crew looked like a group of university students more concerned with
correct ideology than with grasping the importance of quickly-
changing conditions of struggle.[46]

In attempting to discredit Tasca, Gramsci also commits a number
of theoretical mistakes. In 'Unions and Councils' of 12 June,
Gramsci explains that the union is neither essentially revolutionary
nor reformist, but fulfills its function in accordance with the level of
class consciousness and militancy attained by the working class. This
would have been consonant with Tasca's views, and constitutes a
refutation of almost everything he had said since May 1919.
Whether remonstrating with the syndicalists or chiding the
reformists, the trade union is the product of an early phase in the
development of capitalism which caused workers to view themselves
as wage-earners within the system, rather than producers in opposition to it. But then Gramsci reverts to his original position in
claiming that 'obviously' the union defends the interests of labour as
a commodity bought and sold on the free market. Gramsci con-
tradicts himself again by affirming the revolutionary potential of the
union, which is fulfilled when union members discard the law to
devote themselves to the 'spiritual preparation' of the working class.
In this instance the trade union becomes a revolutionary institution;
trade union discipline is effective revolutionary discipline. When
Gramsci departs from the will of the union membership to imbue the
workers with a revolutionary class consciousness and returns to the
question of industrial legality, he once again invokes the notion of
the Council as inherently revolutionary against the reformist tendencies of the union:

The Council perpetually strives to break with industrial legality. In the
Council one finds the exploited masses tyrannised and compelled to perform

servile labour. The Council thus tends to universalise every rebellion, and to bring resoluteness and positive value to its every exercise of power. The union, as a responsible agent intimately bound with legality, tends to universalise and perpetuate that legality.[47]

In a society comprised exclusively of producers, all members of the society are members of the basic producers' institution at some level in the hierarchy of Councils. A producer will also have a trade and thus have a union affiliation if he or she wants to. But membership in the State is obligatory, and therefore takes precedence over incidental membership in other institutions. For this reason Council functions cannot be confused with union functions. However, a year after the 'Workers' democracy' article there was no coherent picture of how the Councils might function independently of the unions. Contradictions and reformist implications in 'The Programme', as well as the ultimately unconvincing polemics with Tasca, bear out this point. Continuing divisions within the working class based on regional, religious and party political differences pointed to the fragmented nature of Italian society; a single proletarian institution would not be able to articulate that diversity. Moreover, syndicalists would still proudly maintain that the general strike of 1904 and other instances of mass-scale union co-ordination proved that when acting in concert, the unions could pose an effective challenge to State power. Rather than negating industrial legality, the Councils proved in some cases to be more effective than the trade union in resolving industrial disputes. Even the employers realised that their proximity to the workplace ensured more expeditious treatment of disagreements on wages and discipline. But Gramsci was unable to make explicit how these bodies could leap from taking on arbitration functions to being the basis of a new State.

The occupations of the factories in September 1920 provided further evidence that the Councils were not inherently revolutionary institutions. It could have been objected that conditions were not mature and that therefore the situation was not a true test of their potential, but an important component of Gramsci's argument is that the Council spontaneously tended to develop the revolutionary element in any situation, as the Soviets had done in the October Revolution. The September occupations should have presented an ideal chance for the Councils to exploit any revolutionary opportunities offered by the Italian situation. By 3 September 1920, 185 metal-working factories had been occupied in Turin, including all of

the main vehicle-producing factories and the main coachbuilding
works and foundries. First priority was thus given to co-ordinating
the exchange of goods between factories to maintain a constant
supply of raw materials. The local branch of FIOM set up a Directive
Committee equipped with several highly skilled technicians to super-
vise this exchange of goods. The Committee was charged with the
task of ensuring that all necessary materials for production
circulated amongst the factories concerned. Exchanges of goods
between Factory Councils was restricted according to overall supply,
though exchanges within a given enterprise were facilitated by
allowing the Councils to take direct control of such operations. The
general direction of production was handled by FIOM, which controlled the Directive Committee.[48]

It was hoped that the economic life of Turin could proceed
normally, and to this end the Directive Committee requested the
various Factory Councils to draft a list of all stocks of raw materials,
work in progress, etc. It proved increasingly difficult to maintain
production schedules in the Turin metal works on this basis, however. As a direct result of a lack of raw materials and the need for
supplies from secondary industries, other factory occupations
occured: the Italian Oxygen Company works were occupied on 14
September, and the Michelin Tyre plant seized on 16 September.
These factories contained a small number of FIOM officials, giving
the Turin Chamber of Labour the opportunity to direct the organisation of production in the occupied factories of the city. On 13
September, the Chamber of Labour issued a statement announcing
that it would decide which factories would be occupied and which
would function as they had always done. It was also declared that the
occupations would be managed by the Chamber in conjunction with
the PSI. The FIOM Directive Committee was thus replaced by a joint
body incorporating an FIOM representative and the Executive Committee of the Chamber of Labour. To provide specialised services,
four sub-committees were established: legal, technical, supply and
propaganda. At this time the Chamber of Labour created an
'Exchange and Production Committee' comprised of workers from
FIOM and the technicians' union. The Committee was led by a
member of the Chamber of Labour, who was responsible for co-
ordinating the exchange of raw materials and finished goods.
Factory Councils around Turin intending to sell new products were
obliged to submit a list of their stock to this new Committee. By

mid-September the occupations had generated an intricate network of Councils and committees to maintain the pace of production in the city. This complex productive apparatus was directed by FIOM and the Chamber of Labour through the specialised committees. At the same time the Councils executed directives on distribution and exchange and took on disciplinary functions. The Councils defended the occupied factories from possible government sabotage with a batallion of communist groups and 'red guards'. Since March these groups operated with the consent of the local branch of the PSI.[49]

Historian of the Council movement Martin Clark notes that an article in the Turin section of *Avanti*! of 2 September cautioned against any direct analogy between the occupations and an experiment in direct communist management. The bourgeoisie continued to control State power, and the proletariat could not yet be certain of the reliability of technicians and clerical staff, who might run out on the working class in the advent of State violence. Finally, it was unreasonable to expect production to continue as usual when the occupied factories could not obtain necessary raw materials in sufficient quantities or sell the goods produced.[50] Gramsci hoped that the occupations would confirm his prediction that the unions would prove themselves incapable of leading the masses, who would then turn to the Councils. In the *Ordine nuovo* article 'Red Sunday' of 5 September, he discounted the possibility that technicians and other highly skilled workers would abandon the Councils, which he claimed had already been successful in uniting workers of all levels of training and diverse backgrounds. However, this turned out to be a rather cursory analysis of the very real problem of overcoming divisions in the working class based on craft distinctions and varying levels of skill – divisions which Gramsci insisted were obviated by the Council structure. After citing a passage from *The Civil War in France* to invoke the authority of Marx's Paris Commune writings, Gramsci compares each factory to an isolated 'factory-republic' maintaining its autonomy from the bourgeoisie and capitalist State: 'Today, with the occupations, the despotic power of the capitalists is broken, as the right to elect industrial officials has passed over to the working class . . . In the factory-republic, there exists only one class – the proletarian class.'

Council democracy cannot be compared with bourgeois democracy, where electors vote once in every five or seven years to decide which members of the ruling class will exploit the people in Parliament. The Council system emulates the Paris Commune to the extent that the workers elect their own government in the workplace, subjecting their representatives to the stringent conditions of recall on demand. For Gramsci this amounts to a direct assault on both capitalism and the parliamentary State. Thus he advised the Councils to elect local soviets which could organise militias to defend the factory republics.[51] In reality the Councils were subordinate to the unions, however, especially FIOM, which continued to lead the occupation production drive in concert with the Chamber of Labour and the local branch of the PSI. Highly skilled workers and technicians did in fact abandon the factories when they concluded that they had less to gain than the rest of the workers there, which greatly slowed down the production effort in a number of factories. The Councils were unprepared to act as the central unifying force in the Italian socialist movement, contrary to what Gramsci had always asserted. Moreover, the fact that workers were electing their own officials on the shop floor according to highly democratic criteria did little to alter the fact that military power remained firmly in the control of the existing State apparatus, as the article in the Turin section of *Avanti*! noted. Gramsci called for the establishment of a soldiers' Soviet as a response, but the balance of forces were nonetheless highly unfavourable for the workers. To make matters worse, the rural masses who constituted the majority of the Italian population remained under the ideological influence of the Vatican and the bourgeoisie, outside of Council, Party or union organisation.[52]

Following the September occupations Council activity was rejuvenated in other parts of Italy, though it was impossible to set up an adequate co-ordination between the centres of unrest. In the syndicalist stronghold of Genoa local agitation committees had great difficulty persuading workers to record who had been elected to which post. In Florence and other cities the former CI continued to oversee production and discipline in conformity with past practice, i.e., with the help of local FIOM officials. The Turin Committee of Study attempted to issue instructions explaining the most appropriate method of electing factory delegates, but these were largely left out of consideration in individual factories. In Turin *L'Ordine nuovo* had undeniably contributed to the management of the factories during the occupations. But Gramsci was eventually forced to concede that the uniquely centralised structure of Turin industry had played a large part in explaining the successes of the Councils in that city, and that it was unreasonable to expect the rest of Italy to react like its most advanced industrial centre.[53]

As the occupations lost momentum, Giolitti played a shrewd waiting game, and was able to bring all sides of the conflict to the bargaining table before any major violence took place. In the final settlement between business leaders, union leaders and the government, FIOM leader Bruno Buozzi insisted that trade union control meant worker control over industry in general. Control of the labour process was to be exercised by the trade unions, while the Councils looked after dismissals, suspensions, etc. Buozzi was aware of the influence of *L'Ordine nuovo* and did not want to stray too much from the system of Factory Councils that had developed during the occupations. Gramsci took the opportunity to express his conception of worker control in the first issue of *L'Ordine nuovo* to appear after publication was resumed at the end of the occupations. He insisted that control must always be exercised by Workshop Commissars as the revocable delegates of the Factory Councils; anything short of this was unsatisfactory. The trade union control of industry called for by the Giolitti Plan was merely an olive branch to the industrialists.[54]

The September occupations had completely removed any doubts in Gramsci's mind about the possibility or desirability of immediately forming a new Party. His proposal for the spread of communist groups could only provide an interim measure. Would such groups take over the right to call strike action, thus usurping the original function of the Councils? Were they more closely linked to the Councils or to the Party? In July these were still open questions. When the PSI renounced its role as vanguard and put the entire question of reform versus revolution to a general vote for the whole world to see, Gramsci had nothing but contempt for the lamentable old dog of Italian socialism. How could it have been otherwise than that the majority would opt for compromise with Giolitti? A Party that allowed the most important question in its entire history to be decided by a referendum was not worth saving. Why had the occupations failed to ignite the spark of the Italian revolution? Why had the leadership vacillated on the most important questions of theory and practice?

The tactic followed until the present, which culminates in the referendum, can answer these questions. The leaders of the proletarian movement base themselves on the masses, that is, they demand that their action receives the prior consent of the masses . . . A revolutionary movement cannot but found itself on a proletarian vanguard, it must be conducted without prior consultations or an apparatus of representative assemblies . . . Assemblies are limited to ratifying what in effect has already happened.[55]

It appeared that Gramsci had swung all they way over to Bordiga's position to embrace the Lenin of *What is to be Done?* Yet as late as October 1920, Gramsci was still insisting that 'The Factory Councils have demonstrated themselves to be the historically most vital and necessary revolutionary institution of the Italian working class.'[56] Even though he was now reconsidering the role of the vanguard Party, he was clearly not in favour of Bordiga's Party-State. Gramsci attempted to define his position with greater precision in the *Ordine nuovo* article 'The Communist Party', which was written during the occupations and reprinted in October. Although he remained faithful to his view that the Italian revolution could not be the work of elites alone, the events of July–October 1920 could not have but profoundly shaken his initial assumptions. A workers' democracy overcoming the limits of a 'politically configured society' had to be based on producers' institutions. But given the continued dominance of the repressive apparatus of the State and the ideological immaturity of the masses of peasants, it seemed that there was little hope of overthrowing the existing order. Gramsci directed his inquiry back to Sorel, who had intuited the proper direction of research, even if Italian syndicalists had committed fundamental errors in his name. Sorel believed that the history of Christianity demonstrated that new civilisations are not created by small groups of intellectuals who disseminate ideology. Rather, it is only when a group of leaders establishes an organic relation between itself and the masses that new institutions, a new philosophy, new myths – in short, a new culture – can emerge. Christianity was successful because it did not seek to replace one small hierarchy with another, but strove instead to change the way all of society looked at the world. The implications were not only religious, but political and artistic as well. This project entailed the creation of new institutions and new practices which formed the basis of an entirely new *civiltà*. Gramsci had long ago rejected the notion that socialism is achieved when a group of leaders calling themselves socialists assume political power formerly held by people calling themselves liberals or democrats. The lesson of the Commune and the Russian Revolution was that the working class could not wield the ready-made State machine in its own interests; it followed that everything else associated with the bourgeois world-view had to be jettisoned as well. If the crisis of the capitalist system had been hastened by the World War, it remained to build the proper institutions to create the faith and discipline required to provide the subjective conditions. It was painfully clear in this context that the organic link between leaders and led characteristic of the early Christians was absent from the Italian socialist movement.[57]

Sorel thought he had seen such organic unity forged in the daily struggles of trade union militants. With his experience of the CGL and FIOM in particular, Gramsci could not place the same confidence in the Italian trade union movement. By the time of the *Ordine nuovo* writings, the Factory Council seemed to be the historically new revolutionary institution which the trade union appeared to be at the turn of the century. But specific conditions of struggle affecting the development of the Italian unions and Chambers of Labour suggested that it was impossible to create an autonomous factory-based institution without it becoming entangled in the politics of the old institutions. Gramsci maintained that this had been borne out during the occupations, when the unions, Chambers of Labour and the PSI smothered the Council in their bureaucracies, thereby depriving it of its revolutionary potential. Italian revolutionaries would have to create something entirely new, with no connection with the failures of the past. In May 1919 Gramsci followed Sorel in his equation of political parties with bourgeois democracy. But Sorel's rejection of political parties as vestiges of the bourgeois social order did not solve the problem of political leadership, nor shed light on the role of elites in a proletarian revolution. Sorel's confusion is manifest in his praise for such different figures as Lenin and Mussolini. Gramsci's changing positions during July–October 1920 indicate that he rejected the traditional institutions of the socialist movement in favour of the radical democracy of the Councils. But he could not ignore the fact that the vacillation of the PSI had condemned the Factory Council movement to a reformist solution; without political leadership outside of the factory, producers' institutions would not have the necessary liberty to flourish within the factory. The April strike and the abysmal performance of the PSI in September resulted in an extremely important development in Gramsci's ideas. While he had previously assumed the basic similarity of all political Parties, he now envisaged not only a new type of State based on the Factory Council, but also a new type of political Party – the Communist Party.

3

The Italian Communist Party and the fight against Fascism, 1921–1926

Writing in the columns of *L'Ordine nuovo* in May 1920, Gramsci predicted Italy's immediate future in ominously accurate terms:

The present phase of the class struggle in Italy is that which precedes either the conquest of political power by the revolutionary proletariat for the transition to new modes of production and distribution which will make productive growth possible once again, or we will see a tremedous reactionary movement by the property-owning class and the governing caste. No amount of violence will be spared in forcing the industrial and agrarian proletariat into servile labour. The reactionary forces will seek inexorably to smash the institutions of political struggle of the working class (The Socialist Party) and to incorporate its institutions of economic resistance (the unions and the co-operatives) into the bourgeois State machine.[1]

In January 1921, after the PCd'I split from the PSI at Livorno, Gramsci resumed leadership of *L'Ordine nuovo*, which had been transformed from a weekly into a daily newspaper. It was in these articles of 1921 and 1922 that Gramsci produced his first tentative explanations of the origins and likely future development of Fascism. At this stage Fascism had taken hold only in Italy, so it was difficult to assess its long-term significance. On 24 October 1922 an enormous Fascist rally took place in Naples, where Mussolini declared that the Fascist Party wanted to 'become the State'. That afternoon he inspected 6,000 Fascists who paraded in military formations, and proclaimed that 'either the government will be given to us or we shall descend upon Rome and take it'. His enthusiastic troops replied 'To Rome! To Rome!' Mussolini met with his leading paramilitary chiefs to decide the fate of the nation. He declared that the immediate aim of the 'March on Rome' was a Fascist seizure of power and the establishment of a new Cabinet with at least six Fascists in the most important posts. On 27 October the Fascist militia were assigned the task of occupying all anti-Fascist prefectures, police stations, radio stations, newspapers and Chambers of Labour within marching distance of Rome, to prepare for the assault on the capital. During 26–29 October Mussolini negotiated the possibility of forming a new government in Milan. The leaders of the General Confederation of Industry, the Bankers' Association and the Confederation of Agriculture telegraphed Prime Minister Luigi Facta asking that Mussolini replace him as Prime Minister.[2]

King Victor Emmanuel III returned to Rome on the evening of 27 October, where he received Facta's resignation. However, perhaps fearful of a general insurrection, the King did not at first accept Facta's intention to withdraw. Though the King had been told by his generals that 100,000 Fascists were on their way to Rome, in reality there were some 20,000 poorly-armed and badly-organised Black Shirts which approached the city from the north-west, north and east. Had it wanted, the army could have easily repelled the attack.[3] In any case, on the night of 28 October the King asked the former Prime Minister Antonio Salandra to form a government with Fascist ministers; Mussolini insisted that he alone could be Prime Minister. When the King conceded, Mussolini took the night train from Milan to Rome and arrived on the morning of 30 October. Before leaving Milan the Fascist leader ordered his *squadristi* to demolish the *Avanti!* offices. This was the fourth time this had been done since April 1919, forcing the paper to publish out of Turin. This episode had been preceded by many other anti-Socialist gestures which had been tolerated by the authorities; many more were to follow. Few, if any, observers realised that Fascism was a revolutionary force which would sweep away the old order. Gramsci's prescient statement above stood out as a marked exception to the general state of incomprehension with which the vast majority of the Left confronted its most violent and aggressive political opponent in the history of the class struggle.[4]

Gramsci quickly recognised that Fascism represented an important innovation in the political reorganisation of capitalism. This led to a highly variegated analysis of the movement's protean forms. His articles of this period reflect this diversity: Fascism appears at times as simply an extreme form of bourgeois reaction, at other times as a specifically Italian phenomenon deriving from problems bequeathed by unification, and in other instances it is depicted as a movement of the *petit bourgeois* masses and the agent of the *latifundisti* and owners of capital. He describes Fascism as both an essentially urban phenomenon and as an attempt to subordinate the towns to the countryside. Only gradually was Gramsci able to harmonise these contradictory views into a more coherent synthesis.[5]

This chapter will show how in the period following the founding of the PCd'I in January 1921 and leading up to his arrest in November 1926, Gramsci was able to reflect upon the weaknesses in his positions during the Factory Council movement. If during the *biennio rosso* Gramsci underestimated the autonomy of politics, his experiences in the Communist Third International and grappling with Fascism forced him to develop a theory of politics adequate to the complexity of Italian realities such as the *Questione meridionale*, the existence of numerous intermediate strata that the working class would need to win over, and the persistent problems impeding Italy's modernization which dated back to the *Risorgimento*. While Gramsci had not given up on the idea of Factory Councils during 1921–26, he now devoted all of his energy to creating a Communist Party which would unite Italy's disparate regions into a cohesive industrial producers' society. If the Councils were to have a central role in this project in 1919–20, it was now the Communist Party that was to be the protagonist of Italy's moral, material and political regeneration. Gramsci had not as yet seen the parallels between Machiavelli's Prince and the Communist vanguard, though these ideas began to germinate during the period we are examining in this chapter.

The Livorno Congress and its aftermath

From the time of the Congress of Bologna in October 1919, Bordiga's group based in Naples around *Il Soviet* advocated splitting the PSI and forming an entirely new Party structure. As Gramsci and *L'Ordine nuovo* struggled through increasing difficulties and isolation in the spring and summer of 1920, Bordiga's influence steadily grew as it became clear that Serrati would be unable to hold the various reformist and revolutionary wings of the Party together. Existing centrifugal forces were given further impetus by the resolutions of the Second Congress of the Communist Third International, or Comintern, founded in March 1919. It was decided at the Second Congress of July 1920 that entry into the Comintern was henceforth to be subject to compliance with the famed 21 Points. These were

twenty-one conditions which each Communist Party had to comply
with in order to retain its membership in political organisation of the
international proletariat. To begin with, all member parties had to
change their names to the Communist Party of the various countries
they represented. Among other stipulations, the 21 Points required
member parties to expel the reformists in their ranks, which had
obvious implications for Turati and his followers in the PSI. The
imposition of the 21 Points marked an important component of the
Bolshevik strategy to model the entire Communist movement on its
own organisational structure, thus enhancing Russian domination
of the International.[6]

In the aftermath of the factory occupations of September 1920,
preliminary meetings were held by the five distinct factions which
composed the PSI to prepare for the seventeenth and decisive Party
Conference in Florence in December.[7] However, the growing
strength of Fascism in the city forced the Party Directorate to move
the Congress to the Teatro Goldoni in Livorno and postpone it until
15 January. The fundamental question for each faction was defining
its position toward the Comintern and its demand for the expulsion
of the reformists. When no compromise between Party factions
could be found, Bordiga called for the creation of an intransigent
revolutionary Party based on Leninist principles of organisation and
adhering completely with all of the Comintern's 21 Points. Those
that supported Bordiga's motion then followed him out of the Teatro
Goldoni to the nearby Teatro San Marco, to hold the First Congress
of the Italian Communist Party.[8]

The sixty-seven articles which were drawn up at the first Congress
of the PCd'I reflected the desire irrevocably to break with past PSI's
reformist traditions. Party historian Paolo Spriano described it as the
document of an army whose most important principle was the
subordination of the single militant to the will of the collective and
the decisions of the directing organs of the Party. It was decided that
each new member be given a trial period of six months during which
he or she could not miss three consecutive meetings without being
expelled except in cases of grave illness or other extenuating circumstances. An extremely tight control of the Party press was immediately established, along with the strictest control of the youth
sections by the Central Committee. The Executive Committee of
each federation was to be directly accountable to the National
Executive Committee, comprised of five members. Gramsci's role at

Livorno and the subsequent founding congress was small, which was reflected by the fact that he was not elected to the first National Executive Committee. Indeed, the first PCd'I document is characterised by a notable absence of any of the themes dear to the *Ordine nuovo* group, such as the need to combine vanguard activity with the creation of institutions with a mass base, such as workers' and peasants' Councils or trade unions.[9]

The crucially important question at Livorno was clearly that of ascertaining how much of the PSI centre and centre left would follow Bordiga into the PCd'I. Serrati's Maximalists refused to accept all of the 21 Points, and the International was unwilling to compromise. Matters were further confused when the reformists decided to move to the left to accept the Maximalist position. The Comintern's intransigence reflected its belief that Bordiga would be able to swing the vast majority of the PSI to his side, which proved to be a gross miscalculation that would have tragic consequences in terms of organising a united front against Fascism. The split isolated the extreme Left, leaving 14,000 reformists and the bulk of the Maximalists together in the PSI. The new PCd'I had 58,000 or about one-third of the votes at Livorno, but only 42,000 later joined the Party. It seemed that the only victor was Bordiga, who had always stressed the need for an ideologically pure Party – even if this was at the expense of mass popular support. In the pre-World War II period the combined membership of the new parties of the Italian Left never reached the 220,000 of the PSI before Livorno.[10]

The PSI and PCd'I competed for the same electorate and the same support from Moscow in a spirit of bitterness and hostility. The PSI entertained the hope that it might convince the Comintern to change its decision and admit the Socialists, which seemed plausible given their persistent electoral strength. In the parliamentary elections of May 1921, the Socialists won 122 deputies while the Communists managed only sixteen. Bordiga and the majority of the PCd'I firmly believed that the PSI was the single most important obstacle to the unification of the Italian working class and its assault on State power. By June 1921 Gramsci even suggested that PSI passivity contributed to the success of Fascism. In 'Socialists and Fascists' he writes that:

The fascist *coup d'état*, based on the army, the *latifundisti* and the bankers is the ominous spectre which has threatened this legislature from the outset. The Communist Party has its own position: the necessity of an armed insurrection leading the people to the liberty guaranteed by the workers' State. What is the position of the Socialist Party? How can the masses still have any faith in this party, which restricts its political activity to moaning and the 'beautiful' speeches of its parliamentary deputies[11]

The PCd'I and the Communist International

Although in January 1921 the Comintern supported Bordiga, by the summer of 1921 it became clear that a Communist Party under his leadership would be intractable, especially at a time when some sort of compromise with the Socialists became an urgent necessity. Bordiga and those adhering to similar positions had already received a stern warning in the debates following the publication in April 1920 of Lenin's *Left Wing Communism: an Infantile Disorder*.[12] The failure of the March 1921 insurrection in Germany convinced Lenin of the need for electoral alliances between Socialists and Communists throughout Europe. Yet Bordiga maintained that the Italian situation demanded intransigent PCd'I opposition to all other parties – especially the Socialists. This ran directly counter to the united front strategy that the Comintern was developing at this time.[13] At the first enlarged plenary session of the Executive Committee of the Communist International (ECCI) in February and March 1922 involving 105 delegates from thirty-six parties, the Italian, French and Spanish delegates refused to support the united front theses, which nevertheless were passed by 46 votes to 10. Bordiga's refusal to accept the united front policy marked a decisive stage in his conflicts with the Comintern which would eventually lead to his removal from the leadership of the PCd'I.[14]

Immediately after the First Plenum of the ECCI, the PCd'I held its second congress in Rome from 20 to 24 March 1922. The main question to be settled was clarifying the Party's position on the united front tactic, to which end Bordiga drew up a series of resolutions which have gone down in Party history as the "Rome Theses". They are a direct attack on the united front tactic, which he insisted could only have been followed at the trade union level. Party historiography is fairly much in agreement on the importance of the Theses, but there is still some controversy concerning the extent to which Gramsci supported Bordiga at this point. This is not merely a point of detail, since it helps complete our picture of Gramsci by portraying both the political leader as well as the theorist. At a certain point it became clear to Moscow that Bordiga was not the ideal leader to build the united front against Fascism, and by 1922–3 the Comintern was looking for possible alternatives. After Bordiga was muscled out of the Party leadership in 1924, it became imperative that future leaders not be tainted with *Bordighismo*, an infantile disorder. Togliatti, who succeeded Gramsci as PCd'I chief when the Sard was imprisoned in November 1926, as well as Spriano and other Party historians, claim that Gramsci was already distancing himself from Bordiga at Rome.[15] Tasca denies this in his book *The First Ten Years of the PCI*. The fact that Tasca, like Bordiga, would later be expelled from the Party must certainly have influenced Tasca's account. However, it might be added that in his introduction to Tasca's book Luigi Cortesi notes that not only were the contributions of Tasca and Bordiga belittled in the historical record, but anything that could not be seen as directly descended from the Togliatti line was systematically ignored during the period of Togliatti's leadership, which stretched from 1926 until his death in 1964.[16] There can be no doubt that pressure from Moscow played a large part in this tendentiousness, and without Moscow's aid the PCd'I might have perished in its incipient years.[17] Moreover it will be seen that Bordiga's refusal to engage in class alliances eventually did convince Gramsci that a new Party leadership was imperative. Yet if Gramsci did abandon Bordiga when it looked as if the Comintern was turning against him, we wonder what Gramsci would have done if he had escaped Italy to live under the hegemony of Stalin, as Togliatti had done, which practically eliminated Togliatti's margin for critical analysis. It is possible that we would have been deprived of the precious patrimony of critical Marxist thought bequeathed in Gramsci's *Quaderni del carcere*. Unfortunately no adequate answers can be found to this extremely important question.

In any case Gramsci did not appear to have withdrawn support for Bordiga by March 1922. His invectives against Serrati and Turati in *L'Ordine nuovo* carried on apace in increasingly strident tones.[18] But these polemics were soon to stop as Gramsci was chosen as the PCd'I delegate to the ECCI in Moscow, probably because of his ability to work with the Comintern's representative at the Congress of Rome, Vasilii Kolarov. Gramsci left for Moscow in May 1922, and although he was very ill, he participated in the Second Plenum of the ECCI of 7–11 June. After the session he was on the point of physical collapse, so he went to a rest home at Serebryanyi Bor on the outskirts of Moscow, where he remained for about six months. He suffered a complete breakdown, with constantly high fever and tremors in his arms and legs, and even after his recovery he was plagued by exhaustion, amnesia and insomnia. Despite these grave physical problems, this was also an extremely happy time for Gramsci. In Serebryanyi Bor he met his future wife Julia Schucht, with whom he had two children, Delio and Giuliano. Gramsci's *Letters from Prison* reveal the deep affection he felt for her until his death.[19]

Meanwhile the crisis of the Italian parliamentary regime entered the final stages which ended in Mussolini's march on Rome. Giolitti's government fell in June 1921. His successor was the ex-socialist Ivanoe Bonomi, who led a weak government which gave way to an even more unstable coalition headed by Luigi Facta in February 1922. The Left watched passively, while its isolation and impotence became increasingly apparent. In July and early August 1922 the unions called a protest strike against Fascist violence which was easily crushed, contributing to a declining spirit of resistance within the PSI and CGL. Turati's effort to convoke the leaders of the other parties for consultations with the King during a mid-summer crisis of the Facta government failed, as he was denounced by the Maximalists and forced to withdraw. By November 1922 Gramsci was well enough to attend the Comintern's Fourth Congress. Two important developments in October informed the resolutions regarding Italy: the Fascist March on Rome, and the Rome Congress of the Socialist Party, in which the PSI finally complied with the most important of the 21 Points by expelling the reformists. This precipitated the formation of the United Socialist Party of Italy (PSUI), whose ranks were composed of notable reformist leaders such as Turati, Treves, and Giacomo Matteoti. The PSUI had sixty-one parliamentary deputies to the thirty which remained in the PSI. The Fourth Congress went beyond the united front theses by proclaiming that communists had to declare themselves ready to form workers' governments with non-communist proletarian parties. In Italy this signalled the demand for a rupture with the Rome Theses of the PCd'I. The Comintern went as far as calling for the merger of the PSI and PCd'I on the basis of the Socialist Party's expulsion of the reformists.[20]

Bordiga maintained that any fusion was impossible and produced further evidence of the Comintern's reformist tendencies and its incapability of understanding the Italian situation. Tasca, representing the right of the Party, accepted the plan, while Gramsci insisted that fusion was only possible with Serrati's 'Terzini' faction. Soon after, however, Gramsci accepted the Comintern plan and was assigned to the joint committee charged with organising the merger. Gramsci later asserted that the extremely difficult situation of the PCd'I at this time made any break with the Comintern impossible, yet it was also impossible to reject Bordiga, who may well have been the only single leader capable of unifying the various factions in the Party. In this situation it is not surprising that the Comintern President Grigori Zinoviev complained that Gramsci was constantly tergiversating and prone to making vague promises he could not keep. In any case the impetus for a merger was dashed when Pietro Nenni, who had taken over the editorship of the PSI daily *Avanti!*, secured a majority within the Socialist Party against fusion. Serrati was arrested immediately after his return to Italy after the Congress, which prevented him from taking any counter measures. Zinoviev called for a bloc between the two parties if a fusion was absolutely unfeasible, but once again the majority of the PCd'I resisted.[21]

On 3 February 1923 Bordiga and Ruggero Grieco, the principal opponents to the Comintern line on the PCd'I Executive Committee, were arrested. Terracini, acting as the third leading member of this body, appointed Mauro Scoccimarro, Camilla Ravera, Tasca and Antonio Graziadei to the Central Committee, and brought Togliatti and Scoccimaro into the Executive Committee itself. Togliatti denies that this was a deliberate attempt to rid the Party of Bordiga's leadership, though he acknowledges that it did create some of the necessary preconditions for a major change of direction.[22] In April, while still in prison, Bordiga circulated a letter calling for an unequivocal break with plans for united front action, with alliances with non-communist parties, and with Comintern-orchestrated attempts to merge the PCd'I with other parties. Despite Togliatti's suggestion that Gramsci sign the manifesto, Gramsci refused, thus opening up a debate between the original *Ordine nuovo* group which was not resolved until February–March 1924, when Gramsci won the support of Togliatti, Teracini and Scoccimarro. By the time of the Third Plenum of the ECCI in June 1923, the Comintern decided that Terracini should come to Moscow as the PCd'I representative, while Gramsci was moved to Vienna to facilitate his eventual return to Italy. He left in November, just as Bordiga was released from prison.

Shortly before his departure for Vienna Gramsci wrote a letter to the
Executive Committee of the PCI disclosing his plans for a new Party
daily to be published by the Party and the 'Terzini' expelled from the
PSI. This letter has been regarded as the beginning of the transformation of the Italian Communist Party into a more flexible party
with the potential for a mass membership.[23] This change was
reflected in the proposed name, *L'Unità*, which was to appeal not
only to Italy's industrial workers, but also to the southern peasant
masses. The first issue appeared on 12 February 1924. Its regular
publication was interrupted in November 1926 when all anti-Fascist
parties were outlawed, but it was occasionally published
clandestinely during the Mussolini years, and became the PCd'I (or
PCI as it subsequently became known) daily since the end of World
War II.[24]

Not a great deal is known about the period that Gramsci spent in
Moscow and Vienna between May 1922 and May 1924. In some
ways he was still very much in the shadow of Bordiga. He was absent
from Italy during crucial moments such as the March on Rome,
which cost him some influence within the Party. But it cannot be
doubted that his presence in Moscow and Vienna amidst the most
important Bolshevik leaders and Communists from other countries
gave him a new perspective on the Italian situation. During this
period Gramsci was forced to acknowledge that the present state of
affairs was intolerable: the Left was losing influence in Italy as the
Fascists consolidated their power, and PCd'I fear of the dangers of
PSI reformism paralysed the Communist Party. Under these conditions relations with the Comintern were very poor, while precious
time was lost on futile debates on the merits of fusion versus absolute
autonomy. Gramsci's proposals for the dominant themes for
L'Unità constituted the first major step toward discarding this
straitjacket. His renewed emphasis on the *Questione meridionale*
would be elaborated further in the 'Lyons Theses', to which we will
turn shortly. But what does become clear is that under the pressure of
the Comintern and the long-range perspective provided by his
sojourns in Moscow and Vienna, Gramsci began to realise that an
effective opposition to Fascism could only be formed as a broad
coalition of popular forces – something Bordiga would not accept.
Gramsci's analysis of the failed uprising in Germany and events
elsewhere led him to the conclusion that class alliances, despite the
risks of 'ideological contamination' they implied, were now an abso-

lute necessity. There was no longer any point in furiously opposing the Comintern on the grounds that it did not understand the Italian situation in general, and the social democratic threat of the PSI in particular. Indeed, a much more fruitful approach was to take Comintern slogans on the united front and workers' governments and adapt them to the realities of the Italian situation, which meant allowing for the existence of large peasant strata.[25]

The situation for all Communist parties had already become more complicated at this time because of the growing fissions within the Communist Party of the Soviet Union (CPSU). In a letter to *Pravda* in October 1923 Trotsky raised a number of important questions on Soviet policy and Party organisation concerning the relation between democratic centralism and democracy, the relation between the Bolshevik old guard and the new cadres, criticising the slide toward bureaucratisation, and challenging prevalent strategies for industrialisation. This 'Platform of 46' would eventually draw the charge of fraction-building from Trotsky's opponents, Zinoviev and Stalin. In 1924 Stalin would declare the necessity of building 'socialism in one country' against Trotsky's demands for permanent revolution throughout the West, and it became increasingly clear that Comintern disputes were being shaped by the power struggle within the CPSU. At this time Bordiga was siding with Trotsky, and also attempting to have his manifesto of April publicly circulated at Comintern meetings. From Gramsci's vantage point in Vienna an attack on the Comintern would only be exploited by the enemies of the international Communist movement, and had to be vigorously opposed. On 12 May 1924 Gramsci returned to Italy after being elected to the Italian Parliament as a representative for the Veneto, and prepared to challenge Bordiga's leadership at the Party Congress at Como.[26]

The Party Congress was held in an atmosphere of semi-clandestinity with great concern not to arouse the suspicion of the police, who had already gone to great lengths to disrupt meetings and close down the press offices of the opposition parties, especially those of the Communists. The Congress was attended by sixty-seven PCd'I militants, with texts provided by Bordiga, Togliatti and Tasca, each representing the ideas of the three major components of the Party that had crystallised since the promulgation of the united front tactic. The centre, represented by Togliatti and comprised primarily of the nucleus formed in Turin during the *biennio rosso*, was now acknowledged to be the strongest faction. While Como seemed to provide the possibility for the inevitable break with Bordiga, Terracini came with a message from Zinoviev explaining that a rupture with Bordiga was to be avoided. Zinoviev complained of being overburdened with work for the Comintern, and as such proposed that he have relief help from Bordiga and the Bolshevik Nicolai Bukharin. It was hoped that this would widen Bordiga's perspective and make him see the merits of Comintern policy. But in its text the Left of the Party declared itself ready to re-sign the Rome Theses. This position was rejected by the centre, which called for a re-drafting of the Theses, and the right, which presented a thorough critique of PCd'I policy since Livorno. However, the results of the voting for the various motions revealed that while the centre controlled the Party by keeping it together, the majority of militants still supported Bordiga.[27]

It is against this background of division within the CPSU and intransigence within the PCd'I that the Fifth Comintern Congress of June–July 1924 began. The Congress started on 17 June with 406 delegates from forty-one countries, and was the first without Lenin, who had died in January. The main topics for discussion were the enduring hold of social democracy on the masses and the spread of Fascism.[28] In England the Labour Party formed a government for the first time in its history, while in France a centre-left coalition came to power, obliging the Comintern to have a new look at the power of social democracy. At the Fifth Congress it was decided that the Bolshevisation of the worlds' Communist parties was still partial and needed to be seen through to completion, while Bordiga claimed that the growing success of social democracy directly negated the efficacy of the Comintern. This served to further isolate Bordiga and ensure what had been clear since Como: though the Left enjoyed widespread support in many of the PCd'I federations, it no longer had any hope of reconquering the Party leadership. In fact, Moscow insisted that the Left be excluded from the newly-chosen Central and Executive Committees. The new Executive Committee was thus composed of five members including three centrists (Gramsci, Togliatti and Scoccimarro), one representative from the Right (Gustavo Mersu), and one 'Terzini' (Fabrizio Maffi).[29]

The Matteotti crisis and the Lyons Theses

However, for all its scorn for Bordiga's 'ultra-leftism', the Comintern offered a very similar analysis of the Fascist menace. The third and fourth resolutions of the Fifth Comintern Congress asserted that:

The bourgeoisie can no longer rule by the old methods. That is one of the symptoms of the slow but certain growth of the proletarian revolution. The bourgeoisie makes use of Fascism in some instances, and makes use of social democracy in others. In both cases they are concerned to screen the capitalist character of their rule . . . For a number of years social democracy has been caught up in a process of change; from being the right wing of the labour movement it is becoming one wing of the bourgeoisie, in places even a wing of Fascism. That is why it is historically incorrect to talk of 'a victory of Fascism over social-democracy'. So far as their leading strata are concerned, Fascism and social-democracy are the right and left hands of modern capitalism.[30]

These remarks are indicative of the conspicuously simplistic notion of Fascism prevailing in the international Communist movement, and presage the notorious 'left turn' of 1928, when social democracy was declared to be social Fascism, the proletariat's most dangerous enemy. Like most observers, Gramsci's initial writings on Fascism stressed the leading role of the *petit bourgeoisie* in the assault on both the State and the working class. His 1921 articles in the new Party daily *L'Ordine nuovo* did not depart substantially from the Comintern portrayal of the the *petit bourgeoisie* as a slave to large agrarian and industrial interests.[31] But as time went on Gramsci saw that neither the Comintern nor Liberals and Socialists took sufficient account of the fact that there were 'two Fascisms'. The first was centred on parliamentary tactics and the bargaining skills of Mussolini, and relied on the support of the middle classes, moderate industrialists and other forces willing to compromise with Socialists and Populists. The other Fascism relied on extra-parliamentary violence and intimidation as the armed defence of reactionary agrarian and industrial interests against the gains of the proletariat. After the March on Rome, Gramsci tended towards an increasingly nuanced analysis of the relation between Fascism and the various factions of the bourgeoisie. He conceded that in 1921 and 1922 important organs of the industrial bourgeoisie such as the *Corriere della Sera* and *La Stampa*, as well as some banking interests, refused to let themselves be taken over by the second kind of Fascism, which had already aroused suspicion from all quarters of political opinion. Gramsci noted the tension between the reactionary violence of agrarian Fascism and the reformist syndicalism or nationalism of urban Fascism. Several of the original urban Fascist nuclei resigned as a result of the obvious manipulation of the movement by the landowners. Even Mussolini acknowledged that Fascism only gained real strength when it moved beyond being a purely urban phenomenon and reached the countryside. Indeed, the outbreak of Fascist violence in the Po valley and parts of rural Tuscany in 1921 marked a decisive stage in the growth of the political power of the movement as a whole.[32] At this stage it was not clear if the uneasy alliance of urban, rural, syndicalist, veteran and nationalist elements could work together. Matters were further complicated by the fact that Fascism varied in accordance with its regional leaders, each of whom managed to attract rather different social groups to the movement. Italo Balbo in Ferrara, Dino Grandi in Bologna, and Roberto Farinacci in Cremona were just a few of the many local *Ras* of Fascism that understood and manipulated local political traditions. These charismatic leaders could appear republican, syndicalist, or nationalist, depending on the demands of a given moment in the struggle for power at the national level. Defining Fascism thus proved immensely elusive even for Gramsci, who saw that it was split between military and political wings, rural and urban cadres, as well as regional chiefs and the figure of the *Duce*. In any case it was clear that Fascism could not be explained as simply the armed reaction of capital against labour.[33]

As Fascism expanded and developed from a movement to a Party and began formulating a strategy for the conquest of complete political power, various observers saw the urgency of defining its essence. The most notable analyses concentrated on the conspicuous presence of the *petit bourgeoisie* and the fear inspired by the apparent chaos of the *biennio rosso*. Liberals such as Luigi Salvatorelli and Giovanni Ansaldo and critics of Giolitti such as Salvemini stressed the political tensions caused by the fact that the economic position of the working class and lower middle class had improved considerably since the turn of the century, yet this growth was not reflected at the level of political power. The Italian bourgeoisie continued to be too weak to unite the country, and was continually under threat from the growing importance of the popular classes. Observers such as Alberto Cappa confidently assumed that Fascism would exhaust itself in anti-socialism, while Giolitti would once again be able to piece together some kind of reformist solution.[34] Although unable to solve the country's problems, the bourgeoisie seemed determined to hold on to power, and to find whatever allies necessary in order to do so. But the support of powerful interests backing Mussolini was at least temporarily shaken when the abduction and murder of Giacomo Matteotti in Rome on 10 June 1924 unleashed a chain of events resulting in the banning of all opposition parties and the unrivalled monopoly of power by Mussolini's dictatorship.

Matteotti's murder resulted in a boycott of Parliament and the withdrawal of its deputies to the nearby Aventine Hill until 3 January 1925, when it became clear that they were having little success in persuading either King Vittorio Emanuele, the Vatican or the judiciary to condemn Fascist violence. Various Socialists, Populists and Communists supported a general strike. But such action was opposed by the CGL and PSI leadership. Gramsci shifted the terms of the discussion on Fascism away from those employed by the Comintern, arguing that if Fascism initially served bourgeois interests, it was no longer easily controllable, and indeed seemed to have acquired a certain measure of political autonomy from the social classes which had provided its initial impetus. In November 1924 he wrote:

Let's now come to the second aspect of the problem, to its substance, not the Mussolini Ministry or the military, nor Matteotti's trial or other matters, but the regime the bourgeoisie had to make use of to break the force of the proletarian movement . . . In the last analysis Matteotti's murder is nothing other than the expression and direct consequence of the tendency of Fascism to cease being the simple 'instrument' of the bourgeoisie, but to proceed in a series of abuses, violence and crimes according to its own logic.[35]

The PCd'I was the best organised of the parties of the left at this time. The Party had 12,000 members, while *L'Unità* had a readership of 20,000. Moreover, the Party gained new members following the Matteotti crisis. But since 1922 it had been operating under extremely repressive conditions, and was not in any position to wage a revolutionary struggle on its own. Moreover, the weak reaction to Matteotti's murder gave the dictatorship greater confidence in its ability to continue dismantling what was left of parliamentary institutions. From 14 June the government prepared for what it believed was the inevitable general strike, which was to be suppressed 'without indulgence'. The Communists declared a general strike for 23 June, which had very limited success and was followed only in Rome and a few other cities. In the two weeks which followed there were sporadic demonstrations which were easily controlled by the police. The historian Renzo De Felice reports that while the mood of the vast majority of the population was certainly anti-Fascist, the possibilities for a revolution were slim given the many divisions within the opposition. It is possible that a small, well-organised group might have succeeded in assassinating Mussolini, although with the likely result that the armed gangs of Fascist *squadristi* would have reacted with a determined counter-attack. This almost certainly would have resulted in a civil war whose outcome would have been uncertain. Had all the forces of the opposition united to pressure the King to force Mussolini into some kind of parliamentary compromise, it may have been possible gradually to restore political liberties and defuse the Fascist threat. But the Aventine succession prevented former power brokers such as Giolitti from resolving the crisis.[36]

By now the PCd'I was alarmed by the growing state of passivity amongst the masses, and made a final effort to bring down the government in November and December 1924. The Party proposed that the Aventine opposition had been ineffective, and that it was necessary to form a genuine alternative parliament which could compel Vittorio Emanuele to suspend the financing of the government. When the Aventine leaders rejected these proposals, the Communists returned to Parliament to show the masses that they were not to be confused with the weak and vacillating Aventine group. Though Giolitti and Don Luigi Sturzo, the leader of the recently-formed Catholic Populist Party, advocated that the rest of the opposition follow, the Aventine opposition chose to continue in what had clearly become a moral protest without major political impact. Under these conditions Gramsci realised that demands for revolution were illusory, and that any immediate transformation of the regime in the interests of the proletariat would have to be effected by way of a restitution of democratic and parliamentary liberties. The murder of Armando Casalini in September 1924 and other acts of Fascist violence confirmed Gramsci's thesis that even the forces of reaction that initially supported Mussolini were no longer in control of the Fascist movement. Industrialists such as Olivetti and Pirelli who were alarmed by the growing instability of the country and the obvious economic consequences that followed presented Mussolini with a manifesto demanding political normalisation and trade union rights of free organisation.[37] On 15 October the PCd'I Central Committee met and drafted a resolution for a genuine anti-parliament which might win the support of members of the centre and moderate Left, such as Piero Gobetti, who were dissatisfied by the Aventine protest. Writing in *La Rivoluzione liberale*, Gobetti affirmed that the Aventine succession had not been the Italian Dreyfuss Affair that the non-clerical and republican elements of society had hoped for, and that it was time for stronger measures, including the mobilisation of the working class.[38] The PCd'I initiative called for the resumption of Council activity in the factories and fields, as well as the formation of militias for self-defence. In the *Mezzogiorno* the Association for the Defence of the Peasants was born, which was led by Giuseppe Di Vittorio, who joined the PCI with the 'Terzini'.

Despite such efforts, however, the opposition was far too internally divided to mount a successful challenge to the regime. Mutual suspicion continued to dominate PCd'I–PSI relations and made fruitful collaboration impossible. When the legislature returned from Christmas on 3 January 1925, Mussolini shamelessly asserted that if the Fascists were a bunch of delinquents, he was the head of the group. A brutal repression of the opposition press immediately followed; *L'Unità*, for example, was searched eleven times between 3 and 16 January. A general climate of persecution followed throughout the year. After the failed assassination attempt on Mussolini's life by the Socialist Tito Zaniboni on 4 November 1925, the crackdown on all forms of opposition went into its penultimate phase. Meanwhile matters within the PCd'I were aggravated by the continuing discordance between Bordiga's followers and Gramsci's leadership, which prompted the comparison between Bordiga and Trotsky in the international Communist movement. On 6 February the PCd'I Central Committee passed a motion delaring its solidarity with the CPSU majority and condemning Bordiga's 'personal Aventine', deemed an obstacle to the true Bolshevisation of the PCd'I. Togliatti wrote a letter to the Secretariat of the Comintern warning that there was a pro-Trotsky faction within the PCI comprised of Bordiga's supporters and perhaps even instigated by Bordiga himself. As the year closed and with time clearly running out, it was necessary that the PCd'I decide once and for all what

attitude to take with regard to the Bordiga question and the pros-
pects for the Italian revolution. These questions were at the top of the
agenda for the final PCd'I congress in Lyons, France, before the
outlawing of opposition parties and the Communist Party's plunge
into complete clandestinity until the end of World War II.[39]

The Lyons Congress was held from 21–26 January 1926.
Gramsci's Theses at the Congress and several other articles written
before his arrest in November clearly foreshadow some of the major
themes of the *Quaderni del carcere*: the failure of the *Risorgimento*
and the concomitant *Questione meridionale*, the importance of the
intellectuals in shaping the world-view of the masses, and the necessity of winning non-proletarian strata to the Communist cause figure
prominently in Gramsci's writings of January to November 1926.
These themes would all receive greater elaboration in prison. The
immediate task at Lyons was not only the erasing of the imprint of
Bordiga's group on the PCd'I, but also the need to orient future
policy so as to avoid past mistakes which had allowed Fascism a
greater margin of manoeuvre. The fact that Gramsci's centrist group
now had control of the Party did not relieve him of the responsibility
of clearly formulating how the PCd'I could be a Leninist party in
compliance with the ECCI's resolutions on Bolshevisation, and yet at
the same time place great emphasis on grassroots organizations.
Thus in Thesis 29 Gramsci reintroduces some of the *Ordine nuovo*
ideas which had been absent from Party declarations for some time:
'The organisation of the Party must be constructed on the basis of
production and thus at the workplace (cells). This principle is
essential for the creation of a "Bolshevik" Party, and derives from
the fact that the Party must be equipped to lead a mass working-class
movement.'[40]

An important aspect of the Lyons Theses was the emphasis on
preserving the autonomy of the working class without thereby
isolating it. Gramsci reviled the weakness of the Aventine opposition, yet understood the importance of not alienating possible allies.
In the preamble to the Theses, Gramsci admits that the proletariat in
Italy is a minority of the population, and that vast strata of the
peasantry remained under the ideological hold of the Vatican. This
meant that the battle for Italy would be won by the Communists to
the extent that they were successful in convincing the southern
peasantry that only a permanent alliance between all anti-capitalist
strata could save the country from the tryannical rule of the northern

industrialists and southern *latifundisti*. The wresting of the peasantry from the ideological grip of the Vatican and its intellectuals could only be accomplished if the Communists forged their own intellectual leaders capable of articulating a national vision in which the working class was the motor force, but not the exclusive element, of a truly popular State. The conquest of Turin and Milan had to be complemented by reaching the masses of Campania, Basilicata and Sicily.[41]

The Fascist experience proved that capitalist interests would abandon parliamentary democracy if its vital interests were threatened. While parliamentary democracy allowed different fractions of the bourgeois class to compete without thereby threatening bourgeois hegemony as a whole, the transition to Fascism reflected the fact that the capitalist class could no longer master the productive forces sufficiently to allow its various fractions to coexist within a competitive framework. In Resolutions 15–18 of the Lyons Theses entitled 'Fascism and its Politics', Gramsci explained how the bourgeoisie could no longer grant the semblance of pluralist representation, and was forced into joining previously separate institutions such as the Party, the government and the State in a single centralised organism. Thus the Fascist syndicates, while adopting the language of socialism on issues of workers' control of industry, did nothing to challenge the private appropriation of socially produced wealth, and in fact allowed monopoly capitalism to flourish. The transition to State capitalism and Fascism could not solve the problem of political order for the bourgeoisie, however, which now had to deal with the anger of the numerous *petit bourgeois* strata which had originally seen the new movement as its salvation from proletarianisation. The radicalisation of these strata and their unification with the proletariat and peasantry was thus the Party's immediate political aim.[42]

By the time of the writing of the Lyons Theses, Gramsci had come to a far more sophisticated appreciation of the problems posed by Fascism than he demonstrated in his writings of 1920–21. While he never had the time to devote an entire theoretical work to its explication, he now understood that each national terrain set different problems for the proletarian movement, which put objective limitations on the efficacy of the Comintern. The interests of the Italian proletariat were not best served by Bordiga's politics of class sectarianism, however. The point was to trace the origins of Fascism back to problems bequeathed by the *Risorgimento* concerning the historical weakness of the bourgeoisie and its inevitable search for an authoritarian solution to its economic problems. But Fascism represented more than simply a reactionary manifestation of white terror, and if it had managed to galvanize the *petit bourgeoisie*, this was a vital lesson for the proletariat. The authoritarian solution had only been an option because the proletariat had failed to attract all of the potentially anti-bourgeois interests to the side of the revolution. Why had the Populists and the Catholic Action Party been successful when the PCd'I had failed? The Lyons Theses marked Gramsci's first attempt at these important questions.[43]

As the autumn of 1926 approached, Gramsci had also to deal with an urgent problem which, although outside of the PCd'I, had direct consequences for the worldwide Communist movement – the increasingly tense situation within the Communist Party of the Soviet Union. On 14 October Gramsci left the Italian Parliament to meet the Soviet Ambassador to Italy, M. P. Kerzencev. Gramsci and Kerzencev had been in close contact for some time, and the Russian had been able to get Julia Schucht a job at the Soviet embassy in Rome the previous year. Gramsci decided to wait for Kerzencev at the Soviet embassy, where he wrote a letter addressed to the Central Committee of the Soviet Party about the internecine rivalries between the Trotsky faction and the majority Stalin–Bukharin faction. While Gramsci was on the side of the majority, he cautioned against any intention of Stalin's supporters to be excessive in their countermeasures:

Comrades, in these nine years of world history you have been the organising element and driving impulse behind the revolutionary forces of all countries: the function you have fulfilled is without precedent in human history in terms of its depth and scope. But today you are in the process of destroying your work; you are degrading, and run the risk of annihilating, the leading role that the Communist Party of the Soviet Union had acquired through the work of Lenin . . . Comrades Zinoviev, Trotsky and Kamenev have contributed powerfully to educating us for the revolution. They have at times corrected us with energy and severity; they have been amongst our masters. We turn ourselves especially to them, as they are most responsible for the present situation, because we want to be sure that the majority of the Central Committee of the USSR does not intend to push its power too far in the struggle and is inclined to avoid excessive punitive measures.[44]

The letter was sent to Togliatti with the instruction that it be passed on to the Central Committee of the Soviet Party. But Togliatti refused to hand it over to the Central Committee. It was read by several Bolshevik leaders, including Stalin, who were annoyed by its contents. Togliatti was in full agreement with Stalin on the matter, and reproached Gramsci for his counterrevolutionary stance. This friction between the two former collaborators at *L'Ordine nuovo* marked the start of growing differences culminating in the end of communication between them during Gramsci's prison years, contributing further to the Sard's already acute sense of isolation from the PCd'I during the 1930s.[45]

In Gramsci's final writings before his arrest, such as 'An analysis of the Italian situation' of August and 'Some aspects of the Southern Question' of October 1926, we get a clear idea of some of the major themes of the prison writings. In the first Gramsci notes that:

in the most advanced capitalist countries the dominant class possesses political and organisational reserves that it did not possess in Russia. This means that even the most serious economic crises do not have immediate political repercussions. Politics always lags considerably behind economics. The state apparatus is much more resistant than one would normally believe, and in moments of crisis is successful in organising forces faithful to the regime to a much greater extent than the gravity of the crisis would suggest possible.[46]

The ability of the capitalist State to remain intact during crisis periods was certainly borne out in Italy by the events following the Matteotti crisis. But Gramsci goes on to explain that the countries of the capitalist periphery such as Italy, Spain and Portugal offer revolutionary opportunities not available in more stable liberal regimes like England and the United States. Thus he begins outlining a theory of core and periphery capitalist states on a world scale. In the peripheral states the ideological battle for the intermediate strata of society takes on an even greater importance than in the advanced capitalist countries. This was a tacit acknowledgement of the severe limitations in Marx's theory of the inevitable polarisation of society in accordance with the unfolding of the laws of economic development, and an explicit rejection of Bordiga's insistence that the working class remain separate from the rest of society. Gramsci had by this time fully assimilated the lessons of 1919–20: the emphasis on Councils and other mass organisations of the proletariat remained a necessity, but this was combined with the realisation that political engagement with all of Italian society was indispensable. Seeking refuge in economic determinism or ideological purity allowed the forces of reaction to reorganise their forces on their own terms. The invaluable lesson of Fascism, in Marxist terms, was that political initiatives by the superstructure to reorganise the base were every bit as important as developments within the base itself. If there was no direct causal relation between economic crisis and political revolution, all of the political conditions had to be created autonomously. A Bolshevik party, an extensive network of Councils, and the revolutionary consciousness of the masses would create the revolution; the economic crisis of capitalism would not produce these as by-products.

The invaluable lesson of Fascism, in terms of Italian realities, meant fighting an ideological and cultural battle not only against capital and the State, but also against the Vatican, the school in its present form, and the other institutions of civil society promoting traditional modes of thinking that maintained the gulf between economic crisis and political revolution. For Gramsci it was necessary for the proletariat to develop from its ranks a group of intellectuals capable of articulating a proletarian viewpoint on a national level in politics, the sciences, and the arts. This group would also have the task of winning the allegiance of bourgeois intellectuals who realised that liberal democratic institutions and capitalism would never be able to modernise Italy, and that the future of the country lay with its two progressive forces: the proletariat and the peasantry. Gramsci's remarks in 'Some aspects of the Southern Question' mark the evolution in his ideas. He argues that the southern peasant remains under the dominance of the large landowner because of the enduring influence of intellectuals who encourage the belief that existing social relations are 'natural'. Deference to the Church and the local bureaucracy become virtues of the good citizen. Gramsci reserves especially harsh crticism for Giustino Fortunato and Benedetto Croce for their role in this state of affairs. They had become cosmopolitan intellectuals who separated the radical southern intelligentsia from the peasants by encouraging them to adopt a European standpoint that neglected local problems. But the example of Piero Gobetti and the young intellectuals participating in his journal *La Rivoluzione liberale* demonstrated the possibility of founding new relations between intellectuals and masses. Responding to the charge that communists should have no ties with non-proletarian elements, Gramsci observes that:

We could not fight against Gobetti because he developed and represented a movement that should not have been opposed, at least in principle. To fail to understand this is to fail to understand the question of the intellectuals and the function they perform in the class struggle. Gobetti linked us with (1) intellectuals trained in the rigours of capitalist technique who adopted Left positions supporting the dictatorship of the proletariat in 1919–20; (2) he linked us with a series of southern intellectuals who, in a series of more complex relations, posed the Southern Question in new terms, by accentuating the importance of the northern proletariat.[47]

Gramsci goes on to say that because of the nature of their historical function, intellectuals develop more slowly than any other social group. The Italian revolution would depend on the ability of the Communists to disaggregate the bloc of southern landowners and northern industrialists in order for the peasants to form 'autonomous and independent formations', and this could not be accomplished without the help of intellectuals such as Gobetti and Guido Dorso who championed the cause of the South.[48] To what extent could this happen before the seizure of power? To what extent could the PCd'I respect the autonomy and independence of the intellectuals and social groups of the new historic bloc of proletarian forces that enabled it to organise Italy on Communist principles? Gramsci's arrest in November 1926 allowed him to begin answering these important questions in the now famous *Quaderni del carcere*.

4

The *Prison Notebooks* I: historical materialism and Crocean historicism

The prosecutor at Gramsci's trial called for his incarceration on the grounds that 'We must stop this brain from functioning for twenty years.'[1] Against all the odds, his sentence had exactly the opposite effect. Severely ill, Gramsci experienced great physical suffering in addition to the normal hardships of prison. Only his remarkable intellectual willpower and endurance enabled him to seize upon his imprisonment as an opportunity for sustained reflection. Between February 1929, when he was allowed the necessary materials, and the summer of 1935, when chronic illness finally sapped even his mental and physical resources for writing, he filled thirty-three exercise books with some 2,848 pages of notes. In spite of their often fragmentary character, understandable given the conditions in which they were composed, the *Prison Notebooks* are remarkably coherent. Indeed, following a serious breakdown in his health in 1931, Gramsci began to group them together and rework his ideas in special notebooks devoted to particular topics.[2] Taken together, they constitute one of the founding documents of Western Marxism.

In the tradition of Boethius and his hero Machiavelli, removal from politics led him to want to write about it 'from a disinterested point of view, *für ewig* (for eternity)'.[3] Looking back at his prolific earlier writings, he felt they suffered from being too occasional — consisting, as they did, mostly of journalism.[4] However, it would be wrong to portray Gramsci as devoid of any active political involvement during these years, or to view the *Notebooks* as signalling a complete break with his former ideas and interests.[5] On the contrary, the *Notebooks* represented an attempt to articulate in an organic manner the themes of the pre-prison years in the light of the new political context of the triumph of Fascism and the rise of Stalin

– developments of which Gramsci was all too aware.

As we have seen, Gramsci was preocuppied by these two issues in the period immediately prior to his arrest. The first had led him to rethink some of the assumptions that had inspired his involvement with the Factory Council movement. In particular, the essays on 'The Italian situation' and 'Some aspects of the Southern Question' show he came to a greater appreciation of the need for the Party to construct a genuinely national bloc of support, composed of peasants as well as workers, and of the difficulties hindering such a policy within a developed State. His famous letter of October 1926 to Togliatti, regarding the struggle between the Trotsky and the Stalin and Bukharin factions within the Soviet Communist Party, testified to the fact that he was extremely prescient regarding the second. During the summer of 1930 Gramsci was informed of the drastic policy changes resulting from the International's Sixth Congress via a visit by his brother Gennaro, sponsored by the Party in order to learn his opinion of these changes, and from conversations with other communist detainees in Turi prison.[6] The Congress had inaugurated Stalin's attack on the 'rightist' Bukharin faction, and a reversal of the 'United Front' strategy advocating co-operation with other groups opposed to Fascism. The official line was now that Fascism heralded the imminent collapse of capitalism and would be immediately followed by the dictatorship of the proletariat. As a result, there was no need to work with bourgeois liberal movements for a return to parliamentary democracy. Such ideas were held 'to distract the worker and peasant masses from revolutionary struggle, from their preparation for insurrection and civil war'.[7] For, according to the doctrine of 'Social Fascism', little distinguished even Social Democracts from Fascists. Those who continued to favour the former policy were accused of 'opportunism' and, under pressure from the Soviet Union, first Angelo Tasca and then Alfonso Leonetti, Pietro Tresso and Paolo Ravazzoli and finally Ignazio Silone – all members or former members of the PCd'I Political Bureau – were demoted and finally expelled for this reason. All the evidence shows that Gramsci fiercely opposed these moves. He believed that even under the most favourable circumstances, the Party lacked sufficient support for a proletarian revolution. Rather, means had to be found for the making of class alliances whereby the backward peasantry and the discontented *petit bourgeois* classes in particular could be won over. This process was likely to be lengthy and would

necessitate a considerable transitional period during which the Party
would have to exploit liberal freedoms to transform bourgeois
society from within through political action. In order to ensure the
Communists had this opportunity and were not isolated by other
groups, they should put themselves in the vanguard of a broad,
popular anti-Fascist movement. Gramsci supported the notion of a
constituent assembly as a formula capable of mobilising all the
anti-Fascist forces and of ensuring a central role for the PCd'I in a
reconstructed liberal State.

Accounts differ as to how much the Party knew of Gramsci's
dissent from their new position.[8] He was certainly villified by his
comrades in prison because of his opinions, and for a couple of years
all mention of him disappeared from official Party literature. He was
deeply disturbed by these developments,[9] and eventually felt cut off
and even betrayed by the PCd'I leadership.[10] It was against this
background of increasing isolation that Gramsci threw himself into
work on the *Notebooks*. For much more was involved in these
discussions than immediate tactics with regard to Fascism. Gramsci
linked the increasingly narrow and authoritarian Party discipline
and the abandonment of the United Front policy to the 'Maximalist',
mechanistic and economistic Marxism he had consistently opposed.
As Buci-Glucksmann has rightly stressed, it is no coincidence that he
should have embarked on a detailed critique of economism and
started his rethinking of Marxist theory and practice at precisely this
time.[11] The notes dealing with Machiavelli and the role of the Party,
the critique of Bukharin, the question of the intellectuals, the nature
of the State and the different roads to socialism all date from
1930–31. Underlying them all is his reformulation of historical
materialism so as to allow a greater role for consciousness and
politics in the transformation of society, and the resulting elaboration and stress on the concept of hegemony, or ideological
ascendency, within his analysis of the State and the Party's activity.
The rest of this chapter will be devoted to this theoretical revision of
Marxism, with the practical conclusions he drew from it forming the
centre of attention in Chapters 5 and 6. We will show how Gramsci's
mature work continued to combine Marxist categories with
elements from the Italian political tradition with similarly ambi-
guous results to those we have noted with regard to his early
writings.

Critics and sympathisers alike have attributed Gramsci's break with the mechanical determinism of the orthodox Marxism of his day to the influence of the Italian idealist philosopher Benedetto Croce upon his thought. Some interpreters have gone so far as to see him as a totally subjectivist and voluntarist thinker, who returned to Hegel by turning Marxian categories on their head and prioritising the superstructure over the economic base. Such views assume the very dichotomies between idealism and materialism, subjectivity and objectivity, State and society that it was Gramsci's desire to overcome. As his critiques of Bukharin's *The Theory of Historical Materialism: a Manual of Political Sociology* on the one hand, and of Croce's historicism on the other show, Gramsci's aim was to supersede the antinomies between theory and practice characteristic of empiricist and speculative forms of thought respectively. We shall therefore examine each of these critiques in turn and then outline his attempt at synthesis.[12]

Historical materialism

Gramsci used Bukharin's *Popular Manual* as a stalking horse to attack what he regarded as the worst features of vulgar versions of historical materialism. Such theories reduced all existence to matter. Even human thought merely reflected biochemical processes within the brain and their response to external material stimuli. Change occured through a dynamism within nature itself, a process linked with evolutionary doctrines – notably Darwinism. The social world operated literally, rather than merely by analogy, according to the laws of the natural world. Marxism so conceived presented itself as a complete science, which extended the methods and causal logic of the natural sciences to the analysis of society. On this basis, Marxists could claim to have formulated a body of empirically-grounded scientific laws of social development. These laws explained how changes in the material base caused certain kinds of society and class relations to form, which caused in turn class conflicts, which promoted further social and economic changes until the achievement of Communism. A vulgarising of Engels had made such views practically the norm in many Marxist circles at this time. In Italy they were very common, having mingled with the native positivist tradition – particularly in the writings of Achille Loria and Enrico Ferri. Both Croce and Antonio Labriola had already engaged in a critique of Lorianism (to which Gramsci also devoted a whole notebook) – a fact that led to Engels' denunciation of Loria in the preface to the third volume of *Capital*. Gramsci acknowledged his debt to Labriola in particular in this regard,[13] but believed that his assault on naturalist forms of determinism within Marxism had not gone far enough so as to question the whole deterministic conception of history.[14]

Gramsci contended that Bukharin and traditional materialism more generally had illicitly conflated the ontological primacy of matter as the essence of things, with the epistemological and social dimensions of human experience whereby we come to understand and to change the world and ourselves. As a consequence, he criticised both materialist associationist and sensationist psychologies and the positivist epistemologies which accompanied them on the one hand, and the resulting conceptions of social laws on the other other. The view of the human mind and knowledge as a mere reflection of sense impressions transmitted from nature ignored the fact that human beings stood outside natural processes, moulding them to their will. In Gramsci's words: 'Man does not enter into relationship with nature simply, by virtue of being himself a part of nature, but actively, by means of labour and technique. Moreover, these relations are not mechanical. They are active and conscious, that is they correspond to the greater or lesser level of intelligence that the individual man has of them.'[15] Crude materialism originated from ignoring the role of labour within the cognitive process, whereby nature was not merely reproduced but transformed within distinctive social forms or, in Marxist terms, relations of production. Marx's doctrine had nothing to do with the metaphysical materialism of the seventeenth and eighteenth centuries, therefore, which saw matter in quasi-theological terms as an ultimate cause of everything else.[16] Marxism considered matter not in itself, but as it was mediated and socially and historically organised as an economic and productive force. Thus:

the philosophy of praxis does not study a machine in order to understand and establish the atomic structure of its materials, the physical-chemical-mechanical properties of its natural components . . . but in so far as it is a moment of the material forces of production, in so far as it is an object of property of determinate social forces, in so far as it expresses a social relation and this corresponds to a determinate historical period.[17]

Gramsci was not thereby denying the independent existence of the natural world, merely insisting that we both know it and modify it in the course of social and particularly productive activity. As a result, talk of us being materially determined can only make sense in some extremely qualified way.

This argument had important consequences for the positivist conception of natural science and its extension to the understanding of human societies. Positivism appeals to the 'bare facts' of a self-evident external reality. However, such facts are identified and their import explained within the context of a theory. As Gramsci put it:

> the enquiry into a series of facts to find the relations between them presupposes a 'concept' that permits us to distinguish that series from other possible series: how can there take place a choice of facts, to be adduced as proof of the truth of one's own assumption, if there is no pre-existing criterion of choice? But what will this criteria of choice be, if not something superior to each single fact under enquiry? An intuition, a conception, which must be regarded as having a complex history, a process to contect with the development of culture etc. . . .[18]

Positivism's reliance upon a simple-minded empiricism was entirely circular, assuming that the facts were self-choosing and self-validating. Natural science could not simply mirror nature in a neutral manner, it too was necessarily a consciously informed social practice. For 'in spite of all the efforts of scientists, science never presents itself as a bare objective notion: it always appears clothed in an ideology and concretely science is the union of objective fact with an hypothesis or system of hypotheses that transcend the mere objective fact.'[19] It followed that the facts of science were never definitive, but historical categories that altered with changes in scientific knowledge.[20] The methods of the natural sciences had no inherent claim to primacy over other fields of endeavour, such as the humanities, therefore. Like all types of research, it involved applying certain theoretical assumptions and took place within the constraints of a particular social context. From this perspective, positivism largely reflected the dominant structures of the scientific community and bourgeois society.

Gramsci now went further, to argue that all human activity, including the most everyday, was concept-laden – even if the ideas involved were no more than the assumed verities of common sense.[21] Our very use of language implied the possession of a philosophy.[22] This theory-imbued nature of all human practice upset the notion of sociological laws. Whereas he believed the processes of the natural world taken in themselves formed a relatively closed system and unfolded in a constant and potentially predictable manner, the element of consciousness within human action disturbed the regularity of the social world and rendered it radically open. Natural science, on Gramsci's interpretation, constructed theorums on the basis of a series of statistical uniformities. Although human action displayed such tendencies, they amounted to simple empirical generalisations, not laws. Their value was explanatory rather than predictive. This was because purpose and meaning intervene in human affairs and influence our actions in ways which could not be derived in a determinate way from antecedent conditions. Different people, holding different values, were likely to respond to similar situations in different ways. As a result, a purely quantitative analysis of human history broke down because it was unable to explain the qualitative variations and disjunctions brought about by alterations in human will, goals and more than occasional lapses into error and irrationality. The interpretation of human behaviour involved an understanding of the inner feelings, intentions and beliefs of the persons involved as much as an analysis of the external circumstances within which they acted. Indeed, since social institutions embodied particular ideologies, such inner motivations formed part of those external circumstances. Action would only prove predictable, therefore, in periods of conformity and passivity.[23]

Thus, no mechanical formula could be found to explain the whole course of history without abstracting from the human capacity for free will and thought. A completely causal and determinist account of social development deformed reality by excluding its voluntarist elements and ignored 'particular facts in their unique individuality'. Covering laws did not not operate with the same constancy for human evolution as they did for other species. For we consciously altered our environment and with it ourselves in ways which could not be artificially isolated within laboratory conditions and extrapolated from and extended to the whole human race at all times and places.[24] Hence prediction only made sense as an act of will. It was 'the abstract expression' of the effort to bring about a desired change and only true to the extent it was successful, not a 'scientific act of knowledge'.[25] These criticisms did not mean that Gramsci excluded any attempt to posit likely tendencies from observing certain intelligible connections within social phenomena. On the contrary, he regarded Marx's economic theory in just this light – as a set of generalisations of given relations within the productive process derived from Ricardian political economy. However, their worth rested on their ability to illuminate past and contemporary events. They were not law-like predictions of the future based on assumed constant conjunctions of events.[26] In this respect at least, he agreed with Croce's famous designation of Marxism as a historical methodology rather than a philosophy of history.[27]

Gramsci's critique of the 'scientific' pretensions of Bukharin's Marxism had repercussions for the claim that the material base determines the superstructure. Gramsci regarded the belief 'that every fluctuation of politics and ideology can be presented as an immediate expression of the structure' as 'primitive infantilism'.[28] The cause and effect model of the base-superstructure relationship rested on the pseudo-scientific mechanistic materialism whose foundations he had so devastatingly undermined. Once again, it passed over the independent role played by human consciousness. Gramsci pointed out that institutions and belief systems often had internal dynamics of their own, which had no direct connection with economic developments. Ideological disputes within political parties or the Catholic Church, for example, frequently reflected little more than 'sectarian and organisational necessities' and attempts to find 'the immediate and primary explanation within the structure' would be pure 'fantasy'.[29] More important, the influence of the base was mediated through particular superstructures. For we engaged with the structure and partially constituted it through our activity within superstructural institutions and ideologies. Consequently, events such as the French Revolution were not the mere mechanical results of changes in the economic base. Rather, as recent historians have argued with regard to revolutionary France, struggles and alterations within the superstructure could be seen as indirectly or directly facilitating and partially shaping such changes. This point will be developed below to show that it involved no denial of the reality of such basic structures, merely that their effects and operation included intentional human activity. The principle issue that concerns us here is Gramsci's conclusion that the superstructure could not be reduced to a mere epiphenomenon – it was 'objective and operative' providing, in a paraphrase of Marx's words, the 'ideological terrain' on which 'men become aware of their social position and hence of their tasks'.[30] Thus, superstructures do not present a mere photographic image of the structure; they provide the arena within which we acquired knowledge and labour. Structure

and superstructure form part of a dialectical process whose development is 'intimately connected and necessarily interrelated and
reciprocal'.[31] We shall return to the full implications of this thesis
when considering Gramsci's conception of hegemony in the next
chapter.

Far from offering a value-free, 'scientific' theory of society,
Gramsci looked on 'economism' as a return to theological modes of
thought which negated the agents freedom of choice and action.
Matter replaced God as the final cause and the 'assured rationality of
history' became a 'substitute for predestination, for Providence',
with human beings mere pawns of some cosmic grand plan. He
robustly attacked the 'worse the better' school of Marxism for their
naive view that economic crises would automatically give rise to
progressive historical change.[32] For the dogmatic belief that the
proletariat would triumph in the end regardless of their own efforts
had much the same effect as the Christian doctrine that the meek
shall inherit the earth. It offered a certain consolation in times of
adversity but essentially encouraged 'passivity' to the blind forces of
history and 'mental laziness'. It also fostered a dangerous elitism,
turning the Party cadre, like the Catholic priesthood, into an elite
group possessing knowledge of the natural laws of an inner reality
distinct from the merely derivative experiences of ordinary believers.
The latter had only to trust in the scientific prescriptions of the
former to achieve salvation. The rejection of mechanical Marxism
was therefore a necessary preliminary for the development of a
'philosophy of praxis' – a Marxist theory which emphasised the role
of politics and popular participation.[33]

Crocean historicism

Gramsci's abandonment of determinist conceptions of Marxism has
frequently been interpreted as evidence of his idealism. We have
already noted the influence of both Croce and Gentile on his youthful
thinking, the importance of which Gramsci acknowledged in his
prison writings.[34] However, he also made clear that whilst he continued to regard the Neapolitan philosopher as a major figure com-
manding the attention of all serious thinkers, he had become considerably more critical over the years. He now insisted that Marxism
had not only to incorporate Croce's insights, but transcend them. He
believed Croce's thought was of considerable significance both in

itself and as the most sophisticated and, in Italy at least, dominant cultural expression of liberalism. Indeed, for Gramsci the substantive and socio-historical aspects of Croce's work, like that of any thinker, were intimately connected. Intellectual progress, therefore, required an 'Anti-Croce' along the lines of Engels' *Anti-Duhring*. He thought this project was potentially so crucial that 'it would be worthwhile an entire group of men dedicating ten years of activity to it'.[35] His own reflections were intended as merely the first salvo of a much more concerted campaign by others.

It is hard to exaggerate Croce's cultural influence in Italy during his own lifetime. Outside Italy, he remained relatively obscure and today he is largely unknown. A brief sketch of Croce's ideas is needed, therefore, to help explain just why Gramsci looked on his compatriot as so crucial and to provide a useful reference point for when we discuss his criticisms of the philosopher.[36] Croce's copious writings on aesthetics, history, ethics and politics were intended to constitute a comprehensive humanist philosophy, capable of answering the basic human need for a framework of meaning, value and certainty in a disenchanted age no longer satisfied with the consolations of religion. His *Philosophy of Spirit* aimed at encompassing human activity in all its aspects. Although the term 'spirit' originated with German idealism, Croce (arguably unsuccessfully) tried to rid the concept of the metaphysical and abstract connotations he associated with Hegel's conception of *Geist*, and to treat it as simply coextensive with the evolving collective human consciousness. Croce divided spirit into its theoretical and practical dimensions. The former was further subdivided into intuition and logic, the latter into economic and ethical action, the various parts being so related that the second and third implied the first and second respectively, but not vice versa. These four subdivisions corresponded to the four aspects of spirit – the beautiful, the true, the useful and the good. Croce did not believe that these concepts consisted of eternal ideals by which all human actions and beliefs could be judged, a position he thought inherently at odds with human creative freedom. On the contrary, they were 'pure concepts' which derived their content from the very activity of human beings. We were moved by the intuition of the moment and, if the stimulus was genuine, elaborated in the process a thought which expressed both beauty and, by virtue of being an appropriate expression of the demands of spirit at a certain time, truth as well. Similarly, by

performing actions with regard to their utility in certain circumstances, people also furthered the unfolding of spirit and contributed
both to the useful and, indirectly, to the good. Croce's dialectic of the
distinct moments of spirit was meant to correct Hegel's notion of a
dialectic of opposites. For he believed Hegel's failure to observe these
distinctions accounted for his lapse into panlogism and the consequent subordination of empirical reality to a preconceived theoretical schema.

Croce's argument derived from the German neo-Kantians, particularly Windelband and Rickert. Like them, he denied there were
any fixed *a priori* categories for interpreting the world, as Kant had
argued. The content of the forms of consciousness varied according
to the needs of individuals in particular periods and places. Croce
sought by this argument to avoid the twin perils of positivism and
'abstract' idealism. The chief problem relating to the first was its
reduction of questions of value to questions of fact, thereby denying
the human capacity to appraise and revise beliefs and desires, and act
in a free and responsible, as opposed to a determined and mechanical, manner. 'Abstract' idealism was equally at odds with human
autonomy, because it assumed a 'transcendent' morality separable
from human activity and to which it should conform. Instead, Croce
concentrated on the ways in which people develop and use value
judgements in everyday life. The emphasis was away from the notion
of reality as a given – either abstractly or positively conceived – to
reality as it was thought, acted upon and created by humanity. The
conception of human beings as either vainly seeking the approval of
a transcendent deity or determined by natural laws, was replaced by
that of the individual creating reality by his or her thought and
action.

Croce had not avoided the dangers of positivism and trans-
cendence in order to fall into the equally perilous clutches of
relativism. To avoid this pitfall, he maintained that all human
thought and action could be regarded as the manifestation of a single
entity, namely spirit, and its development in history. Yet in so
arguing, he risked committing the very error he accused Hegel of
making, that of seeing all human history as part of some pre-
programmed metaphysical design. True, Croce firmly insisted –
particularly in his later writings – that spirit evolved within the
world, through human activity, rather than existing above the world
and manipulating human beings like some grand puppeteer. How-

ever, he still felt the need to believe in some form of providence guiding us to avoid a sense of the worthlessness of all human endeavour. The ambivalence of his position can be seen from his varying interpretations of the Hegelian motto that 'What is rational, is real; and what is real is rational',[37] which became the keystone of his doctrine. The German term rendered here as 'real' is *wirklich* and derives from the German term to act, *wirken*. By playing on the double sense of *wirlich*, either as a given reality or as what has been made actual by action, it was possible to argue either that history *per se* was rational, or that it became rational through action. Croce vacillated between the two interpretations. He consistently mis-quoted Hegel by reversing the order of this sentence so that the real became identified with the rational.[38] Although this was often done with the intention of attacking the German philosopher, Croce frequently adopted the somewhat conservative position himself of arguing that we must all trust in the inherent rationality of the historical process. For example, his riposte to his collaborator Giovanni Gentile's highly subjective form of idealism, which significantly was termed actualism, consisted largely in the resolu-tion of philosophy into history.[39] However, when Croce found himself in the position of having to attack the present, as he did during the Fascist era, he tended to adopt the more activist stance.[40]

These vacillations were related to Croce's various shifts at different stages of his career between the view that politics belonged primarily to the realm of the useful, judgements of good and evil being largely resolved by the course of history, and the idea that human practical activity was ethico-political in nature, involving the attempt to realise certain moral ideals. Although these changes in emphasis can be linked to the internal dynamics of Croce's philo-sophy, the main impetus came from outside. For the ambiguity of his theory on this issue became a matter of some political concern once Gentile and others began to employ his philosophy to interpret and justify events such as the First World War or the rise of Fascism. Needless to say, his own ideological preferences played an important part in orientating his response. In general, when he approved of what was happening he adopted the more passive 'economic' stance, and when he was critical of the dominant political trend he leaned towards the more 'ethico-political' view.

It was the latter position, developed in response to Fascism and brought to maturity during the period Gramsci was writing in prison, that most interested the Sardinian. In earlier writings, Croce had identified the individual with spirit, so that history was seen as 'the work of that truly real individual which is spirit eternally indivi-dualising itself'.[41] In Hegelian manner, he regarded all 'real' successful actions as necessarily 'rational' developments of some inner essence – *Geist* or the Idea. In his 'ethico-political' conception of history, in contrast, he gave primacy to the ideals individuals set themselves as makers of history. He now argued that whilst all individuals were necessarily products of the past and hence condi-tioned by it, they were capable of seizing the initiative by becoming conscious of these conditions. This knowledge provided the basis for self-directed, as opposed to passively determined, future action.[42] Seen in this light, history became the story of liberty – the never-ending struggle consciously to transform the world through the creation of the artifacts and institutions of human society. Croce was not thereby advocating a form of voluntarism, so much as an idealist version of compatibilism. For theory only gave way to action to the extent that it took hold of the real conditions of our existence. Vital to this process, he argued, were intellectuals. In his view, they formed a privileged class who should, like himself, be unconnected either with the State or with economic activity. It was by virtue of this relatively detached position that they were able to promote, through their cultural activity, new ideals which opened up alternatives to the present.

Croce's attraction for Gramsci lay in the stress he placed on human ideals, culture and will, the function of intellectuals and on the role of what Gramsci would call hegemony.[43] He appreciated too Croce's historicism and his antipathy to system-building – his insistence 'that philosophy must resolve the problems that the development of the historical process presents from time to time', rather than offering definitive solutions to the supposedly eternal questions of the human condition.[44] Croce remarked that he had arrived at his realist version of idealism because of having approached Hegel and the German idealist tradition through his early studies of Marx.[45] Indeed, Gentile had criticised his earlier economico-political theory for being more Marxist than Hegelian.[46] In seeking to overcome the continuing metaphysical and determinist features of this position with his ethico-political conception of his-tory, Croce provided the conceptual tools Gramsci required for his own battle against these elements within orthodox Marxism. He even believed Croce had brought to light the genuine conceptual status of Marxist categories because the best in his own theory involved 'retranslating' them back into the language of Hegelian idealism from which Marx had derived them.[47] Thus, one way of rebutting the charge that Gramsci's Croceanism led to an excessively subjectivist and intrinsically anti-Marxist position involves pointing out that Croce's historicism did not possess this highly abstract and idealist character and emerged itself from an engagement with Marx. However, Gramsci also felt that Croce's philosophy had severe defects of its own, that only a revised form of Marxism drawing on his insights could overcome.[48]

Gramsci attributed the chief defect in Croce's doctrine to what he called its continuing 'speculative' nature.[49] This weakness arose principally from the Crocean distinctions, particularly between theory and practice, though his continued reliance on the notion of spirit was also to blame.[50] Croce argued that all practical action, including science, was in his terminology 'economic'. It was a first order activity, employing categories of a largely empirical, instrumental and *ad hoc* character. The validity of these rules of thumb with which we orientated ourselves in everyday life could only be ascertained by applying criteria derived from a second-order theory. In the economico-political phase of his writing, this validation came about through the unfolding of spirit within history itself, whereby the truth and goodness of acts arose from their proven contribution within specific contexts. In the ethico-political phase, in contrast, Croce shifted to arguing that the moment of conceptual clarification, of reflective thought and hence of knowledge, prepared the way for constructive action by imaginatively transcending its past historicity to create new history. In both cases, Croce insisted that the process of critique arose out of the immanent dialectic between thought and action. As such, he hoped to avoid the errors of on the one hand an uncritical positivism, which takes things as they are, and, on the other, a transcendent idealism involving the application of pre-formed concepts and categories of a supposedly universal and trans-historical and hence totally ungrounded kind. Gramsci, in contrast, argued that because of the distinction between theory and practice at the heart of his philosophy, he could only avoid the one by falling into the other. He either subordinated the 'economic' to the 'ethical' moment or *vice versa*; he never established a properly dialectical relationship between the two. As a result, the latter phase of Croce's thinking was theological and speculative in the very pejoritive sense used by the Neapolitan, for it assumed some ultimate entity outside of humanity which provided the source of value.[51]

Gramsci observed that proof of the inadequacy of Croce's conception could be found in the ethico-political histories themselves. Croce sought to demonstrate the explanatory worth of his new position in a series of historical works, the most important of which were the *History of the Kingdom of Naples* and the *History of the Baroque Era in Italy*, published in installments between 1922 and 1926, and the *History of Italy from 1871 to 1915* (1928) and the *History of Europe in the Nineteenth Century* (1932). Due to their obvious actuality, the last two drew most of Gramsci's attention. He found Croce's starting-points, 1871 and 1815 respectively, highly significant, for they involved excluding the dramatic moments of the *Risorgimento* and the French Revolution respectively. Yet how, he asked, could one disregard 'the moment in which an ethico-political system dissolves itself and another is elaborated in fire and with iron? in which a system of social relations falls apart and decays and another system rises up and affirms itself? and instead placidly assume as the whole of history the ethico-political moment of cultural expansion?'[52] Gramsci maintained that Croce was unable to account for the interplay between theory and practice which lay behind such momentous changes, whereby the viability of a whole society and hence of a whole way of thinking became called into question. The primacy of theory within his argument meant that its situation within a given set of social relations went unexplored. Indeed, Croce regarded such explorations by Marxist historians of philosophy as irrelevant to the ideas of the great philosophers under examination and essentially unphilosophical. The validity of a philosophy's truth claims belonged to the realm of theory alone, and therefore could only be tested out against other philosophies. From this view flowed Croce's account of the development of the different branches of philosophy, appended to each of the volumes of the *Philosophy of Spirit*, in terms of a chain of systems, whereby the incoherences of each preceeding philosophy generated the solutions of its successor.[53] Even his narrative histories presented a series of disembodied figures whose thought remained abstracted from the concrete situations and engagements which prompted it.[54] In sum, Croce's histories did not live up to his historicist ambition of relating ideas and their development to the requirements of thought within particular historical conditions. Instead, he continued to portray them as emanations of some meta-idea – spirit.

Croce's mistake arose from ignoring the interplay of theory and action within history. For: 'if it is necessary, in the perennial flux of events, to establish concepts, without which reality could not be understood, it is necessary also . . . to establish and remember that reality in movement and the concept of reality, whilst they can be logically distinct, must be conceived historically as an inseparable unity.' Failure to appreciate this necessity had resulted in Croce's histories degenerating into a purely formal history of concepts and of the supposedly Olympian intellectuals who had devised them.[55] But in presenting his parade of theorists, Croce could offer no real explanation of why ideas change other than the internal dynamics of thought. But this was a thoroughly vacuous notion. For 'ideas are not born of other ideas, . . . philosophies have not come forth out of other philosophies, . . . they are the ever renewed expression of real historical development.'[56] Croce's formulation of history as the story of liberty, for instance, could not be understood as an unfolding of some abstract concept of freedom. No such entity existed. Any definition needed to be related both to specific practices and particular traditions of thought and to the way the one informed the other. We explained the shift from a negative to a positive conception of freedom within Europe at the end of the nineteenth century, for example, through the evolving interrelationship between these two aspects – to the manner in which practice and theory played off each other, not as a logically entailed extension of idea of freedom itself.[57] Croce only surmounted the problem of change by either passing over periods of transition altogether, or by attributing them to the evolution of spirit.

In Gramsci's opinion, Croce's conception of spirit formed the counterpart to Bukharin's notion of matter and gave rise to a correspondingly idealist variety of determinism and sociology.[58] Like Bukharin's philosophy, Croce's also encouraged a conservative politics. At best, his intellectual aloofness condemned him to practical impotence. At worst, he ended up offering legitimation of the powers that be. For if theory ceased to engage actively with the world it became either irrelevant or slavishly uncritical. Instead of being a militant founder of a new secular religion which formed the world view of the masses, as Gramsci thought he desired, Croce became at different times either a latter-day Erasmus,[59] equivalent in Gramsci's view to being an academic in the worst sort of ivory-tower sense of the term – a posture he associated with the Renaissance – or a 'sort of lay Pope',[60] the unofficial ideologue of the establishment – a role assumed officially by Gentile under Fascism. Thus, Croce may have regarded his histories of Europe and Italy as providing a philosophy, but in reality he had offered an ideology, that of the liberal bourgeoisie and its period of dominance.[61]

Croce's difficulties arose from his unwillingness explicitly to acknowledge the political function of philosophy.[62] However, in advocating the identity of philosophy and politics, Gramsci was not suggesting that philosophy ought to serve pre-set political ends. Rather, he was pointing out that the status of philosophy, as the discipline with the role of validating the truth claims of rival theories, could not be divorced from its place within a broader social division of labour. As we saw with Croce, to separate the two was to render philosophy either pointless or ideological in the pejoritive sense. Philosophy only escaped this dilemma when it was conceived as part and parcel of the society whose practices it sought to understand. When philosophy was so understood, epistemological questions necessarily raised social questions and vice versa. Or as Gramsci put it, paraphrasing the poet Carducci, Robespierre and Kant, politics and philosophy were synthesised in a dialectical unity.[63] It was this conception of philosophy as intrinsic to and involving the immanent critique of social practice, which distinguished Gramsci's historicism from Croce's.[64]

Gramsci's distance from Croce was evident. To have shown this, however, does not automatically clear him from the accusation of voluntarism. Not only was Croce's idealism not subjectivist in nature, but the grounds on which Gramsci criticised the Neapolitan bore a certain resemblance to the arguments of Gentile, whose actualism could be much more plausibly labelled as 'voluntarist'. A number of commentators have argued from these parallels that Gramsci can be seen as a sort of Gentilian of the Left – a thesis given some support by the fact that certain of the Sicilian philosopher's disciples, such as Ugo Spirito, claimed an affinity with orthodox Marxism.[65] We remarked in Chapter 1 that the idealist elements of Gramsci's pre-prison writings arguably owed more to Gentile than to Croce. As we saw, Gentile drew on Marx, and the *Theses on Feuerbach* in particular, to stress the unity of thought and action within the process of the 'pure act of thought', whereby the conscious ego constitutes itself and its ethical ends. Consequently Gentile, like Gramsci, believed the Crocean distinctions to be the source of his errors, and affirmed that 'every political conception worthy of the name is a philosophy'. Gramsci devoted relatively little attention to Gentile's ideas in the *Prison Notebooks*, but what he did say was almost wholly negative. Of course, given Gentile's close association with Fascism, there were obvious reasons why Gramsci might have taken this stance. However, he was not usually averse to engaging with authors of opposed views and even learning from them – indeed, he advocated such openness in order to liberate oneself 'from the prison of ideologies (in the worst sense, of blind ideological fanaticism)'.[66] There seems little reason for not taking his antipathy to Gentile's actualism at face value, therefore. Although there are various points of comparison to be made concerning the formal structure of their thought, most notably a shared organicism and holism which we shall examine in Chapter 6,[67] Gramsci regarded Gentile's idealism as infinitely more 'speculative' and academic than Croce's.[68] He argued that Gentile had simply identified theory and practice, will and action, to turn philosophy explicitly into a mere ideology of the State.[69] Gentile's famous identification of force and morality reached its apogee in his defence of the Fascist State as 'a completely spiritual creation'.[70] For Gramsci, in contrast, the unity of theory and practice had to be dialectical – allowing mutual criticism – rather than the simple identification of the one with the other. He looked on Gentile's political philosophy as little more than a 'sophisticated disguise' for 'opportunism and empiricism' – the justification of whatever exists as right.[71] Croce's distinction represented an advance on Gentile's position, therefore, since he at least attempted to achieve a modicum of critical distance, albeit of a typically liberal kind based on a falacious notion of detachment and neutrality.[72] In this area at least, Gentile's influence largely consisted in offering Gramsci a salutory warning of the difficulties attending certain forms of thinking, and hence a critical stimulus to avoid these problems when employing superficially similar lines of thought in the elaboration of his own doctrine.

The philosophy of praxis

Gramsci's criticisms of Bukharin's mechanistic Marxism and Crocean and Gentilean idealism were even handed. In different ways, Bukharin, Croce and Gentile were all guilty of reification. He wished to avoid both the determinism of a particular kind of materialism and the subjectivism and transcendentalism of a pure idealism. He sought to achieve this result by synthesising materialist and idealist philosophies in a way which avoided the various dichotomies that had built up within Croce's historicism. He claimed that Marxism, properly understood, accomplished this synthesis when conceived as a 'philosophy of praxis'. Gramsci used this term in order to get around the prison censor. However, it was more than a convenient prison code word, since it accurately reflected his whole approach to Marxist theory. Significantly, Antonio Labriola, whose influence we noted above, also employed this term in preference to historical materialism to denote Marxist philosophy.[73]

The two key texts for Gramsci's view of Marx were the *Theses on Feuerbach* and the 1859 'Preface' to *A Contribution to the Critique of Political Economy*, both of which he translated into Italian whilst in prison and to which he referred throughout the *Notebooks*.[74] These writings need to be always kept in mind when reconstructing Gramsci's ideas. Perhaps the most succinct expression of Gramsci's conception of praxis can be found in the eighth thesis on Feuerbach, namely: 'That social life is essentially practical. All the mysteries, that divert theory towards mysticism, find their rational resolution in human praxis, and in the concept of this praxis.'[75] The centrality of praxis within the production and transformation of social life involved a concomitant emphasis on labour, whereby nature was progressively organised through the mediation of social relations. This conception depended in turn on a view of human nature as neither instinctually determined, like that of other animals, nor unchanging or individualist in character. Rather, the humanity of each individual consisted of a 'series of active relationships' with other people and the natural world, whereby we make ourselves. We may have begun with certain basic material needs for food and shelter etc., but we had the ability in co-operation with others to meet them through labouring on the material world. In the process, we developed both new wants and new methods of meeting them. Human nature was thus historical rather than given, evolving out of the continuous dialectical creation and satisfaction of needs.[76]

A corollary of this historicist conception of humanity was to bring together the materialist insight – of the independent reality of things from thought – with the idealist insight – of thought as an activity through which we know that reality – within a general view stressing the social practices and relations through which we assimilated our environment. Whilst Gramsci held this view to be present within the *Theses on Feuerbach*,[77] he believed 'the most important and authentic source for a reconstruction of the philosophy of praxis' was the 'Preface'.[78] He paraphrased the salient passages as follows:

1. Mankind only poses for itself such tasks as it can resolve; . . . the task itself only arises where the material conditions for its resolution already exist or at least are in the process of formation.
2. A social formation does not perish before all the productive forces for which it is still sufficient have been developed and new, higher relations of production, do not take their place, before the material conditions for their existence have been developed in the womb of the old society . . .[79]

These two points, frequently alluded to in the *Notebooks*, should be read together with the thesis, also drawn from the 'Preface' – 'that men become conscious (of the conflict between the old and the new material forces of production) on the ideological level of juridical, political, religious, artistic and philosophical forms' and Engels' statement that the economic base is only determinant in the 'last analysis'.[80] These quotations contain the core of Gramsci's social philosophy. They show the essentially Marxist origins of his thought – the emphasis on material conditions as the underlying reality of social formations. However, the base did not mechanically determine the superstructure – it provided the 'real' conditions which a 'rational' theory would correctly capture. Thus, Gramsci's conception of praxis contained three separate components which not all commentators have kept distinct, namely: the 'material conditions' presupposed by all action; the 'social formation' corresponding to the relations through which the forces of production were organised; and the 'ideologies' which sustained and allowed the possibility for challenging those relations. Gramsci regarded social structures as dependent upon, but not reducible to, human consciousness. Social formations had both a material and a conceptual dimension. The unity of theory and practice resulted from the manner in which theory was simultaneously practically conditioned by and a practical force in society.[81] All three elements formed distinct but related parts of a totality. These distinctions allowed for the existence of false consciousness and its criticism – both vital aspects of Gramsci's Marxism.[82]

Implicit within this formulation of Marxism was the rejection of any attempt to explain causally historical change through either autonomous alterations in ideas (the error of idealism) or in the material base (the error of materialism and economism). With regard to the latter, it is worth noting that Gramsci was as antagonistic to technological determinism as he was of the more traditional kinds of materialist determinism examined above.[83] A view he associated with Achille Loria, Gramsci not only disputed Loria's reduction of the 'material forces of production' to technology as too narrow, but he specifically denied that economic development could be explained via the 'metamorphosis of the technical instrument'.[84] Economic techniques did not exist in a vacuum, but formed a part of a complex of human relations through which we engaged with nature. As such, they incorporated amongst other things "mental" instruments, philosophical knowledge'.[85] Once again, he insisted that structure and superstructure were indissolubly intertwined, with technology incorporating aspects of both.[86] Fordism, for example, was largely a superstructural phenomenon, which revealed how technological innovations might serve as reinforcements of regressive social relations, rather than forming the motor of progressive change.[87]

What did he mean, then, when he insisted on the primacy of the material forces of production?[88] If the 'material conditions' did not exist apart from human will and cognition, then how could they determine the superstructure? At one level, Gramsci simply denied that they did since, as we noted, he disputed the existence of any causal relationship between the two. But, at another level, he clearly wanted to maintain that, in a weaker sense of the term, material conditions did determine what forms of consciousness were possible. He even contended that these preconditions for action could be described in a 'quantifiable' way and with a 'mathematical' accuracy.[89] Gramsci got over the apparent contradictions of his position by pointing out that most individuals were born into given social structures and fulfilled the duties of their station within them in an unconscious manner. Whilst human agency remained vital to the continuing reproduction of these structures, once they existed they constituted *vis à vis* any given individual objects of constraint and facilitation, operating with certain tendencies. As he put it, 'every social aggregate is something more than (and different from) its component parts'.[90] Human consciousness could form a vital part of the material forces of production, therefore, without undermining their status as the vital processes determining in the weak sense each individual's possibility for action. For our ability to act in an autonomous manner rested on our power to produce a human environment. In the first instance, this required control over nature, which reflected the level of development of productive forces and hence our capacity to exploit existing natural resources. However, this fact did not negate the importance in the second instance of our being able consciously to control those forces. For 'the existence of objective conditions is not yet sufficient: it is necessary to "know" them and know how to use them. And to want to use them.'[91] Numerous superstructural influences intervened to shape our capacity and desire to employ such forces.

Prioritising the base did not entail any negation of Gramsci's insistence on the interplay of structure and superstructure, therefore. Consciousness can play a part both in the development and the exploitation of the productive forces without denying their primacy. In certain circumstances, the base – superstructure model could even be inverted. For example, in Italy during the *Risorgimento*, a contingently favourable international situation gave the progressive class of entrepreneurial landowners in the North their opportunity to unite the country and, by borrowing ideas and institutions from more advanced countries, artificially to promote economic and social development from above. In this instance: 'the problem was not so much one of liberating the already developed productive forces from the fetters of an antiquated legal and political system, as of creating the general conditions so that these economic forces could be born and develop on the model of other countries.'[92] At other times, as in liberal Italy, an entrenched system of superstructural institutions and customs could prop up outmoded relations of production. However, in most cases the superstructure asserted a number of contradictory influences, a point he stressed by consistently referring to a plurality of superstructures. Some worked towards the maintenance of the existing relations of production, others to their supercession. Gramsci claimed that to make new history we had to think through and overcome, in the Hegelian sense of *Aufgehoben*, these contradictions by uncovering those social relations which were sources of oppression, alienation and domination and identifying the changes necessary to realise the maximum emancipatory potential of the material base. Gramsci argued that we achieved this knowledge through history, in other words by studying and becoming conscious of the level of development of the productive processes within a society and understanding the rationale of the prevailing power structures. The premise for social change was of a dual nature, involving both the necessary material conditions, and a degree of awareness of the possibilities they created and a desire to exploit them.[93] The task of politics was to organise the latter.

Underlying this argument was a link between knowledge of the objective forces influencing our lives and human emancipation. Gramsci maintained that what he called the 'cathartic moment', when 'the structure from being an external force which crushes man, assimilates him to itself, renders him passive, transforms itself into a means of liberty, an instrument to create a new ethico-political form, a source of new initiatives',[94] involved a passage from 'objective' to 'subjective'. This thesis, together with a number of notes on the 'so-called "reality" of the external world', have provided further fuel for the idealist and voluntarist interpretation of Gramsci. He argued that objective 'always means "humanly objective", that which can correspond exactly to "historically" subjective, that is objective would mean "universally subjective"'. By this and other similar statements, Gramsci invoked neither a correspondence[95] nor a consensus theory of truth,[96] as has been maintained. His epistemology would be better termed pragmatic – the product of the interrelationship between theory and practice remarked on above.

According to Gramsci's pragmatic view of Marxism, the 'philosophy of praxis' differed from both idealism and 'mechanical materialism' in being predicated upon a theory of rationality which assumed that people could not only share the same empirical judgements in given situations, but act upon them as well. Rationality was not just a matter of the coherence of the beliefs concerned, nor of agreement about their validity, but of their practical efficacy.[97] They gave us a common orientation in the world, 'indissolubly linked to a certain organised (historicised) "matter"'.[98] Gramsci illustrated his argument with an interesting gloss on a famous example of Bertrand Russell's. Russell had argued that whilst London and Edinburgh would be unthinkable without human beings, one could think of two points – one to the North and another to the South – corresponding to the location of these cities in such circumstances. Gramsci remarked that knowledge of any kind – even of North and South – involved the existence of the knower, human beings. For:

it is evident that (they) are arbitrary, conventional, that is historical, constructions . . . And yet these references are real, they correspond to real facts, they permit us to travel by land and by sea and to arrive exactly where one has decided to arrive, to "foresee" the future, to objectivise reality, to understand the objectivity of the external world. Rational and real identify with each other.[99]

The objectivity of the world was in a sense a non-question for Gramsci, since truth only emerged through practice. However,he fact that knowledge was a human construct did not mean that we only knew knowledge. Rather, knowledge developed as a historical process through our practical grasp of the material world. As a result, Gramsci could still talk of our 'relative ignorance' of reality, for example.[100] Extrapolating from the *Theses on Feuerbach* a Marxist reading of the eighteenth-century Italian philosopher Giambattista Vico's dictum that we can only know what we have made,[101] Gramsci maintained that through the making of human history, theory and practice mutually and progressively informed each other. The current conflicts and incommensurabilities between different systems of belief had a 'practical origin' in the 'internal contradictions which tear apart human society'. They reflected the self-interested views of different social groups. The struggle for objectivity was *ipso facto* part and parcel of the class struggle. 'To free oneself from partial and fallacious ideologies' went hand-in-hand with the transformation of the conditions which rendered them possible so as to arrive at 'the cultural unification of the human race'. Thus, 'what the idealists call "spirit" is not a point of departure but of arrival, it is the ensemble of superstructures moving towards concrete and objectively universal unification, and is not a unitary presupposition.'[102] The passage from objectivity to subjectivity, therefore, occurred when human beings were capable of collectively taking control of the forces of production in a self-conscious and autonomous way. In Gramsci's opinion, this only proved possible once the universal system of production created by capitalism was organised by the universal class, the proletariat, under Communism.[103] The philosophy of praxis fostered this outcome by explaining the contradictions within people's current experience and making them aware of the existence of the conditions necessary to overcome them.[104] It offered a 'total' explanation, capable of moulding a collective will out of a number of diverse aims.[105] Summarising his argument in a famous passage, he wrote:

The structure and the superstructures form an 'historical bloc', that is to say the ensemble of complex, contradictory and discordant superstructures are the reflection of the ensemble of the social relations of production. From this it follows: that only a totalitarian ideology rationally reflects the contradictions of the superstructure and represents the existence of the objective conditions for the revolutionising of praxis. If a social group forms itself which is 100 per cent homogeneous on the level of ideology, that means that the premises for this revolutionising exist 100 per cent, that is that the 'rational' is actively and actually real. This reasoning is based on the necessary reciprocity between structure and superstructure (reciprocity which is nothing other than the real dialectical process).[106]

To recapitulate, Gramsci's argument was not that the economic base determined the superstructure, rather that it placed a constraint on what forms of consciousness were possible. Some ideologies were more restrictive than others, and did not allow individuals to become all they could be. The 'philosophy of praxis' was superior because it gave the masses 'the concrete means' to realise themselves:

1. by giving a determinate and concrete ('rational') direction to their own vital impulse or will; 2. by identifying the means which will make this will concrete and specific and not arbitrary; 3. by contributing to modify the ensemble of the concrete conditions for realising this will to the extent of one's own limits and capacities and in the most fruitful form.[107]

It created a new 'historical bloc' of structural and superstructural elements whereby individuals could achieve their potential through the conscious transformation of their relations with each other and nature. It presupposed that discontent with the present already existed, even if only exiguously, and that it had a 'real' basis in the 'material pre-conditions' for social change.[108]

A successful synthesis?

So far we have been concerned to reconstruct Gramsci's position as accurately as possible, saving him from a variety of misinterpretations – notably, the idealist and voluntarist views of his thought. Turning to the assessment of his theory, certain difficulties need to be addressed associated with Gramsci's historicism. These centre on his attempt to synthesise the idealist and materialist aspects of Marxism, represented respectively by the *Theses on Feuerbach* and the 1857 'Preface', through his reworking of Croce and Bukarin. We shall show that whilst the first needed the second within Gramsci's Marxian pragmatism, a tension between the openness of the first and the determinism of the second remained which could not be satisfactorily resolved.

The most obvious doubts concern his pragmatist insistence that the worth of a doctrine arose from its practicality. For a start, this thesis risked equating truth with success. He credited Lenin, for instance, with having 'advanced philosophy as philosophy in so far as he advanced political doctrine and practice'.[109] The danger with this thesis, as the Lenin example reveals, is that it is possible to achieve and impose on others the most unsavoury beliefs and practices. For this reason, both before and after the events of 1989 many Marxists wished to take the very opposite line to Gramsci in this case, and have argued that the Russian Revolution and its aftermath set back Marxist theorising for generations.[110] Of course, this argument is more than a little affected, since it is doubtful that without Lenin's success Marxism would have been taken as seriously as it has been. The essential point that truth and success do not necessarily coincide nonetheless stands.

In Gramsci's defence, it must be remembered that he offered two qualifications to his definition of the practical efficacy of a doctrine which were intended to provide more substantive criteria of truth. First, he equated efficacy with maximising the human possibilities opened up by the available forces of production. An ideology proved its validity to the extent that it led to the maximum freedom for individuals by enhancing our capacity 'to transform the external world' and hence each person's ability 'to potentiate oneself or develop oneself'.[111] To a certain extent, this was capable of quantative measurement, 'since one can measure the degree to which man dominates nature and chance'.[112] However, Gramsci offered a second check of an ideology's truth in this regard stemming from the degree of support it achieved. He contended:

Mass adhesion or non-adhesion to an ideology is the real critical test of the rationality and historicity of modes of thinking. Any arbitrary constructions are pretty rapidly eliminated by historical competition, even if sometimes, through a combination of immediately favourable circumstances, they succeed in enjoying a certain popularity, whilst constructions which correspond to the demands of a complex and organic period of history always end up by imposing themselves and prevail even if their affirmation only occurs in more or less bizarre and heterogeneous combinations.[113]

As we shall see in examining Gramsci's conception of hegemony, he was fully aware of the subtle and not so subtle ways in which liberal and authoritarian regimes can inculcate a distorted view of the world. Nevertheless, he denied that a situation could ever arise where a false ideology could combine with a set of extremely repressive social institutions in such a way that all critical discussion was prevented. He believed that a state of repression always generated criteria for its own criticism, albeit in 'embryonic form', in the agents' sense of frustration and suffering. This experience might well go unarticulated for some time, but it gave rise to a contrast between thought and action which was 'the expression of profounder contrasts of a socio-historic order'. It meant that a social group 'manifests in its acts' a different conception of the world from that which, for reasons of 'intellectual subordination', it articulated in words. The task of the social theorist was to make the implicit explicit through a process of immanent critique which enabled the masses to build on this dissatisfaction.[114]

Both the above criteria of truth formed part of Gramsci's more general historicist doctrine. Gramsci rejected any notion of eternal or transcendental standards, be they God or an objective reality beyond human volition, to determine the nature of truth. Marxism had no need for a metaphysical grounding of this nature, since the 'philosophy of praxis is self-sufficient and contains in itself all the fundamental elements to construct a total and integral conception of the world'.[115] The criteria for judging a theory were fashioned along with the theory itself through its dialectical union with practice in the making of history. In other words, a theory proved its truth through its ability to give voice to and critically extend the human needs and aspirations of a particular time and place and so to prevail historically. 'In Crocean terms: when one succeeds in introducing a new morality in conformity with a new conception of the world, one finishes by introducing the conception as well, in other words, one determines a reform of the whole of philosophy.'[116] From this perspective, even the validity of Marxism was one of degree. It offered the best guide to emancipation available to agents at the current time in much the same way that liberalism had done in the past, and so would alter or disappear along with the conditions which made it possible and which it in turn transformed.[117] However, Gramsci's historicism did not issue in a total relativism, although he acknowledged that avoiding this conclusion might prove 'a somewhat arduous and difficult operation'.[118] Since the present is child of the past, he maintained that at the level of both theory and practice, a doctrine only proved itself as capable of making new history if it managed to unravel and supersede the lacunae and contradictions of all previous practices and the theories which had supported them. It achieved this result through a process of immanent critique issuing in the most comprehensive and coherent doctrine available. Marxism's superiority rested on having managed just such an all-encompassing total point of view. Gramsci's historicism allowed for the possibility for engaging with and criticising the philosophical systems of other periods, therefore, whilst acknowledging that they had a relative validity at the time.[119]

Three main difficulties arise with this argument, however. First, its linking of the real and the rational within history relied on a largely unacknowledged progressive teleology, akin to Croce's religious faith in a providential spirit, whereby the present is necessarily superior to the past. Michael Rosen has shown how the internal logic of immanent critique is vulnerable to what he calls the '*post festum* paradox', namely the paradox of only being able to evaluate the results of immanent critique by depending upon these same results' validity.[120] The sole escape from the circularity of this argument is to assume history to involve the progressive unfolding of truth. In Gramsci, this teleology rested in turn on a belief in the related Marxian theses concerning the progressive unfolding of different modes of production, the eventual crisis of capitalism and the status of the proletariat as the universal class embodying human emancipation. Gramsci may not have interpreted these orthodox Marxist tenets in a mechanical manner, but their presence as tendencies continued to ground his doctrine.

His reliance on this teleology explains why he was never troubled by the second main potential difficulty with his theory – its conflation of cognitive and ethical rationality and of instrumental and substantive reason. Gramsci assumed differences over values and goals ultimately reflected an inadequate grasp of our historical situation or of the best means for exploiting it to the full. He had no sense of what Weber called 'the ethical irrationality of the world'.[121] The fact that good does not always follow from good or evil from evil (the road to hell being paved with good intentions); that irrational or at least non-rational forces frequently lie behind much that is worthwhile in human life and art (as when, to the bafflement of amateur eugenicists, beauty loves the beast); and that tragic and painful choices between incommensurable goods form part of most people's everyday experience and most of the major decisions of government.

These lacunae in Gramsci's thought were related in turn to the third main difficulty in Gramsci's position – his advocacy of a 'total' view point. Gramsci's essentially holistic outlook worked against any recognition of the complexity and pluralism of human existence, and the resulting opaque and conflictual as opposed to transparent and harmonious character of much social life. Even when rational cognitive agreement is possible about the state of the world, rational ethical agreement on what purposes should be pursued need not follow. Gramsci, for example, assumed that enhanced productiveness would always prove emancipating. Yet efficiency and productivity can and frequently do inhibit and destroy other goods making for a worthwhile life. Gramsci believed the question of the uses to which the enhanced forces of production might be put would be answered in the process of evolving the theory and practice of their enhancement. The virtue of a theory of praxis lay in putting these two elements together – in unifying cognitive and ethical, instrumental and substantive issues. He had an almost Millean belief in the value of discussion and argument, particularly between the party leaders and led, in achieving this consensus.[122] He thereby avoided the authoritarianism implicit in a pseudo-scientific belief in knowing the laws of history implicit in Marxist-Leninism. However, striving for a 'totalitarian' perspective, no matter how openly, always tends towards closure and a dull, imposed conformity.

Gramsci took from Croce many of the most attractive elements of his theory. His appreciation of the relative autonomy of ideas and the way values and will shape human action all stem from this source, as does his antipathy to vulgar forms of 'economism'. As we shall see, these features are reflected in the emphasis in his politics on the mobilisation and organisation of consent, both in upholding existing States and in their revolutionary overthrow and the creation of a new order. But he was equally insistent that, to be valid and operative, our ideas and ideals had to relate to the sphere of production and the satisfaction of our material wants. In certain respects this represented a laudable desire for ideas to engage with empirical reality. His pragmatic synthesis of these two elements, in spite of its coherence, has certain drawbacks, however. For it risked degenerating into an instrumentalist justification of social engineering to produce a totally organised world in which the true and the productive were one and the same. These are the features of Gramsci's thought that have attracted criticism as giving rise to an authoritarian or totalitarian politics in the usual, pejoritive sense of these terms. Both these strengths and weaknesses are evident in his conception of hegemony, examined in the next chapter.

5

The *Prison Notebooks* II: hegemony, State and Party

Gramsci's emphasis on the role of will and consciousness within any defensible materialist account of history was intrinsically connected with what most commentators regard as his most important contribution to Marxist theory – his concept of hegemony. Gramsci employed this term in two related ways within the *Prison Notebooks*. Hegemony in the first sense denoted the consensual and ideological, as opposed to coercive, basis of a political system. This attention to the role of ideology and consensus as elements of political domination and social cohesion led in turn to a concentration on the importance of organising class consciousness when seeking to transform and overthrow the State. Hegemony in the second sense referred to the concomitant cultural and educative task of the Party and ultimately the revolutionary State in the formation of a coherent moral awareness and political will amongst the proletariat. This chapter will examine each of these meanings of hegemony in turn.

Once again, Gramsci's stress on the subjective, intellectual and voluntaristic elements of human agency has been variously credited with either creatively revising and adding to Marxism, or of corrupting it with idealist motifs. However, as we noted in the last chapter, Gramsci's argument was underpinned by an insistence on the primacy of the development of the forces of production in determining social and political change typical of, if more sophisticated than, the orthodox Marxism of his time. In his political as in his methodological writings, he attempted to marry historical materialism and Crocean historicism. Once again, we shall contend that this proved a difficult relationship to sustain and that the second was ultimately subordinated to the first with unfortunate results.

'State' and 'civil society'

As Norberto Bobbio pointed out in an important article,[1] Gramsci's analysis of the political system in terms of the balance between force and consent both arose out of and produced a significant reworking of Marx's assimilation of Hegel's conceptions of civil society and State to the Marxian distinction between base and superstructure. Indeed, Bobbio went so far as to credit Gramsci with being more Hegelian than Marxist. The starting-point for any discussion of Gramsci's conception of hegemony in its first sense, therefore, must be a brief examination of the relationships between these three pairings of force/consent, State/civil society and base/superstructure in Hegel and Marx.

Hegel and Marx[2]

Bobbio has observed that the view of politics found in the natural law tradition of Hobbes, Locke, Rousseau and Kant turned upon a crucial distinction they made, albeit in divergent ways, between natural and civil society, the latter including (or being coextensive with) political society. Hegel broke with this line of reasoning by downgrading civil society to the status of a pre-political society distinct from the State. In performing this operation, Hegel continued and united two trends within modern political thought. The first, deriving from realist theories of politics such as Hobbes's and Machiavelli's, conceived the State as a product of rational calculation by self-interested individuals. The second, represented by Rousseau and Kant, saw the State as, in Bobbio's words, 'a product of reason, or as a rational society, the only one in which human beings can lead a life which conforms to reason, that is which conforms to their nature'.[3] Hegel's *Philosophy of Right* produced a synthesis and transformation (*Aufhebung*) of these two processes, whereby the State was perceived as both the result of instrumental reason and as the construction of a rational society.[4]

Hegel distinguished between the natural society of the family, civil society and the political society of the State. In the first, people were united by the particularistic attachments, inclinations and passions with and into which they were born. In the second, we began to fashion these impulses and desires according to our individual will and engaged in commerce and exchange for their satisfaction. Through the manufacture of goods, the division of labour and the exchange of commodities we left the natural state and became civilised. This 'system of needs', as Hegel called it, produced the compacts, agreements and organisations of the pre-State – for example, private property rights and the law of contract, occupational groupings and the administration of justice and welfare – what Hegel, following eighteenth-century usage, termed 'police'. However, in contrast to the realist tradition, Hegel regarded these instrumental settlements as essentially unstable, emerging from the partial perspective of individual interests and hence liable to dissolve when they were not satisfied. Although their inner rationale, as ethical norms providing the framework for a fully developed life, was partly perceived within the associational life of the corporations, it was only consciously grasped in the political institutions of the State – the legislature, government and monarchy. Only at this level could the common good be fully acknowledged and a rational society, in the second sense of Kant and Rousseau, be achieved.

Marx's conception of politics built upon a critique of Hegel's and both extended and simplified it. Commenting on his early critical re-examination of Hegelian philosophy, Marx recalled how it led him to the view:

> that neither legal relations nor political forms could be comprehended whether by themselves or on the basis of a so-called general development of the human mind, but that on the contrary they originate in the material conditions of life, the totality of which Hegel . . . embraces within the term 'civil society'; that the anatomy of this civil society, however, has to be sought in political economy . . . The general conclusion at which I arrived . . . can be summarised as follows. In the social production of their existence, men inevitably enter into definite relations, which are independent of their will, namely relations of production appropriate to a given stage in the development of their material forces of production. The totality of these relations of production constitutes the economic structure of society, the real foundation on which arises a legal and political superstructure and to which correspond definite forms of social consciousness.[5]

Marx followed Hegel in placing the economic system of needs within civil society. However, he characterised it in terms of the Hobbesian natural society of mutually warring individuals. He associated this state of war with the capitalist phase of the economy, which perverted the collaborative nature of production into a nexus of asocial relationships between the buyers and sellers of labour and commodities. Moreover, he removed law and administration from the civil sphere to the superstructure, along with political institutions, ideology and social consciousness. His view of civil society was consequently much narrower than Hegel's. Finally, he denied Hegel's claim that the State genuinely overcame the tensions of civil society by providing people with a fuller understanding of the social relations governing their lives and reconciling them to abiding by the norms and customs necessary to achieve the common good.

Marx argued that the State had been abstracted from civil society, this process of abstraction mirroring and facilitating the manner in which under capitalism human labour was stripped of its specific qualities and rendered 'abstract'.[6] Capitalism involved the free exchange of commodities produced by free contractual labour, both elements entailing abstracting labour power from the concrete social context of production. The State–civil society divide was intimately involved with this development, since the granting of universal equal rights regardless of any determinate social status provided a legal precondition for individuals selling their labour and exchanging goods. Their proprietorship over these objects became in this way a matter of pre-social 'natural' right.[7] These rights were equally abstractions. In part, this was because the exercise of these liberties remained constrained by the continuing differentials of wealth and position in society. The apparent fraternity of our political existence was illusory, being totally subordinated to the relationships of civil society. Marx's principal point, however, was that they were only necessary within a capitalist system of private property requiring the legal emancipation of the worker as a 'free' seller of labour. Hence Marx's debunking of the 'so-called *rights of man*' as universally valid principles applying to humanity as such, and his contention that they were rather 'the rights of the *member of civil society*, i.e. of egoistic man, of man separated from the community'.[8] For Marx, rights were merely the legal counterparts of a society of 'abstract' individuals alienated from their labour within an exploitative system which had abstracted from the essentially collective circumstances of production.

Marx regarded the Hegelian conception of the State, as the rational culmination of the ethical life implicit within the family and civil society, as a confidence trick – a regressive and anachronistic attempt to return to the organic harmony between State and society characteristic of feudalism. The Hegelian State did not reconcile the conflicts of civil society; it legitimised them. It achieved this by giving the coercive character of capitalism, whereby workers were exploited and alienated from their labour, the semblance of a consensual relationship between legally free and equal individuals. As a result, the instrumental and individualistic relations of civil society acquired the form of universal and rational relations, so that the class interests of the bourgeoisie were generalised so as to appear those of humanity.

Marx contended that the function of the State mirrored that of religion, its heaven of free and equal citizens offering a transcendent consolation and justification for the oppressions experienced by individuals within society.[9] The critique of the State similarly paralleled that of religion. Just as 'the abolition of religion as the *illusory* happiness of the people is the demand for their *real* happiness', so that 'to call on them to give up their illusions about their condition is to *call on them to give up a condition that requires illusions*'. So the abolition of the illusions represented by the State called for the transformation of society in order to remove those conditions which made them necessary.[10] Such change came from the formation of a revolutionary consciousness amongst the proletariat stemming from their growing awareness that their emancipation entailed the overthrowing of capitalism. As a truly universal class, the proletariat had no vested interests to defend, and hence had nothing to gain from the protection afforded by the bourgeois legal system. Their oppression stemmed from the very logic of capitalist production and could only be ended when the development of productive forces made possible the creation of an authentic communal existence which had no need for the bourgeois State and its false heaven.[11] As capitalist relations of production based on private property gave way to a community of self-regulating producers, so the State gradually withered away as its functions were absorbed into society.[12]

We have already noted in Chapter 1 how Marx's analysis of the Paris Commune as an example of this reabsorption of the State into civil society influenced Gramsci's early writings. We shall discuss its continued hold on his imagination in the *Prison Notebooks* at the end of the next chapter. For the present, we shall simply make two general remarks concerning Marx's account of the State–civil society relationship which are particularly pertinent to Gramsci's own analysis. First, many commentators have argued that Marx, unlike Gramsci, failed to examine the role of consent in the maintenance of capitalism, regarding the State as merely a coercive instrument of the ruling economic class. Now it is undoubtedly true that quotations abound in which Marx talked of the State as but 'the organised power of one class for oppressing another'.[13] However, it is clear from Marx's remarks about the quasi-theological character of the State that he regarded the illusion of consent as a vital aspect of this oppression. In his eyes, the achievement of the modern State had been to gain general acceptance for the social coercion of the capitalist economy, whereby workers must sell their labour power or starve. A corollary of this development was that the capitalist, unlike the feudal landowner, did not directly control the instruments of explicit political coercion. These too had been monopolised by the State and were similarly legitimised as upholding the interests of all citizens. Coercion and consent were therefore intimately connected in Marx's account of the State, reflecting their similar admixture within the capitalist economy.

Marx's linking of the State to the requirements of a class-divided society in this way has brought a second objection – namely, that he denied the autonomy of politics. Once again, many believe Gramsci supposedly went beyond him in this respect. However, in its crudest form at least, this criticism misses Marx's point that the autonomy of politics is precisely what the abstraction of the State from civil society achieved, with the result that political questions appeared totally divorced from social and economic questions. As a consequence, the view of politics as autonomous need not be opposed to the view of politics as an epiphenomenon of the economic base, as his critics assume, since for Marx the autonomy of politics derived from the nature of the capitalist economy. Moreover, as historical writings such as the *Eighteenth Brumaire* (another of Gramsci's favourite texts) revealed, the derivative character of the State involved no denial of its independent identity on Marx's part. On the contrary, the separation of the State from social control turned it into just such an independent force – a process that for Marx had reached an acute phase in the tyrannical rule of Louis Bonaparte. For this reason, revolutions were necessarily political since they involved the dissolution of the old order, even though he maintained that within the new socialist society there would be no such separate sphere.

To sum up: Marx regarded base and superstructure, State and civil society, force and consent as intimately related elements of the capitalist system and its most distinctive feature – the exploitation and alienation of human labour. As a consequence, human emancipation necessarily involved the overcoming of the dichotomies between State and civil society, politics and economics, public and private, general and particular interests within a democratic and non-exploitative form of society which no longer required such abstractions. For:

> Only when real, individual man resumes the abstract citizen into himself and as an individual man has become a *species-being* in his empirical life, his individual work and his individual relationships, only when man has recognised and organised his *forces propres* as *social forces* so that social force is no longer separated from him in the form of *political* force, only then will human emancipation be completed.[14]

In Chapter 2 we saw how during the *biennio rosso* Gramsci had interpreted this requirement in terms of a workers' democracy centred on the Factory Councils.[15] Imprisonment gave him the opportunity to deepen his examination of the limitations of that movement. Two new features concerned him in particular. First, the resilience of the capitalist State – examined below – and second, the resulting need for the political organisation of the proletariat within a Communist Party – the subject of the next section.

Gramsci

Gramsci's analysis of the State–civil society relationship followed on from his critique of economism and his insistence on the reciprocal influence between base and superstructure. As we noted, the motivation behind this rethinking was political, stemming from the failure of the revolutionary movements in the West after the First World War and the subsequent rise of Fascism. These events prompted him to consider the impact and nature of the political forces stabilising and sustaining the capitalist system. For the experience of the Factory Councils had convinced him that although the economic preconditions for a transition to communism existed, the social and political preconditions did not.

Gramsci linked the continued survival of capitalism and the problem of its revolutionary overthrow directly to his discussion of the interrelatedness of base and superstructure, examined in the last chapter. He divided the latter into two levels:

> the one that can be called 'civil society', that is the ensemble of organisms commonly called 'private', and that of 'political society' or 'the State'. These two levels correspond on the one hand to the function of 'hegemony', which the dominant group exercises throughout society, and on the other hand to

that of 'direct domination' or command, expressed through the State and 'juridical' government.[16]

The two functions were connected. The first set of institutions consisted of organisations such as schools, the media, churches, trade unions and political parties. They obtained 'the "spontaneous" consent given by the great masses of the population to the general direction imposed on social life by the dominant fundamental group, a consent that derives "historically" from the prestige (and consequent confidence) which the dominant group enjoys because of its position and function in the world of production.' The second set of institutions comprised 'the State coercive apparatus' – the forces of law and order, such as the judiciary, the police and the military. These organs ' "legally" assure the discipline of those groups which do not consent, either actively or passively'. Although the latter were always in readiness, they were only employed in times of crisis. Hegemony provided the normal form of ascendency of one or more groups or classes over others. Through this influence, exerted via a series of ideological mechanisms, the class antagonisms between rulers and ruled were overcome, with the result that the latter manifested a degree of conscious and willed attachment to the values and interests of the former.[17]

In later notes Gramsci insisted that this distinction was essentially 'methodological' rather than 'organic'.[18] All of the civil and consensual organisations he mentioned have coercive and political elements, just as the mechanisms he associated with the State contain social and consensual elements. For example, against the anarcho-syndicalists Gramsci pointed to the statist and political elements of trade unions. They may be voluntary but they discipline members, can operate closed-shop practices and have a role through government consultation in the formulation and, in corporatist regimes, even in the implementation, of State policies.[19] Similarly, he noted how it had been the achievement of modern representative parliamentary institutions to attain consent by transforming political parties into elements of the State apparatus.[20] Hence, Gramsci criticised the 'narrow' view of the 'night-watchman' State propounded by certain liberals as naive.[21] As he remarked, even a so-called free market involved direct and indirect forms of State regulation, and could not be regarded as simply a policy of leaving people to themselves as the doctrine of *laissez-faire* would have us believe.[22] Consequently, a full definition of the State involved both these elements. As Gramsci variously put it:

State = political society + civil society, that is hegemony armoured by coercion.[23]

State in the integral sense: dictatorship + hegemony.[24]

The State is the whole complex of practical and theoretical activities whereby the ruling class not only justifies and maintains its domination but succeeds in obtaining the active consent of the governed.[25]

(The State is) an equilibrium between political Society and civil Society.[26]

Those who complain about the 'oscillation' and 'conceptual slippage' of Gramsci's view of the State fail to pay sufficient attention to either the context or chronology of his argument.[27] When these are taken into account, it emerges that having made the original analytical distinction, Gramsci then proceeded to employ consistently the broader view.[28]

Gramsci made clear that the nature of the relationship between these two superstructural levels reflected in turn the character of their relationship with the base. Analytically, he portrayed this connection in terms of a tripartite schema between the economic structure on the one hand and the superstructures of civil and political society on the other. This formulation led him sometimes to talk in terms of civil society as the mediator between the State and the economy,[29] a point which has resulted in critics accusing him of inadequately exploring the social and political nature of economic relations.[30] This criticism needs qualifying. The *Ordine nuovo* writings made clear that he fully appreciated the extent to which 'at the basis of every serious problem of production, there lies the political problem, i.e. of social relations, of the organic functioning of society'.[31] However, the impact of social and political relations on the development of production, whilst relatively autonomous, did not shape the structure in Gramsci's view in the manner argued for by those Marxists who regard class struggle rather than the forces of production as the motor of history.[32] Rather, they merely served to accelerate, stabilise or inhibit the basic trajectory of economic and technical development. This position can be seen most obviously in his comments in the *Prison Notebooks* on 'Americanism and Fordism', where he remarked on the socio-political aspects of Taylor's management techniques. He observed how these had been so effective in indoctrinating the worker that in the United States 'hegemony is born in the factory' and hence required 'for its exercise only a minute quantity of professional political and ideological intermediaries'.[33] The absence of an old establishment class in North America and the relatively liberal and individualist nature of its economy and society had enabled entrepreneurs to restructure production without the direct intervention of the State – at least at first. Here, therefore, a change in the base had resulted in a direct alteration in the superstructure. However, he believed that the failure of the Factory Councils had revealed that in Europe matters were more complex. Although employers such as Agnelli at the Turin Fiat works had introduced Ford-style methods of production and management, which in the hands of the workers provided the basis for a new order, their reception was mediated by a whole series of other cultural and political forces arising out of Europe's richer past historical traditions, semi-feudal class structure and more developed State. Some of these influences weakened the worker's susceptibility to a purely factory culture, others – such as the existence of a parasitic *rentier* class – the capacity of industrialist entrepreneurs to impose it. Indeed, these factors severely constrained the ability not only of capitalists, but of the communists, to organise production along rational lines.[34] For Gramsci took for granted that Fordist methods were required to overcome the crisis tendencies of the capitalist pattern of accumulation. As such, they formed a part of the historical transformation of capitalism towards communism. Thus, changes in production provided the starting-point for Gramsci's analysis of the State. One of his chief aims in the *Prison Notebooks*, therefore, was to examine the broader West European context of the capitalist exercise of power in order to understand the ways the restructuring of production in response to the post-war economic crisis were both mediated by and altered the nature of the State and society.

Gramsci distinguished two broad phases in the development of the State, in the full sense of the term, corresponding to two broad types of 'historical bloc' or forms of integration between political society, civil society and economy. These were the 'economic-corporative' and the 'ethical' State. Gramsci argued that the character of the State reflected the quality of leadership exercised by the ruling class within the economy. In the 'economic-corporative' phase, the interests of the primary productive class were conceived in essentially narrow and purely 'economic', in the sense of material and self-interested,

terms. As a result, they failed to convince subordinate groups of the
identity of their interests with those of the dominant group. This
failure resulted in an imperfect and merely 'mechanical' social and
political unity, such as existed under feudalism, the Italian Renaissance communes and, in Gramsci's opinion as we shall see, even
contemporary Italy.[35] These regimes had little territorial or social
centralisation and consisted of a loose agglomeration of a variety of
social and ethnic groups with no common identity or purpose, and
even possessing institutions of their own. Such social and political
systems lacked flexibility, since little mobility or contact existed
between the different social groupings. What consent existed was
largely passive. They were held together more by external forces
'within the sphere of political-military compression', although
general inertia meant that this was 'exercised in acute forms only
occasionally' at times of crisis.[36]

Within the ethical phase of the State, in contrast, the prime social
group asserted its supremacy not just as 'domination', but through
'intellectual and moral leadership' as well.[37] It achieved this
ascendency by presenting and conceiving of the pursuit and development of its interests on a 'universal' rather than a 'corporate' plane.
This task involved opening itself up to the subordinate groups and
showing a willingness and capacity for incorporating them.[38] Addi-
tionally, some economic sacrifices and compromises might even be
required from the leading group, although never any that jeop-
ardised its pivotal position within the productive process.[39] Cultural
and educational institutions helped it reach this end, by disseminating the ethos of the dominant group amongst the masses.
This education was accomplished not simply through the 'positive'
work of the schools and the various associations of civil society, but
'negatively' through the law.[40] Adopting Hegelian language,
Gramsci described these as the 'private woof' and the 'public warp'
respectively of the ethical State.[41]

Gramsci associated this ethical phase of the State with the bourgeoisie. Their ability to transcend their narrowly economic-
corporative interests in these ways had dramatically transformed the
modern State. Summarising this process, Gramsci observed how:

The revolution brought about by the bourgeois class in the conception of law
and therefore in the function of the State consists especially in the will to
conform (hence the ethicity of law and the State). The previous dominant
classes were essentially conservative in the sense that they did not tend to

allow an organic passage from the other classes into their own, that is to enlarge their class sphere 'technically' and ideologically . . . The bourgeois class poses itself as an organism in continual movement, capable of absorbing the entire society, assimilating it to its own cultural and economic level: the whole function of the State is transformed: the State becomes an 'educator' etc.[42]

On this interpretation, the liberal night-watchman State belonged to the initial stage of bourgeois domination. As industrialism proceeded, however, such minimal government became untenable. As social processes grew in complexity, ever-greater degrees of State regulation were needed, so that State and civil society increasingly permeated each other. The 'active hegemony of the directive and dominant group' replaced the 'outmoded autonomies' of the subordinate groups and incorporated them into the structures of bourgeois rule.[43] Parliamentary regimes represented the climax of this achievement, combining force and consent in such a way as 'to ensure that force will always appear to be based on the consent of the majority, expressed in the so-called organs of public opinion – newspapers and associations – which, therefore, in certain situations are artificially multiplied'.[44]

Although the bourgeois ethical State replaced a mechanical with an organic unity, external compulsion with hegemony and consent, its purposes remained instrumental and fundamentally economic. The 'economic-corporative' phase formed an indispensable element within any political system, since a group's hegemony ultimately depended on the relative importance of their function within the economy. The 'political hegemony' of any new social group seeking to found a new type of State was 'predominantly of an economic order', therefore, involving 'reorganising the structure and the real relations between men and the economic world of production'.[45] This held true for the creation of a proletarian hegemony as well. Consequently, he affirmed that a State was only ethical to the extent that it raised the mass of the population to a cultural and moral level that 'corresponds to what is necessary for the development of the productive forces and hence to the interests of the dominant classes'.[46]

As we would expect given Gramsci's earlier critique of economism, he conceded that the superstructure could not always be related so mechanically to the structure as these remarks suggest.[47] The monopoly of the forces of coercion and consent enabled a ruling class to outlive its economic usefulness. In certain instances, such as Britain and Germany, an economically decadent class – in these cases the landed aristocracy – could continue to hold important positions within political society, whilst being relatively weak as an influence within civil society.[48] In others, such as Italy at the time of the *Risorgimento* (and arguably revolutionary Russia), circumstances arising out of a favourable international situation might place the State in the control of an advanced section of intellectuals and politicians rather than an economic class because the society was economically and socially backward.[49] However, these were exceptions to the general trajectory of social and political development.

Gramsci believed that because 'in the last analysis' the super-structure could not be divorced from the structure, the bourgeois State was doomed. The bourgeois class was now 'saturated', not only unable to absorb other groups, but already splitting up under its own contradictions.[50] Adopting a classical Marxist argument, Gramsci maintained that the capitalist mode of production was finally succumbing to the logic of the falling rate of profit.[51] According to this thesis, at least as Gramsci understood it,[52] competition between producers forced the pace of technological innovation and increased the exploitation of workers, as capitalist manufacturers were driven to cut costs to the bone in order to underprice each other whilst still maximising profits. However, these measures secured steadily diminishing returns. Not only were profit margins gradually whittled away completely, but cutting labour costs progressively eroded the market by reducing or even curtailing the purchasing power of more and more of the workforce. He viewed the economic slump of the 1930s as indicative of a more general crisis of capitalist accumulation.[53] Gramsci contended that these economic developments had precipitated a parallel 'crisis of authority', whereby the hegemony of bourgeois values, ideology and social relations was being undermined so that the bourgeoisie were obliged to resort increasingly to the resources of the State in the narrow sense of the term to maintain themselves in power.[54] He noted how in Italy, for example, traditional party political allegiances had steadily crumbled, with conservative nationalists and progressive liberals losing mass support to increasingly well organised socialist parties. The Italian parliamentary system's capacity to create an equilibrium between State and civil society had commensurately decreased as a result. In an analysis that in many respects paralleled that of Pareto in his *Transformation of Democracy* of 1921,[55] Gramsci diagnosed the lack of effective intermediate institutions as the chief problem of the Italian State, and one which he believed was progressively affecting modern States in general. In consequence, the State in Italy had vacillated between a central despotism relying on bureaucratic, technocratic and authoritarian forms of control on the one hand, and complete disaggregation on the other.[56] Nonetheless, Gramsci did not underestimate the continued ability of the system to adapt to this situation. Unlike many of his contemporaries who believed the crisis presaged the final collapse of capitalism, he maintained that it was merely provoking a significant alteration in the structure of capitalist reproduction and altering the mode of accumulation and the nature of the State in the process. He regarded both the Fordist and the Fascist versions of corporatism as new forms of capitalist expropriation designed to overcome this crisis by monopolising distribution as well as production.[57] He contended that they reflected the need within a complex, international economy for greater regulation of the anarchy of the market.[58] However, their success was necessarily limited. No matter how much entre-preneurial industrialists rationalised the production process, they could not eliminate the specific 'irrationality' of capital arising from the parasitism of speculators and investors. Their 'unwholesome' presence within the economy inhibited the efficient use of resources by promoting profit over use value.[59] Moreover, the continuing exploitative character of these new capitalist formations rendered them necessarily coercive and statist because based on the sub-ordination of the most dynamic element in the new process – the proletarian factory worker. As such, they represented 'regressive' forms of collectivism and totalitarianism, involving the absorption of society into the State.[60]

The true ethical State, in contrast, could only be brought into being by a genuinely universal class 'which presents itself as capable of assimilating the whole of society, and is at the same time really capable of expressing this process' – in other words, the working class.[61] Only 'a social group which proposes the end of the State and of itself as the goal to be attained, can create the ethical State, leading to the end of the internal division of ruled (and rulers) and to the creation of a unitary technico-moral organism.'[62] During the transi-tional stage, the State still needed to take on a regulative role. In both its coercive/legal and consensual/educational dimensions the State became 'an instrument of "rationalization", of acceleration and taylorization' that through a combination of rewards, punishments, and solicitations formed a new type of person and civilisation suited to the maximal exploitation of the productive apparatus.[63] However, this function gradually exhausted itself, having no purpose in a world without class domination and governed by consensual norms. It was replaced by a truly hegemonic 'regulated society'.[64] In this 'State without a State', political and civil society were no longer separated but fused in a way that rendered the individual a producer, citizen and functionary at one and the same time.[65] The members of such a community were united by a total culture rather than a total State to form part of a 'collective will . . . through which a multiplicity of dispersed wills, heterogeneous aims, are welded together with a single aim, on the basis of an equal and common conception of the world.'[66] Thus, the 'regressive' and 'mechanical' totalitarianism of the Fascist State had its putatively 'progressive' counterpart in the 'organic' unity of a totalitarian society in which law had become habit.[67]

We shall detail our reservations concerning Gramsci's 'new order' in the final section of Chapter 6 below. For the present we will return briefly to the comparison with Hegel and Marx. Gramsci referred on a number of occasions to similarities between his own views and those of Hegel. For example, he claimed at one point to have consistently used the term 'civil society' in the Hegelian sense,[68] and he identified Hegel as the chief theorist of the bourgeois conception of the ethical State.[69] However, closer examination reveals Gramsci to have introduced some important modifications to the Hegelian schema.[70] For Hegel placed both economic relations and the apparatus of domination – the law and police – in civil society. Although certain aspects of civil associational life implicitly developed the rational moral norms necessary to regulate our behaviour, Hegel believed these were only made explicit in the ethical consensus generated by the political State. Gramsci reversed this order of things. In Marxian manner he saw such consent as a mask for the force needed in a fundamentally coercive economic system.

Gramsci's reading of Marx was similarly partial, however. We have already remarked that whilst Marx's position was more complex than some commentators (including many prominent

Gramsci supporters) contend, Gramsci's own analysis of the State was more instrumental and firmly linked to the needs of the structure than is often maintained. Nonetheless, Gramsci's theory lacked an important dimension of Marx's analysis – namely, the concern with alienation and any detailed examination of the process of exploitation, elements we linked above with Marx's notion of 'abstraction'. Gramsci, of course, knew neither the 'Economic and Philosophical Manuscripts' nor the *Grundrisse* – key writings for this reading of Marx. Instead, as we observed in the last chapter, his central text was the 1859 'Preface'. Gramsci appears to have derived from this document the view that the chief criteria for judging any social and political order was the extent to which it allowed for the maximisation of production.[71] As he put it:

What is the reference point for the new world in gestation? The world of production, work. The maximum utility must be at the base of any analysis of the moral and intellectual institutions to be created and the principles to be diffused: individual and collective life must be organised for the maximum return of the productive apparatus. The development of the economic forces on the new foundations and the progressive introduction of the new structure will heal the contradiction that cannot fail to appear and having created a new 'conformity' from below, will permit new possibilities for self-discipline, that is liberty even of an individual nature.[72]

Gramsci thought many of the developments of Fordism were to be welcomed as introducing aspects of the new productive morality. He thoroughly approved, for instance, of Ford's policy of policing the private lives of his operatives, his imposition of a puritanical sexual code and the enforcement of temperance. Such measures liberated workers from 'animal and primitive' instincts and rendered them amenable to the 'more complex and rigid norms and habits of order, exactitude (and) precision' demanded by the new mechanised production lines.[73] Whereas for Marx the technological restructuring of capitalism deepened the exploitation and alienation of the worker, Gramsci claimed that 'technical requirements can be concretely thought of separately from the interests of the dominant class'.[74] His chief reservations were that capitalism could not bring this process of rationalisation to completion because of the continuing presence of 'parasitical classes'. Moreover, the production for profit rather than need created a consumption-orientated ethos which moved even the workers off the straight and narrow, resulting in the need for the external compulsion to maintain factory discipline when the incentives of higher wages either could not be maintained or ceased to have any effect. In essentials, though, he believed the formation of a new kind of 'collective worker' involved in Fordism was a 'progressive' move, and the overcoming of proletarian resistance such as that of skilled employees a positive step.[75] The passage to a fully regulated society involved the factory operatives reappropriating this restructuring of the productive process as an autonomous act 'proposed by the worker himself and not imposed from without'.[76] Thus, Gramsci's theory seems more concerned with overcoming *anomie* than alienation. Indeed, his general conception of modern production as giving rise to an 'organic' society requiring a new kind of social morality to the capitalist to regulate it echoes Durkheimian themes.

Two points stemming from the above discussion need emphasising. First, whereas Gramsci's new order had a number of similarities with Marx's vision of the withering away of the State, there were also profound differences. Commentators noticing these have often attributed them to Gramsci's Hegelian reading of Marx. However, Gramsci's interpretation of Hegel appears equally odd. In Chapter 6 we shall endeavour to show that this can be explained in part by situating Gramsci's argument within the context of a peculiarly Italian tradition of theorising the possibility of an ethical State. Second, Gramsci's critique of economism notwithstanding, his own theory frequently came closer to being a sophisticated version of economist doctrines rather than an outright rejection of them. His views on the nature of the capitalist crisis and of the post-revolutionary State were therefore often nearer to those of the Third International, with its similar emphasis on productive efficency, than interpreters have always wanted to admit. Many, if not all, his differences were over tactics rather than substantive strategic matters. It is to these tactical issues that we now turn.

The 'new Machiavelli': intellectuals, the Party and the creation of a revolutionary hegemony

Gramsci's analysis of the role of hegemony within the modern State had important implications for his understanding of the possibilities for revolution and the tactics to be employed to achieve the transition to a communist society. He now had an explanation for why the revolutionary movements in more developed countries such as Italy and Germany had proved less successful than in comparatively backward Russia during the post-war crisis, thereby going against the orthodox 'vulgar' Marxist belief that revolution would occur first in advanced capitalist States. 'In the East,' he now saw, 'the State was everything, civil society was primordial and gelatinous; in the West, there was a proper relation between State and civil society, and when the State trembled a sturdy structure of civil society was at once revealed.'[77] The 'complex structure' of civil society in advanced industrial States gave them ideological and social resources which rendered them 'resistant to the catastrophic irruptions caused by immediate economic factors (crises, depressions etc.)'. Adopting a military metaphor, he compared the influence of 'the superstructures of civil society' with the effects of 'the trench systems of modern warfare':

Just as (in war) it would sometimes happen that a dogged artillery attack seemed to have destroyed the enemy's whole defensive system, whereas in fact it had only destroyed the outer perimeter; and at the moment of their advance and attack the assailants would find themselves confronted by a line of defence which was still effective, so it happens in politics during the great economic crises.[78]

The institutionalisation of hegemony within modern bourgeois States made a revolutionary policy based either on waiting for the moment when crisis would bring them down or solely on a direct assault inadequate. Such tactics, which Gramsci associated with Trotsky's notion of 'permanent revolution', belonged to

an historical period in which the great mass political parties and the great economic trade unions did not yet exist, and society was still, so to speak, in a state of fluidity in many respects: greater backwardness of the countryside and almost complete monopoly of political-state power by a few cities or even a single one (Paris in the case of France); a relatively simple State apparatus, and greater autonomy of the national economies from the economic relations of the world market, etc.[79]

Modern States and economies were more complex than those of the early-modern period, making an assault on the political apparatus far harder to achieve since it was diffused throughout society in a whole range of institutions well beyond the traditional centre of power, such as local government, mass parties, schools, the media, trade unions etc. These institutions socialised the populace into supporting the prevailing system far more effectively than ever before. Moreover, they were often intertwined with international

organizations – multinational corporations and even foreign governments – so that purely national struggles faced extra difficulties. For
revolution to be successful, therefore, it was necessary to penetrate
these social and economic mechanisms first, and win the populace
over to an alternative strategy. It was not sufficent for the economic
preconditions for change to exist; there must be a general desire for
this change and the capacity to engineer it within the nation as a
whole. Continuing the military analogy, Gramsci isolated two
phases of the attack on bourgeois institutions – the 'war of position'
and the 'war of manoeuvre' or 'war of movement'. The former was a
protracted attack on the cultural superstructures. Its purpose was to
create a new hegemony within the institutions of civil society. But
this first phase did not obviate the need, when the time was ripe, for
the second phase – a rapid and no doubt violent revolutionary action
of the usual type, to topple the capitalist leaders when they too
resorted to coercion to maintain their position.[80]

The building of this new hegemony went through numerous stages
in Gramsci's opinion.[81] At the most basic level, it involved the
political organisation of the proletariat and making them conscious
of their class and economic interests. However, as we saw above, to
be truly hegemonic it was necessary to go beyond this stage so that
'one becomes aware that one's corporate interests, in their present
and future development, transcend the corporate limits of the purely
economic class, and can and must become the interests of other
subordinate groups too.' This was 'the most purely political phase',
when economic and political aims achieved an intellectual and moral
unity by 'posing all the questions round which the struggle rages, not
on a corporate but on a "universal" plane'.[82] Gramsci did not believe
that this 'critical consciousness' would come about spontaneously
without organisers and leaders capable of fostering it amongst the
masses.[83] Two groups played an especial role in this task – the
intellectuals and the Party.

Although Gramsci saw all human beings as capable of reflection
and needing to theorise at some level of their lives, so that we were all
intellectuals to some degree, he also recognised that only a few
individuals saw this as being their main role.[84] Gramsci distinguished between two types of such specialist intellectuals: 'traditional' and 'organic'. Members of the former group 'put themselves
forward as autonomous and independent of the dominant social
group'. Examples included self-styled 'detached' scholars like Croce,

and ecclesiastics. But their position was unsustainable. As we saw in the last chapter, Gramsci argued that Croce's detachment was simply a pose. He might act like a 'lay Pope', but 'the most significant character' of his philosophy resided in 'his links with Senators Agnelli and Benni'.[85] 'Organic' intellectuals, in contrast, acknowledged their relationship to a particular social group and sought to 'give it homogeneity and an awareness of its own function not only in the economic but also in the social and political fields'.[86] Gramsci altered the sense of the term intellectual as far as this category went to mean 'not those strata commonly described by this term, but in general the entire social stratum which exercises an organisational function in the field of production, or in that of culture, or in that of political administration'.[87] From this point of view, every specialist group had its own 'organic' intellectuals – they did not form a *cadre* separate from others as the 'traditional' conception of intellectuals assumed.

Gramsci likened the difference between 'traditional' and 'organic' intellectuals to the contrast he drew between the cultural outlook of Renaissance humanism and the Reformation. Croce, for example, he regarded as a modern Erasmus, whose anti-Catholicism and anti-Marxism had served the reactionary function of cutting the intelligentsia off from the bourgeois establishment. The Reformation had succeeded in penetrating down to the masses, providing them with a new world view and creating a unity 'between the bottom and the top, between the "simple" and the intellectuals'. This approach was not to be confused with populism, however. The new culture must show its relevance to ordinary people's needs and desires whilst challenging the traditional nostrums of 'common sense' ways of thinking.[88] This goal involved engaging in a form of internal critique, of the kind described in the last chapter, of the people's everyday beliefs. To achieve this balance, the 'new intellectuals' had to exercise a 'directive' function without becoming an elite group: '[The] need for contact between intellectuals and simple . . . is not in order to restrict scientific activity and preserve unity at the low level of the masses, but precisely in order to construct an intellectual-moral bloc which can make politically possible the intellectual progress of the mass and not only of small intellectual groups.'[89]

The chief means for disseminating this new culture were not individual intellectuals, however, but the 'collective intellectual', the Communist Party. For reasons discussed in the next section, Gramsci likened the function of the Party to that of Machiavelli's Prince. The 'modern Prince' was not 'a real person', though, as those who made a cult of the leader supposed. The contemporary unifier of the nation:

can only be an organism, a complex element of society in which a collective will which has already been recognised and has to some extent asserted itself in action, begins to take concrete form. History has already provided this organism, and it is the political party – the first cell in which there come together germs of a collective will tending to become universal and total.[90]

Gramsci insisted that the political efficacy of the Party was intimately connected to its role as the organiser of a new cultural hegemony. This Modern Prince, he affirmed: 'must be and cannot but be the proclaimer and organiser of an intellectual and moral reform, which also means creating the grounds for a subsequent development of the national-popular collective will towards the accomplishment of a superior and total form of modern civilisation.'[91] The Party's moral reform was not an abstract intellectual construct, however. This programme had to be tied to a policy of economic reform, 'indeed the programme of economic reform was precisely the concrete means by which every intellectual and moral reform presents itself'.[92] For it was the 'economic' force of the Party as the developer of national energies, most particularly in the area of production, which provided the basis for its moral superiority.

Gramsci claimed the Communist Party could repeat the pattern of the French revolutionaries, acting as the historical agents of the proletariat much as they had ushered in the era of the bourgeoisie.[93] It was necessary, therefore, for the Party to develop mechanisms which would link its development to the interests of the masses.

The Party had three elements which worked together to attain this moral unity: (i) a popular base of ordinary people; (ii) the leadership, who co-ordinated activity at a national level; and, most importantly, (iii) 'an intermediate element which articulates the first element with the second and maintains contact between them not only physically but also morally and intellectually'.[94] Thus Gramsci's Party was designed to include all the populace, not just an elite section of it, and to ensure the responsiveness of the leadership to the led as well as vice versa.

Gramsci frequently remarked that his inspiration for this approach came from Lenin.[95] Indeed, the term *gegemoniya* had been coined by the Russian Social Democrats and was often employed by the Comintern after the October Revolution,[96] although we shall see in the next chapter that the concept had distinctive Italian roots as well. Hegemony as used in these contexts shared Gramsci's concern that the proletariat exercise a political leadership over other groups which went beyond a narrow corporatism and hence was capable of appealing to the peasantry in particular as well. But it lacked both the significance of Gramsci's first sense of the term examined above, and the emphasis of his second sense on the role of cultural leadership in achieving such a political ascendency. Moreover, unlike Lenin he did not believe that Party cadres should 'elaborate an independent ideology' without reference to what the workers, deluded by 'bourgeois ideology', actually thought themselves.[97] Gramsci may have held some of Lenin's doubts about 'the spontaneous philosophy of the masses', but he aimed to allow them to criticise it for themselves from within, rather than using the Party machine to impose an alternative upon them.[98] The new ideology was to be formed on the basis of movements and desires which were already expressed, usually inchoately, by the people, not on the basis of scientific laws of economic and social development. The Party sought to bring together leaders and led 'organically', not 'mechanically'. 'Organic' leadership entailed the self-education of the masses, so that 'every leap towards a new "broadening" and complexity of the intellectual strata is linked to an analogous movement of the simple mass'.[99] In addition, the 'educational relationship' existing between them 'throughout society as a whole' developed through a process of mutual dialogue, in which 'every teacher is always a pupil and every pupil a teacher'.[100] Intellectuals and the masses complemented each other, for 'the popular element "feels", but does not always understand or know; the intellectual element "knows", but does not always understand and especially "feel"'.[101] Party organisation reflected this conception of its pedagogical role. Lenin's notion of the vanguard Party and the subsequent elitist and bureaucratic rule of the Party in the Soviet Union resulted from the fact that he had been forced to separate politics and culture, force and hegemony, and postpone the new moral order until after the revolution and a transitionary 'dictatorship of the proletariat'. Gramsci condemned the 'bureaucratic centralism' resulting from such an approach as the 'pathological manifestations' of a 'narrow clique' – a sign of 'the political backwardness of peripheral forces'. In a passage many have seen as being clearly aimed at Stalinism, he observed that:

A party's police function may be either progressive or regressive. It is progressive when it aims at keeping dispossessed reactionary forces within the bounds of legality and raising the backward masses to the level of the new legality. It is regressive when it aims at restraining the living forces of history and maintaining an outdated, anti-historical legality that has become a mere empty shell. When the party is progressive it functions 'democratically' (in the sense of democratic centralism), when it is regressive it functions 'bureaucratically' (in the sense of bureaucratic centralism). In the latter case the party is merely an executive, not a deliberating body; accordingly it is technically a policing organ, and its title of a 'political party' is not more than a mythological metaphor.[102]

Whether in practice such sentiments would amount to anything more than a number of pious platitudes is a different question. Gramsci remained vague on the mechanisms that would square the circle and make the Party both democratic and centralised at the same time. In his definition a great deal seemed to hang on whether one was suppressing 'regressive' or 'progressive' forces, but no putatively left-wing dictatorship has ever admitted to ridding itself of anything but the former. The difficulties inherent in seeking to divide groups into progressive and regressive in the first place are arguably such as to always risk repression of an illegitimate kind. Gramsci attempted to avoid some of the dangers in this way of thinking, but he never doubted its coherence. At best he was a methodological as opposed to an ontological pluralist, for whom debate was but a preliminary to agreement. The Party may have sought to be inclusive and open, but its goal was single-minded to a terrifying degree – the 'total and molecular transformation of modes of thought and being', in which pluralistic discord gave way to a unitary harmony. Moreover, the only measure he gave of the validity of this change was the success of the Party in achieving it. The apparently anti-Stalinist sentiments expressed in the passage cited above found their counterpart in another passage Joe Femia describes as 'worthy of Stalin himself',[103] where Gramsci spelt out the disturbing implications of this position:

As it develops, the modern Prince overturns the whole system of intellectual and moral relations, in that its development means precisely that any given act is seen as useful or harmful, as virtuous or as wicked, only in so far as it has as its point of reference the modern Prince itself, and helps to strengthen or oppose it. In people's consciences, the Prince takes the place of the Divinity or the categorical imperative.[104]

The cause of this worrying aspect of Gramsci's argument becomes apparent once we bring his two senses of hegemony together. For the ultimate purpose of the modern Prince was to mould the new 'collective man' suited to modern production by achieving a unique degree of 'social conformism'. This project required a 'totalitarian politics' whereby the Party members found in the 'Party alone all the satisfactions that previously they found in a multiplicity of organisations'. To achieve this end it was necessary not only to 'break all the threads linking members to external cultural organisations', but eventually 'to destroy all other organisations or to incorporate them in a system of which the party is the sole regulator.'[105] As we saw, the repressive organs of the State performed a similarly totalising and educative role during the passage from capitalism to communism. In the transitionary stage, cultural policy 'will be above all negative, a critique of the past, it will be aimed at erasing from the memory and at destroying'.[106] Even regional dialects must disappear and a common language take their place. However, such measures had the supposedly positive goal of 'creating new and higher forms of civilisation, of adapting "civilisation" and the morality of the vast popular masses to the requirements of the continual development of the economic apparatus of production, and therefore to elaborate even physically new types of humanity.'[107] To this end the conception of law had to be widened to encompass activities traditionally defined as 'juridically indifferent', such as customs, ways of thinking etc., in order to strengthen the sanctions of public opinion.[108] In this way, all dissent would gradually become self-correcting and the system gradually become self-regulating so that the State could finally wither away into a regulative administrative apparatus.

Hegemony and historical materialism

As in his methodological writings, Gramsci's analysis of the State sought to synthesise two aspects of the Marxist tradition: the emphasis on the forces of production as the primary determinant of social evolution on the one hand, and the contention that the primary dynamic of history is class struggle on the other. His originality, encapsulated respectively by the two senses of his conception of hegemony, was to bring out the role played by culture and consent and hence by politics in each of these aspects. As we noted, their importance was implicit in Marx's analysis of the State, but it also owed a great deal to the influence of Croce's 'ethico-political' interpretation of history and the Italian tradition more generally,

examined in the next chapter. However, although Gramsci insisted
on the relative autonomy of politics, he ultimately related it back to
the internal dynamic of the productive forces. In this way, he subsumed the dynamic of struggle and of both senses of hegemony to
certain historical tendencies of the capitalist system. As a result, he
believed political activity would finally be overcome once the
internal contradictions of this system had been fully worked through
and transcended – a possibility he thought to be within reach. At this
stage State, civil society and economy would be fused in a total
political, social, cultural and economic unity. The danger of this
argument is that it can justify not the emancipation, but the indoc-
trination of the working class, and their accommodation through
social engineering to their station and duties within the prevailing
productive process.

We shall consider the disturbing nature of Gramsci's projected
new order at the end of the next chapter. Before that we need to
examine the importance of the Italian political tradition on
Gramsci's thinking. For whilst the impact of the Marxist vision of
communist society on his ideas cannot be denied, his whole emphasis
on building a 'national-popular collective will' can be seen as a
contribution to the contemporary Italian debate on how to create a
nation-State that would be united both politically and culturally.
Elements of Gramsci's linking of the need for moral integration with
the requirments of productivism can undoubtedly be found in the
Marxist tradition – especially in the writings of his contemporaries.
But we shall contend that Gramsci's understanding of this linkage,
which led as we remarked to the exclusion of other equally important Marxist themes such as alienation and exploitation, was largely
formed by his participation in an ongoing discussion on the nature of
the Italian State.

The *Prison Notebooks* III: 'making Italians' – the *Risorgimento* and the new order

We have already noted in Chapter 1 how Gramsci's early political thought involved a creative reworking of the Italian concern with the formation of a new State capable of uniting the diverse classes and cultures of the peninsula. In putting forward his mature ideas, Gramsci also employed the language of the Italian political tradition, assimilating Marxist concepts into its framework. It is to this tradition that we must attribute the peculiar mix of Hegel and Machiavelli that so many commentators have found distinctive about Gramsci's Marxism.

The dialectic of 'force' and 'consent' in the Italian theory of the State from Gioberti to Mosca

The dichotomy of 'force' and 'consent' had been characteristic of Italian thinking since Machiavelli. During the *Risorgimento*, however, this Machiavellian theme became associated with the Hegelian distinction between 'State' and 'civil society' in the writings of a number of politicians and philosophers confronting the problems posed by the unification of the country.[1] These difficulties were twofold. First, there were the cultural and economic divisions existing between both the different Italian territories, particularly the developing North and the undeveloped South, and the educated classes and the unschooled masses. Second, and largely as a result of these differences, there was the tension between 'legal Italy', the set of liberal institutions resulting from political unification, and 'real Italy', the fragmented social reality of divergent regional traditions, economic attainment and polarised classes: a tension epitomised for contemporaries in the 'southern question'.

The *Risorgimento* bequeathed a distinctive intellectual legacy to the Italian thinkers seeking to remedy this situation. Both the Giobertian Catholic-Liberals and the Republican democrats inspired by Mazzini had professed essentially eschatological ideologies, in which the unification of Italy was conceived of as the realisation of a national identity. Both movements had placed great emphasis on the role of the people as the carriers of this national consciousness – they constituted the 'real' nation in contrast to the largely foreign-backed and merely 'legal' regimes then governing the various parts of the country. While effective as a means of legitimising the revolt against *de facto* governments of the time, it had profound drawbacks as a practical strategy, since the Italian people lacked the cultural and social cohesiveness these theories assumed.

The liberals within the Moderate Party appreciated the nature of this dilemma rather better than the Mazzinians, and it was their solution – the unification of Italy by Piedmont – which ultimately set the tone of Italian politics. Vincenzo Gioberti's formulation of this policy following the dashing of his hopes in the failed revolutions of 1848 proved particularly influential. In language explicitly adopted by Gramsci later, he argued that the 'formative principle of nations' consisted of 'what the ancients called hegemony [*egemonia*]': 'that species of primacy, of supremacy, of majority, which is neither legal nor juridical, properly speaking, but consists in the moral efficacy, that amongst many similar provinces sharing the same language and nationality, one of them exercises over the others.'[2] If, he continued, 'every national hegemony entails, at least at the beginning, dictatorship' in order to unite politically the various components of the nation, its legitimacy derived from the 'national-popular' will. Thus Piedmont's unification of the peninsula by force of arms alone and the imposition of Piedmontese institutions on the rest of the country were justified by the belief that its temporary domination would allow the development of an uncoerced moral unity stemming from the people's growing sense of a common nationality.[3]

The Neapolitan neo-Hegelian apologists of the Historical Right, the Cavourian party which governed Italy immediately after unification, refined Gioberti's thesis.[4] They viewed the relationship between force and consensus, State and nationhood, in terms parallel to the earlier philosopher's. Whereas Hegel had regarded the State as the product of the national *Volkgeist*, his Italian followers reversed this formula and argued that the ethos of nationality had to be created within the political organisation of a centralised State. Only uniform procedures and strong central government could prevent regional particularism reasserting itself and dividing the new kingdom. A crucial ambiguity concerning the relationship of politics and ethics thereby entered into Italian political discourse, with Machiavelli supplementing Hegel in their thinking. The Florentine thinker, according to the influential interpretation of De Sanctis,[5] had separated the political means from the ends they served, appreciating that the two operated according to different logics. In so doing, he had not argued that only the means counted; merely that one judged political methods by their efficacy and appropriateness, reserving moral judgement for the goals for which they were employed. 'Knowledge' and 'will' were the prime political virtues, attaining moral status only when they served to promote good. The State added 'moral force' to mere 'political force' when it succeeded in concentrating the energies of the entire nation, disciplining all its members in the performance of their patriotic duty. If a Prince was required to unite the country with the 'legitimate' force of good government, this achievement would only prove durable if the new rulers could foster the 'republican' consensus of the people. The entry of the Piedmontese armies into Rome at the very moment De Sanctis composed his famous chapter seemed to him to mark the close of the first stage. The problem was whether, to echo the famous phrase of the Moderate statesman Massimo D'Azeglio, having 'made Italy' the liberals were capable of 'making Italians'.

It is important to note that, in spite of the Hegelian influence, De Sanctis's view of Machiavelli was oddly Kantian. He sharply condemned 'vulgar' Machiavellianism for analogous reasons to those employed by Kant against the 'political moralist', namely that it subordinates ends to means. The 'moral politician' represented the true essence of Machiavelli's doctrine. He appreciated that it paid not just to appear virtuous, but to be so. Both political expediency and morality coincided in such a statesman, with law being judiciously applied gradually to place all citizens in a position to act morally without precipitately forcing them to do so. De Sanctis's theory differed, therefore, from the more full-blooded Hegelianism of thinkers such as Bertrando and (to a lesser extent) Silvio Spaventa, who aimed at the creation of an 'ethical State'.[6] In their view, the State did not 'restrict itself solely to the administration of justice and the defence of society, but wants to conduct (the people) by those paths which lead to the highest ends of humanity'.[7] Indeed, these ends could only be found within the State, since the individual in him or herself was 'nothing' once cut off from the community which provided the context which gave human lives meaning and value.[8] Extrapolating from this platitudinous observation of the social nature of human beings, Bertrando Spaventa in particular drew the extreme conclusion that the individual and society must be identified. He contended, therefore, that 'the true individual *recognises* and brings about the community as something of *his own*, as the very necessity of his being; and in this necessity he is really free, and truly himself.'[9] Liberty conceived of simply as the capacity for choice was mere licence, and hence 'corresponds to the state of nature, it is that which can be called *the animality* of man'.[10] Separated from the community, we became like beasts and lived in an asocial condition of perpetual war and conflict. We only expressed our genuine, civilized and moral nature when we identified the objective will of the community as the innermost expression of our subjective will. To achieve this result, 'the State must draw and concentrate within itself, in its universal substance, the dispersed and diverse individuals, unite in a single and common end the souls and wills of everyone'. Spaventa insisted this ethical unification of the State was only possible to the extent that it operated not as a '*force* which draws to itself all the individuals and remains external to those it draws' but 'unites them to the extent it is *immanent* in the *whole* understanding, in *all* the activity of the individual'.[11] Thus, although these thinkers gave the State a tutelary function, theoretically at least they distinguished the force of the law from the moral consensus of the citizen body. Unfortunately this distinction was harder to make in practice. Italian politicians and intellectuals did not always resist the temptation to treat the laws of the State as representing the rational will of its members rather than the goals of its rulers, confusing Spaventa's ideal with reality. In this circumstance the force of the State became falsely conflated with the consent of its subjects.[12]

Some historians have blamed the authoritarian nature of Italian liberalism on the supposedly malign influence of Hegelian ideas.[13] Leaving aside the dubiousness of this interpretation of the German philosopher,[14] over-emphasis on this strand of Italian political thought is misleading. We have done so because this current provided the chief influence on Gramsci. However, to a large extent positivism rather than idealism represented the official ideology of the liberal regime. Despite differences in method and approach, the positivists shared remarkably similar beliefs about the difficulties attendant on unification and their solution. Evolutionary theory led them to adopt the same terminology of the 'organic' harmonious State, providing them with spurious scientific laws whereby the social organism might be controlled and the integration of the individual parts of the political 'body' obtained.[15] It was the northern positivist criminologist Cesare Lombroso, for example, who was to provide the cruel repression of so-called 'subversives' with a pseudo-'scientific' basis by identifying criminal and rebellious minds with certain atavistic types.[16] Likewise, a similar Machiavellian strain went through their work, culminating in the elite theories of Gaetano Mosca and Vilfredo Pareto.

Even De Sanctis acknowledged that Machiavelli's theory required certain vital amendments to yield the *Rechtsstaat*, notably with regard to individual rights. Yet popular participation and guarantees of individual liberty remained conspicuously absent from the Right's programme, the southern situation in particular encouraging them to adopt bureaucratic and coercive measures to moderate and control individual claims.[17] The State as conceived by positivist and idealist liberals alike had an undeniably progressive function in building the infrastructure and legal framework required for liberal capitalism. This involved measures to improve communications (the Right fell on the issue of a nationalised railway network), the establishment of a single internal market and the standardisation of currency, patent laws and weights and measures, a secular education system with particular emphasis on primary schools and, of course, laws securing property against threats from below. These policies were pursued in a benevolently paternalistic fashion with the aim of moralising the populace into an acceptance of bourgeois hegemony, but went hand in hand with an attitude towards public order of a potentially authoritarian kind. Initial resistance to unification, particularly in the South – where the Piedmontese lost more troops suppressing the bandits than in fighting the Austrians – resulted in a severe penal code, giving the executive wide-ranging 'preventative' powers which effectively criminalised criticism of the regime under a blanket denunciation of 'subversive' activity. The Right, and the liberal elite more generally, claimed to speak for the nation, but

economic and social change generated dissenting popular movements on both sides of the ideological spectrum which eventually
undermined liberalism as a political force. With the fall of the Right
from power in 1876, Italian politics underwent a marked moral
decline. For De Sanctis, it appeared that the political class had slowly
given up the Machiavellian ideal and adopted the character traits of
what he called 'Guicciardinian man'. Whereas those inspired by the
former were prepared to sacrifice their lives and interests for something that they loved, the latter suffered from 'moral laziness' and
regarded life as a mere 'mathematical calculus'.[18] Far from performing the high moral function which the Historical Right had accorded
it, the Italian State degenerated into a mechanism for the brokering
of interests, with all the corruption that that entailed. Under the
Left's leader Agostino Depretis the pattern of *trasformismo* was
begun, whereby the ruling elites employed State patronage to woo
and absorb the opposition. Governments alternated between the
manipulation of 'consent' by granting favours to important local
clientele, and the application of force, in which the police powers
were used to the full in response to the growing 'social question'.
Despite an initial liberal revolt at the abuses made by the Left under
Depretis' successor Francesco Crispi, these methods remained substantially unreformed by the liberal politician Giovanni Giolitti, who
dominated twentieth-century Italian politics prior to the rise of
Fascism. Italian political life retained a pronounced 'Guicciardinian'
flavour, making the passage to Fascism in the face of mounting social
unrest all too palatable a solution for the ruling liberal classes.

It would be wrong for this brief sketch of the language and nature
of Italian politics to suggest that the rise of Fascism was in some way
ideologically determined. The constraints arose as much from Italy's
comparatively backward economic and social conditions and the
patterns of class allegiance they promoted, which forced Italian
liberalism into a difficult compromise with the traditional hierarchical social relations of the old elites. Moreover, the crisis of the
1920s gave rise to a liberal opposition along side the supporters of
the Fascist regime within both the main schools of thought. Just as
Croce and Guido de Ruggiero offered a liberal idealism in contrast to
the Fascist variants of Gentile and Ugo Spirito, so Gaetano Mosca
and Luigi Einaudi countered Vilfredo Pareto and Alfredo Rocco in
the positivist camp. The debate between these two groups on the
nature of the State provided a constant reference point for Gramsci's

own reflections in the *Prison Notebooks.*

Mussolini opened the debate with a brief article on the Machiavellian theme of 'Force and consent' written a few months after the March on Rome. His target was the typical caricature of the liberal position adopted by positivist and idealist nationalists and Fascists alike, according to which liberals supposedly saw society as a free association between atomistic individuals. Adopting the standard critique, Mussolini argued that such a social order was inherently unstable. 'Liberty,' he remarked, 'is not an end but a means. As a means it must be controlled and dominated. This is where the discussion of "force" becomes relevant.' He rhetorically requested the *signori liberali* to tell him if there had ever been a government that was entirely based on popular consent and totally renounced any use of force:

Such a government has never existed, and never could exist. Consensus is as changeable as the sandy patterns on the sea shore . . . Remove force from any Government whatsoever – and I mean physical force, armed force – and leave only its immortal principles, and that Government will be at the mercy of the first group organised and determined to overthrow it.[19]

Mussolini clearly had no intentions of committing the mistakes of his liberal predecessors!

Gentile as the self-appointed philosopher of Fascism took up the theme in one of his most notorious speeches. Justifying the violence of the Fascist *squadristi* which marked the early years of the movement, he argued that it was impossible:

to distinguish moral force from material force: the force of the law freely voted and accepted, from the force of violence which is rigidly opposed to the will of the citizen. But such distinctions are simple-minded when they are sincere! Every force is moral force, for it is always an expression of will, and whatever method of argument is used – from sermon to blackjack – its efficacy cannot be other than that of entreating the inner man and persuading him to agree.[20]

Gentile based this sophistry on his own reading of Bertrando Spaventa's theory of the ethical State, which he came to identify with the Fascist project.[21] The ethical purpose of the State, he believed, was to reconcile the internal conflicts of the national community in the common will.[22] Like Spaventa, he insisted this unity was presupposed by the particular wills of different individuals rather than being the product of their coming together. The State existed not as a society *between* persons (or *inter homines*, in Gentile's terminology), but *within* each and every one of them (or *in interiore homine*).[23] As a result, one could not talk of the State coercing individuals, since it was not a force external to them but the expression of a will immanent to all their diverse purposes: 'State and individual are identical.'[24] Thus in Gentile's eyes, to revolt against the State was literally to be at war with yourself. Law, from this point of view, had an educative function in bringing the individual back into harmony with him or herself. Because the law represented the individual's 'true' and 'moral' will, force and consent could not be distinguished. The stronger the State, the greater the consent of the populace. 'The art of government' consequently became:

the art of so reconciling and uniting (State and individual) that a maximum of liberty harmonises with a maximum of public order not merely in the external sense, but also and above all in the sovereignty ascribed to law and to its necessary organs. For always the maximum liberty coincides with the maximum force of the State.[25]

Gentile argued that the Fascist corporate system of representation aimed at introducing this inner unity between the constituent parts of the State into its very organisation. The corporations were supposed to organise the moral will of the people within the moral force of the State. The unions or 'syndicates' constituted the corporate personality of the worker, which together with the employer's federations were brought within the national personality – the State. Through these bodies, individuals exchanged the 'abstract', 'empirical' and 'naturalistic' perspective of their particular interests, for the 'universal', 'ideal' and 'ethical' interest of the State *qua* embodiment of society at large.[26] Gentile contended the Fascist State was totalitarian only in the special 'philosophical' and non-pejorative sense he gave to the term, as denoting its capacity to offer a total organisation of the nation's will, thought and feeling.[27]

Gentile's philosophical support for Fascism compelled his former colleague Benedetto Croce to offer a philosophical justification for his own continued adherence to liberalism.[28] Croce's distinction between the Useful and the Good, politics and ethics, meant that he had never accepted the doctrine of the ethical State. In his theory, the State was an 'economic' concept belonging to the realm of practice. Its role was essentially utilitarian and its distinctive characteristic 'force' or 'power'. Croce traced this thesis back to his early writings on Marx. Drawing on De Sanctis's interpretation of Machiavelli, Croce had praised Marx for appreciating the Florentine's lesson that politics was concerned with means rather than ends. Indeed, Croce had gone so far as to call him 'the Machiavelli of the proletariat'.[29] Significantly, Gentile had criticised him as early as 1918 for being more Marxist than Hegelian in his view of the State, and for failing to appreciate Hegel's insight (as he saw it) that 'the force of the State is ethical force'.[30] After the war, Croce had also offered limited support to Fascism. However, in conformity with his political theory, his argument had been based on the inability of the liberals to maintain public order – their lack of 'the force or *virtù* to save Italy from the anarchy in which it was enmeshed'.[31] Although it is true that only a man with Croce's conservative opinions could have regarded the threat of left-wing agitation to be greater than that stemming from the Fascists themselves, there can be no doubt that his aim was to strengthen the liberal State rather than to inaugurate an entirely different sort of Fascist regime.[32] Once it became clear that Mussolini had no intention of restoring the liberal system, Croce began to wonder whether the Machiavellian emphasis on force had not been somewhat overstressed.[33] That the shift in his theory from an 'economic-political' to an 'ethico-political' conception of politics should occur just as he moved from the establishment to the opposition was entirely consistent with his earlier position. For in taking a moral political stand against Fascism he spoke no longer as the upholder of the State, but against it.

In polemic with Gentile, Croce maintained that the State in the strict sense could only mean the government and bureaucracy and the forces of authority. If the Hegelian theory of the ethical State had any meaning at all, then it must include moral life in general which 'embraces the men of government and their adversaries, the conservatives and the revolutionaries, and the latter perhaps more than the others, because they open the paths to the future and procure the advancement of human society'.[34] The State on this narrow reading was a purely political and 'economic/utilitarian' entity, the realm of force. Civil society, in contrast, was the truly moral sphere within which the clash of opposing ideals took place and agreement was consensual. He thereby ethicised economic and social relations, making the State the inevitable organ of force which, given the passional and irrational aspects of human nature, always had to be present in one form or another. The organisation of civil society and the degree of State intervention it required to remain stable reflected the prevailing historical circumstances. The whole debate about force and consent had to be rethought, therefore, in terms of the relationship between State and civil society, the economic and the ethical. Turning to Mussolini's speech, Croce remarked that force and consent were correlative terms:

all consent is forced, forced to a greater or lesser extent but forced, that is it is what emerges from the 'force' of certain facts, and hence is 'conditioned': if the factual condition changes, then the consensus, as is natural, will be withdrawn, debate and struggle break out, and a new consensus establishes itself on the new condition . . . Translating the same terms of this relation into another vocabulary, and calling 'authority' all that which represents the moment of force (be it in the form of promises or threats, the announcement of praise or of punishment), and 'liberty' all that represents the moment of spontaneity and consensus, one must conclude that in every State authority and liberty are inseparable (and this includes the extremes of despotism and liberalism).[35]

Croce contended that liberalism philosophically understood was a 'metapolitical' doctrine, coextensive with a historicist and dialectical conception of reality as the progressive development of spirit.[36] It reflected the human ability to use different types of social and political organisation as the occasion demanded so as to increase the realm of liberty. Arguing against the liberal economist Luigi Einaudi, Croce contended that philosophical liberalism had no necessary connection with the normal liberal practices of democracy and the free market. For human progress called for different political programmes in different situations. Even Communist measures might be appropriate in certain circumstances. Genuine liberalism consisted of a conception of history as a process of free and creative human development and the consequent recognition of the historically contingent nature of all political programmes.[37] He went so far as to claim that so long as *trasformismo* was understood in philosophical terms and separated from its pejorative current meaning, then it entirely accorded with a dialectical, historicist and hence liberal position. For according to this conception of liberalism, progress resulted from the fact that every social system threw up an opposition which forced the regime to develop and change. *Trasformismo* on this interpretation signified the capacity of the system to absorb its opponents into a new synthesis.[38]

The debate between the two main proponents of the idealist school was paralleled by a similar discussion amongst positivists. Using the quite different sources of Social Darwinism, for example, Alfredo Rocco offered an alternative to Gentile's theory in his own (arguably more influential) justification of Fascist corporatist doctrine and the reduction of the individual to an organ of the State as force (*Stato-forza*). Luigi Einaudi, in contrast, employed analogous ideas to promote free trade. Gramsci commented briefly on these writings, and often employed the latter as a stalking horse for his analysis of liberal economics. However, he found rather more in the contrasting use of the Machiavellian concepts of force and consent by the elite theorists, Pareto and Mosca.

Pareto's political sociology was built around the thesis that 'in all history force and consent appear as the means of government'. He argued that the composition of the ruling elite oscillated between 'lions' who governed in an authoritarian manner, and 'foxes' who governed through invention and guile. He associated this 'circulation of elites' with social and economic cycles linked to changing sentiments within the populace at large. Crudely put, periods of boom went together with more liberal and in some respects creative views, which governments sought to manipulate with fox-like cunning. However, they inevitably provoked a reaction, usually accompanied by a slump, when people adopted more conservative opinions and called for a return of government authority and the strengthening of law and order. Pareto regarded Fascism as an appropriate response to this second stage of the cycle. He died in 1923, but given his continued adherence to free-market economics, it is doubtful if his support for Mussolini would have lasted long.

Although Mosca engaged in a life-long battle with Pareto to assert his primacy as the formulator of the concept of elitism, his elaboration of it was very different to his compatriot's.[39] The belief in the inevitability of elite rule made him similarly cynical about mass democracy as a system of popular government, but he was ultimately led to adapt rather than reject liberal democracy to take account of this fact and to oppose Mussolini's destruction of the parliamentary party system. For Mosca, the chief element of democracy lay in its ability to obtain and manage consensus. Three features stand out in his analysis, all of which find an echo in Gramsci's writings. First, he stressed the role of parties in helping an organised minority to recruit a following. Through them the elite was able to choose their electors rather than vice versa. Second, he noted how a ruling class legitimated its rule within a given 'political formula' or set of values congruent with its interests and supported by appropriate institutions. He regarded parliamentary democracy in this light as

upholding, in Gramscian terms, the hegemony of the liberal bourgeoisie. Third, via his concept of 'juridical defence' he rethought
democracy to mean an openness of the ruling elite to the rest of the
populace, rather than a system of power-sharing.

These debates and the general problem of devising a revolutionary
strategy suited to the social and political conditions of Italy were a
constant element in Gramsci's prison speculations. He looked on the
discussion triggered off by Mussolini as an indication of the 'relative
advance' of Italian political science. It showed an ability to tackle
head-on the central question of the age: namely, 'how to reconstruct
the hegemonic apparatus of the dominant group, an apparatus
collapsing because of the consequences of the war in all the States of
the world?'[40] In common with most other Italian political theorists,
Gramsci traced the weaknesses and peculiarities of the Italian State
to the limitations of the unification movement. His detailed examination of the *Risorgimento* in the *Notebooks* served not merely to
highlight the origins of the problems present in the Italian situation,
but to rethink the terms in which they were traditionally addressed.

Gramsci and Italy's 'passive revolution'

Gramsci's account of the *Risorgimento* involved an implicit contrast
between his own proposals for a new hegemony and the unity that
was actually achieved by the liberals.[41] The architects of unification
had been the Moderate Party composed of Cavour, the followers of
the Piedmontese monarchy and the agrarian elites. Their sole aim
was to maintain their socio-economic position by securing political
power. They achieved this goal through a mixture of conquest and
power-broking – first with foreign nations, then with the bourgeoisie, and finally with sections of the working class. Instead of
basing their domination on intellectual and moral leadership, which
following Gioberti he regarded as necessary for a genuine 'political
hegemony',[42] they had employed the crudest forms of 'force' and
'consent'.[43] The only possible alternative, the Mazzinian radical-
democrats in the Party of Action, had remained very much a subaltern group, whose 'abstract' and 'international' viewpoint and lack
of organisational skills had inhibited them from making a decisive
contribution to the national movement. To succeed, they would have
needed to offer 'an organic programme of government which
reflected the essential demands of the popular masses, above all of

the peasants'. He argued that a project of agrarian reform could have won over the allegiance of both the peasantry and the intellectuals from the middle and lower strata. This policy would have created a 'liberal-national formation' capable 'at the very least of giving to the *Risorgimento* a more markedly popular and democratic character'.[44] Instead, their advocacy of religious reform mirrored the Italian intellectuals' characteristic divorce from the concerns of the people, for 'not only did it not interest the great rural masses, but on the contrary rendered them open to incitement against the new heretics'.[45] Although individual radicals such as Ferrari, Cattaneo and Pisacane recognised the need for popular support, their advice went unheeded. The opportunity was lost because the Mazzinians were worried on the one hand that a genuine mass movement might lead to a terror, as in 1793, and on the other that the Austrians might exploit the peasantry for a Vendée-type counter-revolutionary offensive. Gramsci acknowledged that the historical precedents existed for both alternatives, but he argued that if the peasants had been offered an amelioration of their conditions they would have actively supported the cause of unification. The mass base could have enabled the Party of Action to resolve the 'military problem' of raising sufficient troops to repel the Austrians without external aid via a 'revolutionary levy' and the formation of peasant militias. When such a possibility offered itself, such as the 'Five Days' insurrection in Milan in 1848, Mazzini flinched from taking it, for the reasons given above, and capitulated to the help proffered by the Piedmontese forces. Moreover, on the one occasion when they succeeded in gaining the initiative, during Garibaldi's invasion of Sicily, the Mazzinians ended up brutally crushing the peasant uprisings against the barons.[46]

Gramsci claimed the Party of Action's approach reflected a long-standing failure on the part of the urban bourgeoisie to engage with the rural peasantry going back to the time of the mediaeval communes, a pattern which was repeated at a different level in the modern North–South divide. In both cases, the bourgeoisie consolidated their power, not by allying with the more dynamic sections of society, but by compromising with the established agrarian elites. Their practical ineffectiveness resulted in the Mazzinian group's absorption into the Moderates and their acquiescence in the purely formal unity imposed by Piedmont. A pattern was thereby set for the subsequent development of liberal Italy, with 'transformism' continuing the process of the 'decapitation' of the elites of potentially disruptive social forces and their temporary 'annihilation'. As Gramsci remarked, such a mixture of bribery and police repression, employed with varying degrees of finesse, characterised the methods of political control adopted by the various liberal regimes, particularly in the South, up to and including Fascism. The latter simply indicated the limits of liberal 'legality' in the face of the mounting organised social unrest in both the towns and countryside following the First World War.[47]

In Gramsci's eyes the *Risorgimento* was a missed opportunity. Instead of a genuine revolution, Italy had undergone a 'passive revolution'. This was a term borrowed from the historian and philosopher Vincenzo Cuoco, which he 'completely modified and enriched'.[48] He employed it to describe the development of a new political formation without any reordering of social relations. It encompassed Caesarist actions from above, such as Mussolini's seizure of power, and certain styles of reformist politics. Adopting De Sanctis's famous comparison, he related it to the politics of Guicciardini as opposed to that of Machiavelli – of diplomacy and management rather than the exercise of *virtu*.[49] Throughout his account he compared the Mazzinians with the French Jacobins, who he regarded as 'Machiavellian realists' rather than 'abstract idealists'.[50] By building a 'national-popular' mass movement on the basis of urban–rural alliances, the Jacobins (at least in Gramsci's view) had succeeded in 'leading', representing not just the the immediate interests of the existing bourgeoisie, a moderate and exiguous class, but 'the revolutionary movement in its entirety, as an integrated historical development'. Consequently: 'they did not only organise a bourgeois government, that is make the bourgeoisie the dominant class, they did more, they created the bourgeois State, they made the bourgeoisie the leading national class, hegemonic, that is they gave the new State a permanent base, they created the compact modern French nation.'[51] The contrast with the 'illicit' union of the Moderates and the Party of Action could not have been greater. Rather than the legitimate modern bourgeois parliamentary State, 'they produced a bastard' which failed to have either 'a diffuse and energetic ruling class' or 'to include the people'.[52] After 1848 the 'real motor' of unity had not been a revolutionary class, but the Piedmontese State. The process of hegemonic expansion which had been such a distinctive feature of the bourgeoisie's rise and transformation of social relationships in France and Britain did not occur in Italy. Piedmont functioned as the ruling class. The Italian liberals conceived 'unity as the extension of the Piedmontese State and of dynastic patrimony, not as a national movement of the base but as a conquest of rulership'. In consequence, 'domination' predominated over leadership, dictatorship over consent.[53] Instead of the organic and truly hegemonic unity characteristic of the genuine modern bourgeois State, the Italian bourgeoisie created a transformist State based on 'the gradual but continuous absorption, achieved by methods which varied in their effectiveness, of the active elements produced by allied groups and even those which came from antagonistic groups which appeared irreconcilable enemies'.[54] *Pace* Croce, Gramsci contended that this was a thoroughly undialectical system, which sought to disarm and neutralise the opposition to prevent change, rather than to adapt in a positive manner so as to take them on board. The contrast between transformism and a genuinely stable hegemonic democracy 'in which [economic development and thus] the legislation [which expresses that development] favours the [molecular] passage from ruled to rulers' could not be greater.[55]

Gramsci traced all Italy's political ills to this failure to develop into a hegemonic State.[56] He identified only one alteration in the transformist system after 1860. Prior to Giolitti's ascendency at the turn of the century, *trasformismo* operated in a 'molecular' fashion to win over particular members of the parliamentary opposition to the 'conservative-moderate "political class"'. During this phase, it was 'characterised by its aversion to any intervention of the masses in State life, to any organic reform which would substitute "hegemony" for crude dictatorial "domination"'. After 1900 it was extended outside the sphere of mere parliamentary management to recruit entire groups of the Left over to the moderate camp. Gramsci gave the formation of the Nationalist Party out of ex-anarchists and syndicalists as an example of this process.[57] Thus, Giolitti's reformist and apparently more democratic policies merely changed the emphasis and methods of transformism to cope with the changing social and political situation. They did not break with it. However, the transformist process could not continue indefinitely. The State remained isolated from civil society and so vulnerable to social change. With the advent of a mass electorate and the politicisation of previously apathetic groups by the war – particularly organised labour, Catholics and sections of the *petit bour-*

geoisie – the parliamentary system began to break down.[58] The opportunistic nature of the Italian parties and their lack of principles prevented them from winning the hearts and minds of the people.[59] Not even the PSI proved capable of marshalling these forces. Bombarded by demands that it could not satisfy, the Italian State experienced a 'crisis of authority'. As the great masses became detached from their old ideologies, the ruling class lost its consensus. As a consequence, they were 'no longer "leading" but only "dominant", living by pure coercive force.'[60] Indeed, these groups could not even be controlled by 'legal' forces. Thus, not only consent, but the legitimate use of State force was replaced by the 'illegal force' of the Fascist squads.[61] With the break-down of the traditional and procedural forms of legitimation, only the violent intervention of a charismatic figure proved capable of filling the vacuum.[62] Such 'Caesarist' solutions were fragile, however.[63] For as with Piedmont's unification of Italy by conquest, they had to build hegemony from the top down to justify their domination, rather than becoming dominant having won a hegemonic ascendency. Fascism continued Italy's passive revolution which sought to reorganize the productive forces with the minimal disruption of social relations.[64] This circumstance made them vulnerable to a counter-hegemonic strategy by rival political forces within civil society.

Gramsci's strategy involved a self-conscious reappropriation of the Machiavellian approach to politics. In keeping with the *Risorgimento* tradition, he drew on the final pages of *The Prince* to read Machiavelli as a theorist of Italian unity. He argued that 'throughout the whole little volume Machiavelli deals with how the Prince must be in order to conduct a people to the foundation of a new State'. He consequently brought 'everything back to politics, that is to the art of governing men, of securing their permanent consent, and hence of founding "great States"'. Gramsci's Machiavelli was no more a complete voluntarist than he was, however. For according to Gramsci, the great strength of the Florentine arose from his perception of the need to address the 'effective reality' of social and economic forces whilst nevertheless appreciating the power of politics to shape them. As a result, he wrote about politics 'neither in the form of a cold utopia nor a reasoned doctrine, but as a creation of concrete fantasy that works on a dispersed and pulvarised people to arouse and organise their collective will.'[65] Machiavelli was 'the first Italian Jacobin',[66] therefore, who saw that

social revolution involved a moral and political capacity to supersede the prevailing economic conditions. Like the French Jacobins,
he had seen what the Party of Action had not: namely, that 'every
formation of a national-popular collective will is impossible, unless
the great mass of peasant cultivators bursts *simultaneously* into
political life'.[67] His militia scheme had been an attempt to address
this question.

In these respects Gramsci appealed to the idealist reading of
Machiavelli of De Sanctis. But in his views on how force and consent
operated in modern societies and might be employed by the 'Modern
Prince' or Party, he had more in common with the elitists. Like them
he accepted the division of society into 'rulers' and 'ruled' as a
'primordial fact' that could not be ignored even, as Mosca's pupil
Roberto Michels had shown, within workers' organisations.
Mosca's work may have been an 'enormous hotch-potch of a
sociological and positivist character', but his thesis had led him as far
back as 1883 to understand better 'the political technique of the
subaltern classes than, even several decades later, even the urban
representatives of these classes understood it'.[68] Parallels could also
be drawn between Mosca's concepts of 'juridical defence' and the
'political formula' and the two senses of Gramsci's conception of
hegemony. Clearly Gramsci's notions of 'organic intellectuals' and
'democratic centralism' modified considerably the cynical and
oligarchical conclusions of the elite theorists. But their work had
raised issues concerning the autonomy of politics and the mechanics
of its operation which could not be ignored.

More generally, Gramsci's view that in Italy State and civil society,
force and consent, had been pulled apart reflected the categories of
the Italian tradition. He explicitly admitted his own debts to Croce's
reworking of these themes in his ethico-political interpretation of
history, praising him for having 'energetically drawn attention to the
importance of cultural facts and of thought to historical development, to the function of the great intellectuals in the organic life of
civil society and of the State, to the moment of hegemony and of
consensus as a necessary form of the concrete historical block.'[69] His
own emphasis on the role of hegemony in both the State and Party
had more than a little affinity with Croce's ideas, although he
criticised Croce for failing to appreciate the economic preconditions
and political organisation required to sustain or change a given
hegemonic social configuration.[70] Similarly, his famous distinction

between the 'two grand superstructural "levels"' of civil society and
State' restated the Machiavellian distinctions of force and consent in
terms of Croce's distinction between the ethical and the political. He
credited Croce with the insight that it was a lack of fit between these
two levels that could provoke a 'crisis of authority', and that in such
circumstances the effective State would be found amongst the
government's social opponents.[71] However, we noted in Chapter 4
that he criticised Croce for failing to explore the dialectical connection between theory and practice, politics, culture and society. He
felt that the Crocean distinctions reflected not only the traditional
aloofness of the liberal intellectual, but the failure of the liberal
political regime more generally to incorporate the people, to unite
State and civil society in the new nation. Croce's insistence on this
distinction committed the same error as free-trade libertarians of
seeing the State–civil society divide as 'organic' rather than
'methodological'.[72] For Gramsci, the creation of an ethical State was
not the abomination Croce feared, so long as it was created from the
bottom up. Fascism involved a governmental morality because it
lacked roots in civil society. He attacked Gentile, who contrary to
Croce regarded history as 'all history of the State', for proposing 'the
(economic-) corporative phase as the ethical phase in the historical
act'. As a result, in his theory 'hegemony and dictatorship are indis-
tinguishable, force is consent pure and simple: one cannot distinguish political society from civil society: only the State exists and
naturally the State-government etc.'[73] The identification of State and
individual made by Gentile and his followers, such as the corporatist
theorist Ugo Spirito, was merely verbal. The consent of citizens was
'passive' and 'indirect', a matter of doing what the State and its rulers
told them.[74] The aim of his own approach, however, was to avoid
such statist consequences by building through the Party the proletarian ethical State within society. Thus, his new order or regulated
society was an 'ethical State' of a supposedly participatory and
democratic kind, in which harmony resulted from the direct and
active involvement and occasional dissonances of single persons. In
other words, he did not so much reject Gentile's thesis, as seek to
invert it and bring it back to its Spaventian roots. The true ethical
State, according to this conception, was, as we saw a 'State without a
State', in which no divide would exist between citizens and administrators.[75]

He regarded Fascism as continuing the tendency for the State to take on the role of a class or party in Italian history. It constituted the culmination of Italy's 'passive revolution', namely 'the integration of civil society in all its forms into the single organisation of the party state'.[76] Gramsci's own strategy was purposely designed to reverse this process and avoid its pitfalls. Rather than seeking to achieve power through seizing the State by force of arms, he insisted on the need to first conquer civil society and win the hegemonic consent of the masses. This conclusion had been one of the main lessons of the *Risorgimento*: 'that a social group can and indeed must lead before conquering governmental power (this is one of the principal conditions for the very conquest of power); afterwards, when it exercises power and even if it holds it strongly in its fist, it becomes dominant but it must also continue to "lead".'[77] He wished the proletariat to emulate the way the bourgeoisie outside Italy had wrested social power from the feudal aristocracy before assaulting the *ancien régime* State. Only in this manner would the transition to communist society be smooth and secure, avoiding the excesses of Fascism and by implication Stalinism.

The weaknesses commentators have noticed with this proposal also mirrored the Italian situation. Critics argue that Gramsci underestimated the degree to which the bourgeois-democratic State engineers the active consent of its citizens through its procedures.[78] They point out that the 'war of position' strategy, whereby hegemonic control of society can be won prior to an assault on the State, depends on the relative autonomy of civil society. Whereas this precondition largely prevailed in the case of the *ancien régime*, the same cannot be said of the States of modern industrial western nations. For a start, today's States are far more powerful and better organised than those of the eighteenth and early nineteenth centuries: not only do their bureaucratic structures stretch into large aspects of economic and social life, they also have highly efficient forces of coercion at their disposal. Both features can block counter-hegemonic projects more effectively than under earlier regimes. More important, bourgeois democracy itself channels potential opposition into supporting and upholding the State, disarming radical calls for change. Gramsci's examination of the development of the modern bourgeois State in France shows that he appreciated these changes, but he was also painfully aware that they had not emerged in his native land. Italian liberals had never felt much allegiance to parliamentary democracy, let alone successfullly constructed such a regime. As Gramsci correctly diagnosed, the resulting divergence of State and society was at the heart of the 'crisis of authority' threatening the liberal regime. His analysis was largely echoed in this respect by the Italian historian of liberalism, Guido De Ruggiero. Writing in 1921, De Ruggiero noted: 'This crisis can only be resolved by the gradual absorption into the State of those forces (the socialist masses) which now express themselves outside it. Only then will we have a strong State – thus enabling us to reduce the immense armies of police that we have today.'[79]

Unfortunately, his was a relatively isolated voice within the liberal camp. Too many liberals shared Croce's initial belief that it was better to use the Fascists to strengthen the coercive force of the State than to win the consent of the people through democratic reforms. Having witnessed the rise of the Fascists, Gramsci's belief that a political party 'carries out in civil society the same function as the State carries out in political society'[80] was not unreasonable. But for all its successes, the Italian Communist Party found this impossible to achieve under a successful parliamentary regime, and in the period following the Second World War was driven ineluctably towards reformism.[81]

Gramsci's picture of the new order was similarly influenced by models of the ideal unified Italian State and was likewise vitiated as a plausible goal for modern societies. At the heart of Gramsci's desire for a fully integrated society incorporating all groups was the belief of Italian political theorists that political unity ultimately required the social and cultural unity of the nation to be legitimate and successful – that Italy would only be truly 'made' when the political class had managed to 'make Italians'. Gramsci was particularly indebted to the Neapolitan Hegelians in this respect, whose conception of the tutelary function of the State and the relationship between force and consent he incorporated into his view of the role of the revolutionary Party and the nature of the 'new order'. He also shared their cynicism and more especially that of the elitists about liberal democracy. For these groups, every bit as much as for Marxists, the separation of State and civil society could only serve a sinister purpose. However, from the liberal perspective this distinction reflects the need for a political mediation between the heterogeneous aims of different individuals. Democracy provides a relationship between the two spheres without dissolving the tension between them – for this very tension provides the guarantee of individual freedom. To submerge the one into the other would be either to plunge society into the anarchy of the war of each against all, or to give rise to a bureaucratic Leviathan in which all individuals were organised by administrative procedures. It is to the question of whether Gramsci's resolution of State and civil society within a cultural totality can avoid this liberal dilemma to which we must now finally turn.

The new order: a 'progressive' totalitarianism?

Gramsci's conception of the 'new order' seems in some respects paradoxical. On the one hand, he stressed a radical theory of democracy and the importance of openness based on immanent critique rather than bureaucratic closure. On the other hand, however, he painted a picture of a closed society based on a 'total' culture reflecting the 'total' organisation of production, in which the individual had become but a disciplined cog in the productive machine. We shall argue that this paradox resulted from the fact that the apparent liberality of the first required the authoritarian structures of the second for its coherence. Gramsci had not thereby resolved the basic liberal problem of how to balance liberty and the need for authority. Rather, like the Italian theorists of the ethical State and many others in the Marxist tradition, he falsely conflated the two. Indeed, the distinctiveness of Gramsci's thesis could be characterised as the result of his grafting the desire for cultural unity of the Italian Hegelians onto the productivism he derived from Marxism.

Gramsci's desire to broaden the role of popular participation to give the masses the power to direct and control social and productive activity went back to his advocacy of the Factory Councils in the early 1920s and was clearly undiminished in the *Prison Notebooks*. Here too he continued to consider the possibility of 'a diverse solution, both from parliamentarism and from the bureaucratic regime with a new type of representative regime'.[82] As before, the inspiration for this new form of democracy was the system of Soviets as idealised by Lenin in *State and Revolution* and the Paris Commune as described by Marx. Unlike parliamentary democracy, consent in such a set up did not stop at the moment of voting:

Consent is presumed to be permanently active, to the point that those who consent are considered 'functionaries' of the State and elections a method of voluntary enrollment of State functionaries of a certain type, that can in a certain sense be linked (at different levels) to self-government. Since the elections are held on the basis not of vague and indefinite programmes, but of concrete immediate tasks, he who consents commits himself to doing something more than the common legal citizen, to realise them, to be that is a vanguard of active and responsible work.[83]

Thus, the creation of a new type of stateless State with which individuals could identify on the basis of 'an active culture' involved the construction: 'within the shell of political society of a complex and well-articulated civil society, in which the single individual is self-governing, without this self-government coming into conflict with political society, but, on the contrary, becoming its normal continuation and organic completion.'[84] Underlying his championing of free discussion and popular involvement, however, lay the belief that opinions and decisions would converge. As he expressed it in a revealing passage: 'A collective conscience, and therefore a living organism, does not form unless a multiplicity is unified through the friction of individuals . . . An orchestra tuning up, each instrument on its own account, gives the impression of the most horrendous cacofony; and yet this tuning is the condition of the orchestra living as a single "instrument".'[85] This quote contains both the liberal and the authoritarian sides of Gramsci's argument – the plea for dialogue and the need for individual experimentation and discovery on the one hand, and the contention that heteronomy must give way to the homogeneity of a single will on the other. This second aspect of Gramsci's argument cannot be detached from the first. For the emergence of a general will and the interchangeability of citizens and administrators presupposed a common interest and a common outlook. Gramsci's 'producers' democracy' was entirely functional in nature and assumed that ethical questions had become technical issues, so that politics could be reduced to administration. The aim of each and every citizen was to maximise productivity through performing his or her job to the utmost.

Gramsci's theory of radical democracy rested on an essentially holistic ontology and a pragmatic epistemology linked to a particular understanding of historical materialism. As we saw in Chapter 4, these were the preconditions for his contention that scientific objectivity corresponded to complete subjectivity of agreement. Similarly, the belief that every citizen could be a functionary,[86] actively involved in the implementation and elaboration of a coherent policy, assumed the interrelated and complementary nature of human endeavours and the belief that decisions could be reduced to easily-resolved technical disputes concerning the maximisation of production. There are numerous objections to be made to this position. First, what role remained for politics or democratic discussion to play in this new order? Consensus on goals and interests would mean that the important questions would have been resolved. Moreover, what value would the consent of Gramsci's Taylorised workers have in any case? Surely the consent of a totally moralised and socialized population, no matter how active in appearance, has about the same status as the consent of a group of brainwashed zombies? Second, even if the discussion of ends could be separated from discussion of means, which is doubtful, agreement on the former would not necessarily reduce the potential for conflict arising from the latter. Apart from anything else, there are constraints of time, information and scale which this model does not take into account. Even with the use of computer technology, the time necessary to decide on an agenda, discuss issues and vote on them will be prohibitive, while making the relevant information available may be both costly and only comprehensible to those with specialist knowledge in any case. How can all play an equal role in the formulation and carrying out of policies in these circumstances? As modern societies grow in complexity and size so that face-to-face relations decline, even common interests and the best will in the world on the part of all participants would not prevent them from making well-intentioned but uncomprehending and ill-informed decisions with potentially harmful effects for unknown others. Radical democracy of the kind espoused by Gramsci would seem to rely on not just shared interests and a common moral code, but omniscience, omnipotence and angelic rectitude on the part of citizens as well.

Gramsci sought to avoid these difficulties by arguing for the need for deference to technical authority. In a fine piece of sophistry, he argued that the discipline such deference entailed might be reconciled with both democracy and individual liberty. So long as the discipline of the new order was understood not as the 'passive and supine acceptance of orders', but 'the conscious and lucid assimilation of the directives to be accomplished' it did 'not annul the personality in an organic sense, but only limits licence and irresponsible impulsiveness.' Thus,

Discipline does not negate personality and freedom; the question of 'personality and freedom' is posed not by the fact of discipline, but by the 'origin of the power that lies behind the discipline'. If this origin is 'democratic', if that is the authority is a specialised technical function and not 'arbitrary' or an external extrinsic imposition, discipline is a necessary element of democratic order, of freedom.[87]

However, this contention merely brought Gramsci's argument round full circle. If radical democracy presupposed common 'organic' interests, moral consensus and the reduction of ethical to technical questions, then administration by a central planning authority might prove more efficient yet just as 'democratic' as self-government. For the rationale for the latter had all but passed away. Democracy of the kind desired by Gramsci was only possible to the extent that it involved a rigorous self-discipline arising out of the assimilation of norms generated by the mode of production and handed down by technical experts.

Gramsci's difficulties mirrored those of Marx in these respects. Marx wrote little on what the reabsorption of the State into society involved, deriding such exercises as unscientific and 'utopian'. However, as we noted, he regarded the Paris Commune as offering a possible model. He believed that this movement had demonstrated that 'the working class cannot simply lay hold of the ready made State machinery and wield it for its own purposes'; real change required 'a revolution to break this horrid machinery of class domination itself'.[88] A transitory period of class dictatorship consolidated the social transformation of society by removing the vestiges of bourgeois social power, e.g. their monopoly of the technical skills and administrative positions vital for the running of the economy, and the continued prevalence of bourgeois ideology in such matters as incentives for work. The elimination of class divisions, however, would finally allow the 'narrow horizon of bourgeois right' to be crossed under Communism.[89] According to Marx, these circumstances laid the basis for a 'true democracy', in which 'government' gave way to 'administration'. This involved society becoming self-administering in deciding questions concerning the allocation of goods and the planning of production. Specialists in charge of these functions were not to be free agents, but bound by the formal instructions, or *mandat imperatif*, of the people.[90] Marx held that the division of labour, necessary for running a complex economy even under Communism, was a 'business matter that gives no-one domination'. All the different functions within society would be on a par with each other and appointments made on purely technical considerations. Indeed, technology will have so simplified the different tasks that jobs could be interchangeable and in principle performed by any of the citizens. Elections for these various posts and the making of decisions generally will have lost in consequence their 'present political character'.[91] Yet if matters could be as cut and dried as this, what purpose would elections serve? As numerous recent commentators have pointed out, this vision of the future seems to rely on much the same assumptions we have noted in Gramsci's new order: first, that members of the new community have internalized the social norms regulating conduct within it to the extent that no enforcement of them is necessary; second, that the collective nature of labour can in some sense render the self-realisation of each the condition for that of all; third, that resources are sufficiently abundant for conflicts over their use not to be problem; fourth, that humans have been transformed into a race of super-beings lacking all the usual tendencies to error, etc.[92]

The weaknesses of such arguments are self-evident.[93] The historical record, for example, belies Gramsci's optimism in the liberating potential of integrated work processes for the many-sided development of the individual. In this area at least, self-realisation and co-operative production have tended to conflict rather than to complement each other. Those who worked on the Fiat assembly line, rather than theorised about it, appreciated how the new techniques achieved the maximum integration with the minimum of individual autonomy. His faith that the evolution of productive forces would bring about the coincidence of the rational and the real seem equally flawed. The processes of functional differentiation have enhanced both cognitive and moral pluralism. People can not only rationally desire diverse and often incommensurable goods; they also frequently adopt distinct and occasionally contradictory kinds of reasoning in the different contexts within which they operate. As a result, the identities and loyalties even of single individuals can become divided between the membership of different groups – their professional, neighbourhood, family, sexual, ethnic and religious ties can all clash at times. Needless to say, these tensions between the various spheres of social existence are exacerbated when seeking to produce a rational consensus between individuals and groups. For the division of labour and the fragmentation of our lives not only splits up our own sense of personal identity, it also seriously weakens our ability to relate to others as members of a common moral, social and political world. The size of modern societies and the concomitant absence of face-to-face relations; the growing complexity and technicality of many social and economic tasks and the resulting reliance on experts, including a permanent professional bureaucracy; the intrusion of new technologies into all areas of life, including leisure as well as work, and especially new information technology; and the enhanced functional differentiation and specialisation which accompanied these innovations – all these forces have progressively weakened the individual's capacity for autonomous rational action and choice. The dependence on unknown, unpredictable and uncontrollable others involved in an integrated global economy; our containment within managerial hierarchies of various kinds; the proliferation of sources of information and persuasion resulting from the technological revolution within the media, etc. have rendered it increasingly hard for us to make reasoned judgements of our own about the world, since we cannot reduce its complexity to manageable levels.

A number of consequences follow from these circumstances. First, as the ability of individual citizens rationally to comprehend their place in the whole progressively decreases, increasing participatory democracy is likely to enhance rather than reduce this complexity by increasing the number of decisions and augmenting particularist sentiments. The homogeneity required for collective deliberation on the common good no longer exists and could only be reintroduced at the drastic cost of a gross simplification and curtailment of human creativity and interaction. Second, in such conditions no ethical code exists capable of rationally integrating the diverse dimensions of human life into one scheme of values. Attempts to produce a 'total' perspective risk becoming 'totalitarian': even a socialised community of individuals, if they remain individuals in any meaningful sense, will contain a diversity of different types of relationship operating at a variety of levels. The relations between friends, workmates, lovers, neighbours, other citizens and strangers – all of which would presumably persist under Communism – are not of the same quality, and with the best will in the world cannot always be brought into harmony with each other. Choices between incommensurable goods, sometimes of a tragic kind, could only be eliminated in a behaviourist utopia of the most deadening type. Finally, the openness and unpredictability of complex social systems render the historicist faith in either a single subject, teleology or a meaning of history highly dubious. Such conceptions could only be pronounced upon by bringing history to a premature close – a prospect which seems as stultifying as it would necessarily be coercive.

Once Gramsci's assumptions become called into question, then so does his desire to absorb the State into civil society. He showed no awareness of the role the State plays in protecting individuals from the coercion of others by upholding the rule of law, or of its function as an arena for political debate about the distribution of resources and the priorities of the social union binding together its constituent members. To achieve these goals, the State must be responsive to civil society whilst remaining a co-ordinating entity in its own right. In modern conditions, the purpose of the democratic State cannot be the expression of the general will of autonomous individuals. Rather, it provides the institutional context for the maintenance of an equitable *modus vivendi* between individuals by offering mechanisms for exercising control and influence over the authoritive laws and regulations needed for a degree of security in our mutual relations. The democratic State, in sum, represents a response to the perennial need in human societies to find a balance between liberty and authority. That the first proves impossible without the second does not diminish the degree of tension between the two. To seek, as Gramsci did, to resolve this tension by identifying them leads to simple authoritarianism. That Gramsci's intentions were 'progressive', the absorption of authority into liberty rather than vice versa, cannot be doubted. But this circle cannot be squared – only confronted and negotiated. In the tension between State and civil society, liberty and authority lies the essence and necessity of politics and hence of democracy. It was the tragedy both of the Marxist and the Italian political traditions on which Gramsci drew to have denied this fact. As a result, both gave rise to some of the most repressive State systems of recent times.

Conclusion

On 7 March 1933 Gramsci collapsed in his cell. Two weeks later he was examined by a doctor, Professor Arcangeli. He certified that 'Gramsci cannot survive long in present conditions: I consider it necessary for him to be transferred to a civil hospital or a clinic, unless he can be granted conditional liberty.' Gramsci refused to submit a plea for mercy to the Fascist authorities. However, Arcangeli's statement was published in May by *L'Humanité* and led to an international campaign for Gramsci's release. In December he was transferred to a clinic at Formia. Here he began the process of rewriting and grouping together various of the notes into a series of 'special' notebooks on particular themes. In October 1934 he submitted a request for conditional release, which was granted. A further crisis in his health in June 1935 led the authorities to grant his request to be moved to a clinic in Rome, where he went in August. Exhausted and still under surveillance, he had ceased work on the *Notebooks* but was able to resume correspondence with his wife and children in 1936. In April 1937 he was finally granted unconditional freedom, but was too ill to move. On the 25th of that month he suffered a cerebral haemorrhage and died two days later.

As a result of the foresight and care of his sister-in-law, Tatiana Schucht, who had supported Gramsci throughout his incarceration, the manuscript of the *Notebooks* and many of his letters were preserved and ultimately sent to Togliatti and the PCd'I leaders in Moscow. So began the plundering of Gramsci's writings to legitimise every twist and turn of the Italian Communist Party's policy. Thus, in different phases of the Party's history Gramsci has been a Stalinist, a mere Leninist, a post-Leninist Eurocommunist and, most recently, the first proponent of the Party's split with Communist ideology. An implicit purpose of this study has been to show that little evidence can be found in Gramsci's writings for any of these positions. His ideas must be examined in relation to the debates of his contemporaries on the appropriate institutions for the unification of Italy, not in relation to the strategy of the PCI within the secure parliamentary system of an advanced industrial nation.

What then remains of his legacy – in Crocean terms, 'What is living and what is dead in Gramsci's philosophy?' The living to a large extent resides precisely in what Gramsci took from Croce and reworked in his own terms – his historicism. It is from this source that all the most attractive features of Gramsci's theory flow: his belief in creative human agency and his concomitant concern with the role of human will and consciousness; his appreciation of the complexity of forces in play in a given historical moment and of the necessity for theory to address these empirical features of our political life; his interest in popular culture and the importance of the masses developing a critical consciousness of their own from within, rather than having one imposed on them from without; his rejection of dogmatic systems and attentiveness to the need for theories to address and partially shape a changing social and political reality; his opposition to the mechanistic economism of many contemporary Marxists and his insights into the relative autonomy of the State and the hegemonic power of civil society and the consequent part to be played by intellectuals and the Party in shaping a counterhegemony. This study has sought to emphasise these strengths by placing Gramsci's writings firmly in the political and ideological context of his times, and showing the degree to which Gramsci's theory grew out of a practical engagement with the ideas and politics of his age.

However, we also have the advantage of the standpoint of history to reveal the weaknesses which resulted from this approach. For it led Gramsci to make assumptions and work within traditions we find questionable, and to see trends and draw empirical conclusions that have proved unfounded. Above all, it resulted in him transforming a justified critique of the Italian State into an attack on the idea of the State *tout court*, and misinterpreting the particular trends of his age as linear developments of a universal logic. Gramsci's linking of the Italian ethical State tradition with a Marxian productivism and faith in the universality of the proletariat proved particularly pernicious in this respect. Whilst this mixture helped Gramsci appreciate the importance of obtaining hegemonic control over civil society and of providing a cultural unity to an increasingly diverse working class within advanced western societies, it also led him to underestimate the problems involved in these operations. For the very forces that had spread political power throughout society as a whole had also increased the State's ability to block counterhegemonic movements and enhanced the fragmentation of the proletariat. These developments also weakened the plausibility and desirability of Gramsci's projected totally harmonious 'regulated society', within which each individual is absorbed into his or her role within the productive process. As we observed at the end of the last chapter, the historical record belies Gramsci's optimism in the liberating potential of integrated work processes to unify the real and the rational, to overcome the tensions between authority and liberty, central planning and spontaneous self-government, and to reconcile each person to his or her station and its duties. In modern conditions, this drive to encompass diversity within some kind of higher unity risks becoming totalitarian in the pejorative sense. Far from being overcome, the role of the State as the guarantor of an increasingly pluralistic society seems ineliminable. Our central concern can no longer be with the withering away of the State, so much as ensuring its democratic character. Both the difficulties concerning the organisation of an effective counterhegemonic movement and the implausibility and unattractiveness of the goal of social emancipation (at least as traditionally conceived) continue to bedevil democratic socialists.

If a historicist critique of Gramsci reveals many of his ideas to belong inextricably to a past we can no longer share, why study him at all? First, because Gramsci's desire to relate theory to the understanding and making of history retains its validity even if the terms in which he conceived this relationship do not. That philosophical enquiry needs to be located within the world rather than beyond it, to avoid vacuity on the one hand or dogmatism on the other, is an important lesson for political philosophy above all. Contemporary political philosophers are all too prone to falling into one or other of these traps in seeking to divorce a philosophical grounding of politics from a philosophical understanding of and involvement in politics. Gramsci's life and thought offer a salutary reminder of the importance, as well as the pitfalls, of linking theory and practice. Second, whatever the weaknesses of Gramsci's own analysis, the dialectic between State and civil society to which he drew attention continues to be of fundamental importance for understanding the nature and exercise of political power within industrial societies. Existing State formations are currently undergoing dramatic and often contradictory transformations, assailed as they are by international pressures from without and increasingly localised national pressures from within. Gramsci's own categories and solutions may not be of much help in this situation, but the general problem he sought to address – namely, the construction of a viable democratic political culture suited to a socially and economically diverse society – is more pressing than ever. Finally, his writings remain of interest because an historical engagement with them, which examines the various forces moulding and motivating them, in showing the distance which separates Gramsci's world from our own also teaches us about ourselves. To be aware of the contingency of many of his assumptions has the beneficial effect of forcing us to criticise them and to come up with new ideas – an attitude far more in keeping with the whole spirit of Gramsci's work than the slavish dedication shown by many of his devotees. Those who have sought to transport Gramsci willy-nilly from the 1930s to their own times have clearly failed to interrogate his texts sufficiently closely or to learn this most important lesson from them.

Notes

Notes to chapter 1

1 Dante Germino, *Antonio Gramsci: Architect of a New Politics*. Baton Rouge: Louisiana State University Press, 1990, pp. 2–6.

2 Giuseppe Fiori, *Vita di Antonio Gramsci*. Bari: Laterza, 1966, pp. 11–16; John Cammett, *Antonio Gramsci and the Origins of Italian Communism*. Stanford: Stanford University Press, 1967, pp. 3–4; Anne Showstack Sassoon, 'Gramsci's life' in Anne Showstack Sassoon (ed.), *Approaches to Gramsci*. London: Writers and Readers Cooperative, 1982, p. 150, and Tom Nairn, 'Antonu su Gobbu' in Sassoon, *Approaches to Gramsci*, pp. 159–160.

3 Giuseppe Fiori, *Gramsci, Togliatti, Stalin*. Bari: Laterza, 1991, pp. 108, 169–70.

4 Fiori, *Gramsci, Togliatti, Stalin*, pp. 170–73.

5 Cammett, *Antonio Gramsci and the Origins of Italian Communism*, pp. 16–17.

6 James Joll, *Gramsci*. Glasgow: William Collins Sons and Co., 1977, pp. 21–5.

7 Walter Adamson, *Hegemony and Revolution*. Berkeley: University of California Press, 1980, pp. 29–30; Cammett, *Antonio Gramsci and the Origins of Italian Communism*, p. 18.

8 Joll, *Gramsci*, pp. 18–19.

9 Emilio Gentile, *Il mito dello stato nuovo: dell' antigiolittismo al fascismo*. Bari: Laterza, 1982, pp. 3–4. For problems concerning popular estrangement from the post-*Risorgimento* state, see Sidney Sonino in his speech to the Camera dated 30 March 1881, quoted in Federico Chabod, *Storia della politica estera italiano del 1870 al 1896*, Volume I. Bari: Laterza, 1965, p. 589.

10 Richard Bellamy, *Modern Italian Social Theory*. Cambridge: Polity Press, 1987, pp. 4–5.

11 Guido Oldrini, *La cultura filosofica napoletana dell'ottocento*. Bari: Laterza, 1973, pp. 188–90.

12 Bellamy, *Modern Italian Social Theory*, p. 5.

13 Emilio Gentile, *Il mito dello stato nuovo: dell' antigiolittismo al*

fascismo, pp. 5–9; Emilio Gentile, *La Voce e l' età giolittiana*. Milan: Pan editore, 1972, pp. 7–9. David Roberts, *The Syndicalist Tradition and Italian Fascism*. Manchester: Manchester University Press, 1979, pp. 26–8. As Roberts shows, fragmentation, atomisation and lack of a sense of civic virtue amongst Italians were important concerns of Francesco de Sanctis, Giustino Fortunato and Guido de Ruggiero. De Sanctis had an important influence on Gramsci during his university studies in Turin immediately preceding the *L'Ordine nuovo* period. See Gramsci, *Scritti giovanili, 1914–1918* (here after *SG*). Turin: Einaudi, 1975, pp. 376–7.

14 Gramsci, *Quaderni del carcere* (four volumes), edited by Valentino Gerratana. Turin: Einaudi, 1977, p. 1233; Emilio Agazzi, 'Filosofia della prassi e filosofia dello spirito' in Alberto Caracciola (ed.). *La Città futura*. Turin: Einaudi, 1959, p. 256. On the problems presented by Croce's separation of theory and practice see Eugenio Garin, *Intellecttuali italiani del XX secolo*. Rome: Riuniti Editore, 1974, pp. 53–65.

15 Nicola Badaloni, 'Filosofia della praxis' in *Gramsci: le sue idee nel nostro tempo*. Rome: Editrice l'Unità, 1987, pp. 93–5.

16 Benedetto Croce, 'Per la a rinascita dell'idealismo' (1908), in *Cultura e vita morale*. Bari: Laterza, 1926, pp. 35–6.

17 Benedetto Croce, 'La morte del socialismo' (1911) in *Cultura e vita morale*, p. 155.

18 Benedetto Croce, 'Per la rinascita dell'idealismo', p. 40; 'La morte del socialismo', pp. 156–9.

19 Eugenio Garin, *Cronache di filosofia italiana, 1900–1943*. Bari: Laterza, 1955, pp 366–71.

20 Bellamy, *Modern Italian Social Theory*, p. 103; *Marx and Engels Selected Works in 1 Volume*. London: Lawrence and Wishart, 1968, pp. 29–30; Emilio Agazzi, *Il giovane Croce e il marxismo*. Turin: Einaudi, 1962, pp. 235–7.

21 Gramsci, 'Il socialismo e la filosofia attuale' (1918), in *La Città futura*. Turin: Einaudi 1982, p. 650; Giovanni Gentile, *Teoria generale dello spirito come atto puro*. Florence: Sansoni, 1916, pp. 93–105; *I fondamenti della filosofia del diritto*. Florence: Sansoni, 1916, pp. 41–66. For an analysis OF Gentile's influence on the young Gramsci and some of the similarities in their views up until 1921, see Giancarlo Bergami, *Il giovane Gramsci e il Marxismo*. Milan: Feltrinelli, 1977, pp. 82–4, and Darrow Schecter, 'Gramsci, Gentile and the theory of the ethical state in Italy' in *History of Political Thought*, 11 (1990), pp. 491–508.

22 Paolo Spriano, *L'Ordine nuovo e i consigli di fabbrica*. Turin: Einaudi, 1971, pp. 30–31; Zefiro Ciuffoletti, 'La fondazione del Partito Socialista Italiano e l'azione di Filippo Turati' in Gaetano Arfe (ed.), *Lezione del PSI, 1892–1975*. Florence: Cooperativa Editrice Universitaria, 1976, pp. 12–13. Ciuffoletti also provides a useful historical account of the phenomenon of *trasformismo*.

23 Paolo Spriano, *Storia di Torino operaia e socialista da De Amicis a Gramsci*. Turin: Einaudi, 1972, pp. 195, 262–3; *SG*, p. 154.

24 Gramsci, *Scritti 1915–21*, edited by Sergio Capriolo. Vicenza: 'Il Corpo', 1968, pp. 16–20; *SG*, pp. 31–2.

25 Gramsci, *Scritti 1915–21*, p. 53.
26 Gramsci, *Scritti 1915–21*, pp. 5–6, 11, 16, 18–19, 48, 54, 87; *La Città futura*, pp. 82–3, 118–19, 402–3; Bergami, *Il giovane Gramsci e il Marxismo*, pp. 33, 38–41.
27 Gramsci, *Scritti 1915–21*, pp. 87–8; *SG.*, pp. 140–41.
28 *SG*, pp. 269–75.
29 On the fragmentation of Italian society and the problems of *trasformismo* and the *Questione meridionale*, see Roberts, *The Syndicalist Tradition and Italian Fascism*, pp. 26–48; Giuseppe Galasso, *Passato e presente del meridionalismo. Volume I: Genesi e sviluppi.* Naples: Guida Editori, 1978, pp. 84–5; Alberto Caracciola, *Stato e società civile: problemi dell'unificazione italiana.* Turin: Einaudi, 1960, pp. 111–13, pp. 124–6; Alceo Riosa, *Il sindacalismo rivoluzionario in Italia.* Bari: De Donato, 1976, pp. 16–17, in addition to the already cited references to the works of Emilio Gentile. See also Guido Dorso, *La rivoluzione meridionale.* Turin: Einaudi, 1925, 1972 edition, pp. 77–9.
30 Leo Valiani, *Gli sviluppi ideologici del socialismo in Italia.* Rome: Editore Opere Nuove, 1956, pp. 10–20.
31 Valiani, *Gli sviluppi ideologici del socialismo in Italia*, pp. 23–8; Gaetano Arfe, *Storia del socialismo italiano, 1892–1926.* Turin: Einaudi, 1965, pp. 9–11.
32 Arfe, *Storia del socialismo italiano, 1892–1926*, pp. 74–6; Z. Ciuffoletti, 'La fondazione del Partito Socialista Italiano e l'azione di Filippo Turati', pp. 27–33.
33 Ciuffoletti, 'La fondazione del Partito Socialista Italiano e l'azione di Filippo Turati', pp. 30–31; Gwynn A. Williams, *Proletarian Order.* London: Pluto Press, 1975, pp. 322–33; Arfe, *Storia del socialismo italiano, 1892–1926*, pp. 270–72; Gramsci, *SG*, pp. 321–2.
34 Enzo Santarelli, *La revisione del marxismo in Italia.* Milan: Feltrinelli Economica, 1977, pp. 220–22.
35 It is in this context that Massimo Salvadori correctly maintains that despite syndicalism's failure to win a mass appeal among Italian workers, and the subsequent defection of some of the syndicalists to fascism, the movement challenged PSI strategy on a number of important points and subsequently had a large impact on Italian communism. See Salvadori, *Gramsci e il problema storica della democrazia.* Turin: Einaudi, 1977, pp. 395–6.
36 *SG*, pp. 30–31. Paolo Spriano observes that in addition to the notable influence of Sorel, Gramsci's understanding of syndicalism also came from journals such as *Avanguardia Socialista*, *Il Divenire Sociale*, and *Pagine Libere*. Gramsci first became familiar with the works of Arturo Labriola and the syndicalists in Cagliari, where he read the journal *Il Viandante*. Paolo Spriano, *Gramsci e Gobetti.* Turin: Einaudi, 1977, pp. 10–12; Fiori, *Vita di Antonio Gramsci*, pp. 56–7.
37 Gramsci, 'Alcuni temi della quistione meridionale' in *La Costruzione del partito communista italiano, 1923–1926* (hereinafter *CPC*). Turin: Einaudi, pp. 144–6; Massimo Salvadori, *Gramsci e il problema storico della democrazia.* Turin: Einaudi, 1977, pp. 392–3.

38 Gramsci, *La Costruzione del Partito Communista Italiano, 1923–1926*, pp. 146; Arturo Labriola, *Storia di dieci anni 1899–1909*. Milan: Casa Editrice 'Il Viandante', 1910, p. 10.

39 Labriola, *Storia di dieci anni 1899–1909*,p. 10.

40 Labriola, *Storia di dieci anni 1899–1909*, pp. 305–6. See also S. F. Romano, *Storia della questione meridionale*. Palermo: Edizioni Pantea, 1945, pp. 51–5; Massimo Salvadori, *Il mito del buongoverno: Il questione meridionale da Cavour a Gramsci*. Turin: Einaudi, 1960, pp. 90–91.

41 Gaetano Salvemini, *Scritti sulla questione meridionale, 1896–1952*. Turin: Einaudi, 1958, pp. 152–3; Arturo Labriola, *Sindacalismo e riformismo*. Florence: G. Nerbini Editore, 1905, pp. 14–16; Enrico Leone, 'L'azione elettorale e il socialismo' in *Il Divenire Sociale*, II, (1906), pp. 17–22; Sergio Panunzio, 'Socialismo, liberismo, anarchismo' in *Il Divenire Sociale*, II (1906), pp. 72–4.

42 Labriola, *Sindacalismo e riformismo*, pp. 15–16. See also Arturo Labriola, 'L'onesta polemica contro Giorgio Plekhanoff e per il sindacalismo' in *Pagine Libere*. Lugano: Società Editrice Avanguardia, II (1908), pp. 185–200; Arturo Labriola, 'Sindacati e socialismo' in *Il Divenire Sociale*, I (1906), pp. 259–1; Sergio Panunzio, 'Socialismo, liberismo, anarchismo', pp. 73–4; Paolo Orano, 'Perchè il sindacalismo non è populare in Italia?' in *Il Divenire Sociale*, II, (1907), pp. 225–227. See also Soldani, *La struttura del dominio nel sindacalismo rivoluzionario e nel giovane Gramsci*, pp. 24–9, and Giovanna Cavallari, *Classe dirigente e minoranze rivoluzionarie*. Camerino: Jovene Editori, 1983, pp. 27–32.

43 Sergio Panunzio, *La persistenza del diritto*. Pescara: Casa Editrice Abbruzzese, 1910, pp. x–xxii, pp. 1–64; Giuseppe Prezzolini, *La teoria sindacalista*. Naples: Francesco Perrella Editore, 1909, pp. 103–13.

44 Reformists and revolutionary syndicalists struggled for control of the PSI until 1908, when the General Strike was declared dangerous and syndicalism itself declared incompatible with the principles of the Party. The expulsion of the syndicalist faction from the PSI thus marked the end, until Gramsci and Amadco Bordiga would take up the question a few years later, of any revolutionary strategy within the PSI which included the *Questione meridionale*, and which called for the abolition of the existing state. In the years immediately after the 1904 General Strike, the reformist line gradually gained the upper hand even in Sicily, which had been the scene of a great deal of peasant agitation around the turn of the century. Giolitti's transformist bloc succeeded in binding the economic interests of northern industrial workers with the political interests of northern industrialists and southern *latifundisti*, thus isolating syndicalist currents within the organized labour movement. See Romano, *Storia della questione meridionale*, pp, 55–60, and Melis's introduction to *Sindacalisti italiani*.

45 *SG*, p. 150

46 Preface to the 1872 German edition of the *Communist Manifesto*, in *Marx and Engels: Selected Works in One Volume*. London: Lawrence and Wishart, 1980, pp. 31–2.

47 Marx, *The Civil War in France*, in *Marx and Engels: Selected Works in One Volume*, pp. 287–8.

48   Lenin, *Collected Works*, Volume 27. Moscow: Progress Publishers, 1975, pp. 133, 140.

49   Alaistair Davidson, 'Gramsci and Lenin 1917–1921', in the *Socialist Register, 1974*, pp. 130–39; Carmen Sirianni, *Workers' Control and Socialist Democracy: the Soviet Experience*. London: Verso, 1982, pp. 148–50, 235–9, 301–5.

50   *SG*, p. 106. This tradition of anti-Jacobinism is also salient in the political thought of Mazzini. See Valiani, *Gli sviluppi ideologici del socialismo*, 1956, pp. 10–11. It is widely acknowledged that Gramsci held a much more favourable assessment of Jacobinism in the *Quaderni*.

51   *SG*, pp. 131, 315, 339, 349–50, 355.

52   *SG*, pp. 74–76, 160.

53   *SG*, pp. 280–86.

54   *SG*, p. 25.

55   Gabriele Gorzka, *A. Bogdanov und der russische Proletkult: Theorie und Praxis ein Sozialistischen Kulturrevolution*. Frankfurt: Campus Verlag, 1980, pp. 8–25.

56   *SG*, pp. 73–89; Bergami, *Il giovane Gramsci e il marxismo*, pp. 80–82.

57   *SG*, p. 144; *Bergami, Il giovane Gramsci e il marxismo*, pp. 115–16; Gramsci's letter to Lombardo Radice has been reprinted in *Rinascita*, 10, (1964), p. 32. He praises Viglongo's essay as a 'spiritual cleansing' for the youth of Italy.

58   *Bergami, Il giovane Gramsci e il marxismo*, pp. 52–6.

Notes to chapter 2

1   Paolo Spriano, *L'Ordine nuovo e i consigli di fabbrica*. Turin: Einaudi, 1971, p. 45.

2   John Cammett, *Antonio Gramsci and the Origins of Italian Communism*. Stanford: Stanford University Press, 1967, pp. 71–6.

3   Maurizio Guarnieri, *I Consigli di fabbrica*. Città di Castello: Il Solco, 1946, pp. 11–12.

4   Guarnieri, *I Consigli di fabbrica*, pp. 12–13; Francesco Magri, *La crisi industriale e il controllo Operaia*. Milan: Editrice Unitas, 1922, pp. 24–5; Mario Abrate, *La lotta sindacale nella industrializzazione in Italia*. Milan: Franco Angeli, 1967, pp. 67–8.

5   Martin Clark, *Antonio Gramsci and the Revolution that Failed*. New Haven: Yale University Press, 1977, p. 38; Guarnieri, *I Consigli di fabbrica*, pp. 15–16; Paolo Spriano, *Torino operaia nella grande guerra*. Turin: 1960, p. 299; Paolo Spriano, *Storia di Torino operaia e socialista da De Amicis a Gramsci*. Turin: Einaudi, 1972, pp. 468–70.

6   Gramsci, *L'Ordine nuovo 1919–1920* (hereinafter *on*). turin; Einaudi, 1987 , pp. 297–301.

7   ON, pp. 131–2.

8   ON, p. 128.

9   ON, p. 341.

10   ON, p. 129.

11 ON, pp. 87–91, 619–28. The so-called *coup d'état* was directed against Angelo Tasca, who denies the great significance of the 'Workers' Democracy' article. In his own account of the Factory Council movement he asserts that he had for some time been considering the possibilities of enlarging the sphere of action of the CI. Meanwhile the article did not provoke the kind of rupture Gramsci suggests, since Tasca continued to work with the other members of *L'Ordine nuovo*, including Togliatti and Gramsci, at least until January 1920. See Angelo Tasca, *I primi dieci anni del PCI*. Bari: Laterza, 1971, pp. 98–9. Tasca repeats that he was not unwilling to support the Councils, though he was adamant that the Council could not be the foundation of a new State. Tasca's main concern was to link Council and union activity, not separate them, as Gramsci had wanted to do.

12 ON, pp. 237–8.
13 ON, p. 257.
14 ON, p. 240.
15 ON, pp. 258–9.
16 ON, pp. 487–92.
17 ON, p. 25.
18 Thus in 'The Party and the Revolution' of December 1919, Gramsci assigns the Party the role of 'maximum agent', ON, p. 368. For a look at the debates between *L'Ordine nuovo* and *Il Soviet*, see Paolo Spriano, *Storia del Partito Communista Italiano I: da Bordiga a Gramsci*. Turin: Einaudi, 1967, pp. 37–77; also see Spriano's article, 'Il dibattito tra Il Soviet e L'Ordine nuovo', in *Rinascita*, 1 (1961), pp. 44–5, 47, 50. See also Tasca, *I primi dieci anni del PCI*, pp. 152–60; Franco De Felice, *Serrati, Bordiga, Gramsci e il problema della rivoluzione in Italia*. Bari: De Donato, 1971, pp. 182–83; Antonio Levrero, *La formazione del PCI*. Rome: Editori Riuniti, 1971, pp. 44–5; and Rosa Alcara, *La formazione e i primi anni del PCI nella storiografia marxista*. Milan: Jaca Book, 1970, p. 160.

19 ON, p. 131. For a post-World War II debate between the Italian Communist Party and its opponents on whether or not the parliamentary state must function in the interests of capital, see Norberto Bobbio, *Politica e cultura*. Turin: Einaudi, 1955, pp. 150–60, and Gaetano della Volpe, *Rousseau e Marx*. Rome: Editore Riuniti, 1957, pp. 45–56.

20 ON, p. 341.
21 Darrow Schecter, *Gramsci and the Theory of Industrial Democracy*. Aldershot: Avebury, 1991, pp. 15–20.
22 ON, p. 533. For an analysis of Gramsci's productivism and its political implications, see Schecter, *Gramsci and the Theory of Industrial Democracy*, pp. 138–60.
23 ON, pp.569–74.
24 ON, pp. 88–9.
25 Martin Clark, 'Factory Councils and the Italian labour movement, 1916–1921', Ph.D. thesis in the Department of History, University of Reading, 1966, pp. 67–8. Clark's thesis is easily the best historical account of the Factory Council movement, and is extensively cited both in Schecter, *Gramsci and the Theory of Industrial Democracy* and this book.
26 ON, p. 88.

27   *ON*, p. 88.

28   One of Gramsci's major assumptions throughout the period was that objective economic conditions were tending to homogenise the Italian working class, thus creating a sense of common interest among all workers. However, many workers, especially of southern origin, continued to remain outside of Party and union organisations. During World War I, large numbers of peasants, many of whom had no industrial skills, came to the cities looking for work. In some cases highly skilled unionised workers seeking to defend their gains reacted to this situation by excluding unskilled workers from the unions. Moreover, the increased supply of unskilled labour gave industrialists greater liberty to experiment with new methods of organising the labour process, many of which, such as the implementation of assembly-line techniques, were aimed at breaking the power of skilled labour. This exacerbated existing tensions within the working class. See Tommasso Detti, *Serrati e la formazione del Partito comunista Italiano: storia della frazione terzinternazionalista, 1921–24*. Rome: Editori Riuniti, 1972, pp. 26–7; Magri, *La crisi industriale e il controllo Operaia*, pp. 4, 43–4; Carmen J. Sirianni, 'Workers' control in the era of World War I', in *Theory and Society* 9 (1980), pp. 38–9, 54–9; Emilio Soave, 'L'occupazione delle fabbriche e i problemi del partito e della rivoluzione in Italia', in *Rivista Storica del Socialismo*, 8 (1965), p. 179.

29   These were the views of Ottavio Pastore, the editor of the Turin section of *Avanti!*. Pastore's article is reprinted in Spriano, *L'Ordine nuovo e i consigli di fabbrica*, pp. 161–6. See also M. Clark, 'Factory Councils and the Italian labour movement, 1916–1921', pp. 69–70. Foreshadowing future problems for Gramsci, Pastore explicitly states that union and Council functions must be co-ordinated rather than separated.

30   *ON*, pp. 213–14; Clark, 'Factory Councils and the Italian labour movement, 1916–1921', pp. 97–101.

31   *ON*, p. 238–9; Clark, 'Factory Councils and the Italian labour movement, 1916–1921', pp. 102–3.

32   *ON*, pp. 607–8.

33   *ON*, pp. 432–5; Lenin, *Collected Works*, Volume 27, p. 259; Enzo Rutigliano, 'Gramsci and capitalist rationalization' in *Telos*, 31 (1977), pp. 91–9; Stefano Musso, 'Operai e cultura del lavoro nell' *Ordine nuovo*' in Franco Sbarberi (ed.), *Teoria politica e societa industriale*. Turin: Bollati Boringhieri, 1988, p. 184.

34   That economic centralisation is incompatible with the democratic ideals of the Paris Commune is well argued by Radoslav Selucky in *Marxism, Socialism and Freedom*. London: Macmillan Press Ltd., 1979; see also Paul Hirst, 'The State, civil society, and the collapse of Soviet Communism' in *Economy and Society*, 20 (1991), p. 229.

35   *ON*, pp. 413–16.

36   Bordiga, 'Per la costituzione dei consigli operai in Italia' in *Il Soviet*, 3 (1920) p. 284; Tasca, 'Gradualismo e rivoluzionarismo nei consigli di fabbrica' in *L'Ordine nuovo*, 2 (1920), pp. 220–25.

37   *ON*, pp. 306–11; Clark, 'Factory Councils and the Italian labour movement, 1916–1921', pp. 104–8.

38 Clark, 'Factory Councils and the Italian labour movement, 1916–1921', pp. 108–10; Gwynn A. Williams, *Proletarian Order*. London: Pluto Press, 1975, *op. cit.*, pp. 132–6.

39 *ON*, p. 308; Williams, *Proletarian Order*, p. 135.

40 *ON*, pp. 308–10.

41 *ON*, p. 508;

42 M. Clark, 'Factory Councils and the Italian labour movement, 1916–1921', p. 255.

43 For the history of the Piedmont General Strike, and the events in the Turin metal factories in particular, see Clark's thesis, pp. 140–68; Paolo Spriano, *L'occupazione delle fabbriche*. Turin: Einaudi, 1964, pp. 33–4; Giuseppe Maione, *Il biennio rosso: autonomia e spontaneita operaia nel 1919–1920*. Bologna: Il Mulino, 1977, pp. 116–55; Williams, *Proletarian Order*, pp. 203–9.

44 *ON*, pp. 590–94.

45 M. Clark, 'Factory Councils and the Italian labour movement, 1916–1921', pp. 138–9. For attempts within the PSI to formulate alternative proposals for workers' Councils (most notably the Schiavello and Bombacci proposals), see Clark's thesis, pp. 211–14, and Williams, *Proletarian Order*, pp. 167–8. Gramsci warned the PSI against any attempt to 'create' Councils and soviets as the German SPD had done (*ON*, p. 368), which is in effect what the Maximalists were proposing during January–April 1920. Union leaders also proposed that the Factory Councils be absorbed into the existing union structure, such as the Baldesi project. See Clark's thesis, p. 175. For syndicalist and anarchist support for the Councils, also see Clark's thesis, pp. 178–86. Clark notes that after the failure of the Piedmont General Strike of April 1920, the main supporters of the Council movement were the syndicalists. Indeed, syndicalist participation in the Councils contributed to the association of the Council movement with the tactic of occupying factories.

46 Clark, 'Factory Councils and the Italian labour movement, 1916–1921', pp. 211–14, 216–18, 220–23. Maione, in *Il biennio rosso: autonomia e spontaneita operaia nel 1919–1920*, remarks that adjudicating between Tasca and Gramsci is difficult, since Tasca employs somewhat abstract arguments to argue for the unity of Councils and unions, while Gramsci fails to find an adequate theoretical expression to support his commitment to revolution. Maione mentions that this polemic between two of the founding members of the *L'Ordine nuovo* group carried on until the occupations, losing valuable time for formulating an anti-reformist strategy which gave clear expression to the role of the Councils (Maione, p. 195).

47 *ON*, p. 549.

48 M. Clark 'Factory Councils and the Italian labour movement, 1916–1921', p. 255.

49 M. Clark, 'Factory Councils and the Italian labour movement, 1916–1921', pp. 253–254, pp. 256–7.

50 Turin edition of *Avanti!*, 2 September, 1920; Clark, 'Factory Councils and the Italian labour movement, 1916–1921', p. 258. See also Maione, *Il biennio rosso: autonomia e spontaneita operaia nel 1919–1920*,

p. 243.
 51 ON, p. 669; Clark, 'Factory Councils and the Italian labour movement, 1916–1921', pp. 258–9.
 52 ON, pp. 413–14, 393–4; De Felice, *Serrati, Bordiga, Gramsci e il problema della rivoluzione in Italia*, pp. 227–32.
 53 Spriano, *L'occupazione delle fabbriche*, pp. 70–71, 94, 141; Williams, *Proletarian Order*, pp. 245–8; Maione, *Il biennio rosso: autonomia e spontaneita operaia nel 1919–1920*, pp. 242–7; Clark, 'Factory Councils and the Italian labour movement, 1916–1921', pp. 260–61.
 54 ON, pp. 694–5; Clark, 'Factory Councils and the Italian labour movement, 1916–1921', pp. 273, 276–7.
 55 ON, p. 688.
 56 ON, p. 695.
 57 ON, pp. 651–61. For an analysis of the similarities and differences between Gramsci and Sorel during this period, see Darrow Schecter, 'Two views of the revolution: Gramsci and Sorel, 1916–1920' in *The History of European Ideas*, 12 (1990), pp. 637–53.

Notes to chapter 3

 1 Gramsci, *L'Ordine nuovo 1919–1920* (hereinafter ON). Turin: Einaudi, 1987, p. 511; Angelo Tasca, *I primi dieci anni del PCI*. Bari: Laterza, 1971, pp. 114–16.
 2 F. L. Carsten, *The Rise of Fascism*. London: B. T. Batsford, 1967, pp. 62–3.
 3 Gaetano Salvemini e Bruno Roselli, *L'Italia sotto il Fascismo*. New York: Martello Editrice, 1927, pp. 3–4.
 4 Angelo Tasca, *Nascita e avvento del Fascismo: l'Italia dal 1918 al 1922*. Florence: La Nuova Italia, 1950, pp. 445–7; F. L. Carsten, *The Rise of Fascism*, pp. 63–6. For an account of the immediate post-World War I climate in Italy, Gabriele D'Annunzio's Fiume adventure, and the events punctuating the rise of Italian Fascism, see also Federico Chabod, *L'Italia contemporanea (1919–1948)*. Turin: Einaudi, 1961.
 5 Giorgio Amendola, *Storia del PCI, 1921–1943*. Rome: Editori Riuniti, 1978, pp. 45–6; David Beetham, *Marxists in the Face of Fascism*. Manchester: Manchester University Press, 1983, p. 5.
 6 James W. Hulse, *The Forming of the Communist International*. Stanford: Stanford University Press, 1964, pp. 205–11; Luigi Cortesi, *Le origini del PCI*. Bari: Laterza, 1972, pp. 273–9; Alexander De Grand, *The Italian Left in the Twentieth Century*. Bloomington and Indianapolis: Indiana University Press, 1989, p. 45.
 7 In fact, important steps toward the scission were taken at the PSI Congress at Imola of 28 and 29 November 1920. See Amendola, *Storia del PCI, 1921–1943*, pp. 9–10; Renzo Martinelli, *Il Partito comunista italiano, 1921–1926*. Rome: Editori Riuniti, 1977, p. 112; Luigi Salvatorelli e Giovanni Mira, *Storia del Fascismo: l'Italia dal 1919–1945*. Rome: Edizioni di Novissima, 1952, p. 91.

8   De Grand, *The Italian Left in the Twentieth Century*. p. 45; Paolo Spriano, *Storia del Partito comunista italiano (I): da Bordiga a Gramsci*. Turin: Einaudi, 1967, p. 79; Aurelio Lepre and Silvano Levrero, *La formazione del Partito comunista d'Italia*. Rome: Editori Riuniti, 1973, p. 373.

9   Giorgio Galli, *Storia del Partito comunista italiano*. Milan: Scwarz Editore, 1958, pp. 44–7. The first Executive Committee was comprised of Bordiga, Terracini, Ruggero Grieco, Luigi Repossi and Bruno Fortichiari. Gramsci was elected to the fourteen-member Central Committee which elected the Executive Committee. See Spriano, *Storia del Partito comunista italiano (I)*, pp. 118–19; Cammett, *Antonio Gramsci and the Origins of Italian Communism*, p. 141; Marcella and Maurizio Ferrara, *Conversando con Togliatti*. Rome: Edizioni di Cultura Sociale, 1954, pp. 90–91.

10   De Grand, *The Italian Left in the Twentieth Century*, p. 46.

11   Gramsci, 'Socialisti e fascisti' in *Socialismo e fascismo: L'Ordine nuovo 1921–1922* (hereinafter *SF*). Turin: Einaudi, 1967, pp. 187–8; De Grand, *The Italian Left in the Twentieth Century*, pp. 46–7.

12   James W. Hulse, *The Forming of the Communist International*, pp. 160–64.

13   The united front theses were first enunciated by the ECCI in December 1921. See Jane Degras (ed.), *The Communist International 1919–1943: Documents*. Oxford: Oxford University Press, 1956, pp. 307–16.

14   Andreina De Clementi, *Amadeo Bordiga*. Turin: Einaudi, 1971, pp. 154–5; Cammett, *Antonio Gramsci and the Origins of Italian Communism*, pp. 160–61.

15   Palmiro Togliatti, *La formazione del gruppo dirigente del Partito comunista italiano*. Rome: Editori Riuniti, 1962, p. 11; P. Spriano, *Storia del Partito comunista italiano (I): da Bordiga a Gramsci*, pp. 178–89; Marcella and Maurizio Ferrara, *Conversando con Togliatti*, pp. 90–91.

16   Luigi Cortesi, 'Introduzione' to Tasca, *I primi dieci anni del PCI*, p. 13. Umberto Terracini also avers that although Gramsci was not simply repeating Bordiga's pronouncements, he had not as yet developed an independent position. See Umberto Terracini, 'Come reagirono i comunisti al colpo di statto di Mussolini' in *Rinascita*, 29 (1972), pp. 23–5.

17   Stefano Merli (ed.), *Fronte antifascista e politica di classe: socialisti e comunisti in Italia, 1923–1939*. Bari: De Donato, 1975, p. 247.

18   See especially 'Serrati e il fronte unico', in *SF*, pp. 480–82, of 19 March 1922.

19   Cammett, *Antonio Gramsci and the Origins of Italian Communism*, pp. 162–3.

20   Julius Braunthal, *History of the International, Volume II: 1914–1943*. Bristol: Nelson and Sons, 1967, pp. 211–12; Giuseppe Berti, *I primi anni di vita del PCI*. Milan: Feltrinelli, 1967, pp. 138–9; Cammett *Antonio Gramsci and the Origins of Italian Communism*, pp. 163–4.

21   Cammett, *Antonio Gramsci and the Origins of Italian Communism*, pp. 164–5.

22   Togliatti, *La formazione del gruppo dirigente del Partito comunista*

italiano, p. 51.

23 The letter was seized by the Fascist police, later restored to PCI archives, and finaly published by Stefano Merli in the *Rivista storica dell'socialismo*, 6 (1963), pp. 115–16.

24 Guido Zamus, 'Gramsci a Vienna nel 1924' in *Rinascita*, 47 (1964), pp. 22–3;. Cammett, *Antonio Gramsci and the Origins of Italian Communism*, pp. 165–6; Berti, *La vita di Antonio Gramsci*, pp. 158–60.

25 Spriano, *Storia del Partito comunista italiano (I)*, pp. 291–313; Massimo Salvadori, *Gramsci e il problema storica della democrazia*. Turin: Einaudi, 1977, pp. 336–8.

26 Spriano, *Storia del Partito comunista italiano (I)*, pp. 305–13.

27 P. Spriano, *Storia del Partito comunista italiano (I)*, pp. 352–9.

28 Elfriede Lewerenz, 'Zur Bestimmung des imperialistischen Wesens des Fascismus durch die Kommunistische Internationale', pp. 21–47 in Dietrich Eichholtz and Kurt Gassweiler (eds.), *Fascismus Forschung: Positionen, Probleme, Polemik*. Koln: Pahl Rugenstein Verlag, 1980, pp. 22–5.

29 P. Spriano, *Storia del Partito comunista italiano (I)*, pp. 389–90; Degras, *The Communist International 1919–1943*, pp. 150–54.

30 Degras, *The Communist International 1919–1943*, pp. 146–7.

31 Gramsci, *SF*, pp. 167–9.

32 Tasca, *Nascita e avvento del Fascismo: l'Italia dal 1918 al 1922*, pp. 145–6.

33 Violent disputes between different factions of the Fascist movement on the occasion of the Pacification Pact between Socialists and Fascists of 1921 precluded any such facile interpretation. See Renzo De Felice, *Interpretations of Fascism*. Cambridge: Harvard University Press, 1977, pp. 118–19, 121–2; and S. J. Woolf, 'Italy' in S. J. Woolf (ed.), *Fascism in Europe*. London: Methuen, 1968, pp. 48–9.

34 Alberto Cappa, *Due rivoluzione mancate: dati sviluppo e scioglimento della crisi politica italiana*. Foligno: F. Campitelli Editore, 1923, pp. 168–71.

35 Gramsci, *La costruzione del Partito comunista italiano, 1923–1926* (hereinafter CPC). Turin: Einaudi, 1971, p. 209; Renzo De Felice, *Mussolini il fascista: (I) La conquista del potere, 1921–1925*. Turin: Einaudi, 1966, pp. 619–21.

36 De Felice, *Mussolini il fascista: (I)*, pp. 633–40.

37 De Felice, *Mussolini il fascista: (I)*, pp. 641–2, 677.

38 Piero Gobetti, 'Processo al trasformismo' in *La Rivoluzione Liberale*, III (1924), now in Piero Gobetti, *Scritti Politici*. Turin: Einaudi, 1960, pp. 786–9. Gobetti grew up and went to university in Turin, and profoundly admired Gramsci and the efforts of the *Ordine nuovo* group during the Factory Council movement. When *L'Ordine nuovo* became the PCd'I daily in January 1921, Gobetti was in charge of the cultural section of the paper. He suffered repeated harassment and beatings at the hands of the Fascists until he was forced to flee to Paris, where he died of his wounds on 15 February 1926. See Paolo Spriano, 'Gobetti e i comunisti' in *Rinascita*, 7 (1966), pp. 18–20.

39 Spriano, *Storia del Partito comunista italiano (I)*, pp. 439–42.

40   *CPC*, p. 504; Renzo Martinelli, 'Il PCI al Congresso di Lione: un documento sconosciuto della Centrale' in *Critica Marxista*, 1 (1991), pp. 7–14.
41   *CPC*, pp. 483–4.
42   *CPC*, pp. 495–8; Enzo Santarelli, 'Introduzione' to Enzo Santarelli (ed.), *Sul Fascismo*. Rome: Editori Riuniti, 1973, pp. 19–20.
43   Santarelli, 'Introduzione' to *Sul Fascismo*, pp. 25–31.
44   *CPC*, pp. 128, 130; Giuseppe Fiori, *Gramsci, Togliatti, Stalin*, Bari: Laterza, 1991, pp. 3–9.
45   Aldo Natoli, 'Gramsci in carcere: il Partito, il Comintern' in *Belfagor*, XLII (1988), p. 167; Paolo Spriano, *Antonio Gramsci and the Party: the Prison Years*. London: Lawrence and Wishart, 1977, pp. 40–42.
46   *CPC*, pp. 121–2.
47   *CPC*, p. 157.
48   *CPC*, pp. 157–8.

Notes to chapter 4

1   Giuseppe Fiori, *Antonio Gramsci: Life of a Revolutionary*. London: New Left Books, 1970, p. 230.
2   For details of this decision, see pp. xxiv–xxv of Gerratana's introduction to his critical edition of the *Quaderni del carcere*. (hereinafter *Q*). 4 vols., Turin: Einaudi, 1977.
3   Antonio Gramsci, *Lettere dal carcere* (hereinafter *LC*), new edition by S. Caprioglio and E. Fubini, Turin: Einaudi, 1965, n. 21, 19 March 1927, pp. 58–9.
4   Letter to Tatiana, n. 210, 7 Sept. 1931, *LC*, p. 480.
5   See Joseph Femia, *Gramsci's Political Thought: Hegemony, Consciousness and the Revolutionary Process*. Clarendon: Oxford, 1981, pp. 5–6, 12–13 for these views.
6   For details, see Fiori, *Life of a Revolutionary*, ch. 26; *idem*, *Gramsci, Togliatti, Stalin*. Laterza: Bari, 1991, ch. 1; Paolo Spriano, *Antonio Gramsci and the Party: The Prison Years*. London: Lawrence and Wishart, 1979 and Christine Buci-Glucksmann, *Gramsci and the State*. London: Lawrence and Wishart, 1980, ch. 12.1.
7   Quotation from the PCI journal *Stato Operaio* cited in Fiori, *Life of a Revolutionary*, p. 252.
8   Gramsci's brother Gennaro was commissioned by the Party to visit Gramsci in prison and communicate the policy changes and expulsions to him. He told Fiori that he lied to Togliatti about Gramsci's real opinion in order to save him from being expelled in his turn. Whether or not this is true, the PCd'I cannot have been ignorant of Gramsci's likely response or his general attitude at the time. See Fiori, *Gramsci,Togliatti, Stalin*, pp. 38–49.
9   After his interview with Gennaro he wrote to Tatiana, 'My brother came to visit me a short while ago; since then my thoughts have been zig-zagging wildly.' *LC*, n. 155, 16 June 1930, p. 350.
10   See *LC*, n. 315, 5 Dec. 1932, p. 709; n. 333, 6 March 1933, p. 757. These letters were significantly omitted from the Platone-Togliatti edition of

1947.
11   Buci-Glucksmann, *Gramsci and the State*, p. 240.
12   What follows modifies and extends ch. 7 of my *Modern Italian Social Theory*. Cambridge: Polity, 1987. As I acknowledged there, my debts to Femia, *Gramsci's Political Thought*, esp. ch. 3, are obvious. I have also found Esteve Morera, *Gramsci's Historicism: A Realist Interpretation*. London: Routledge, 1990 very stimulating, as well as the writings of Roy Bhaskar, especially *Reclaiming Reality: A Critical Introduction to Contemporary Philosophy*. London: Verso, 1989, on which she draws. In refining Morera's realist interpretation I have benefited from the following two critiques of Bhaskar: Richard Gunn, 'Marxism and philosophy: a critique of critical realism', *Capital and Class*, 37 (1989), pp. 87–116 and Peter Baehr, 'Critical realism, cautionary realism', *Sociological Review*, 38 (1990), pp. 765–77.
13   E.g. *Q*, pp. 1507–9.
14   E.g. *Q*, pp. 1366–8. See Bellamy, *Modern Italian Social Theory*, ch. 4 for a discussion of Labriola's ideas.
15   *Q*, p. 1345.
16   *Q*, pp. 1410, 1318.
17   *Q*, pp. 1442–3.
18   *Q*, p. 1926.
19   *Q*, p. 73.
20   *Q*, pp. 1456–7.
21   *Q*, p. 1375.
22   *Q*, p. 1330.
23   *Q*, pp. 1326, 1340–1, 1403–4, 1428–30, 1446–7.
24   *Q*, pp. 1431–3.
25   *Q*, pp. 1403–4.
26   *Q*, pp. 1247–8, 1282–3.
27   Croce, *Materialismo storico*, p. 9; Gramsci, *Q*, p. 1402. Of course, Gramsci did not agree with Croce's dismissive use of this judgement, which he felt reduced Marxism to economism, e.g. *Q*, p. 1214.
28   *Q*, p. 871.
29   *Q*, pp. 872–3.
30   *Q*, p. 1319.
31   *Q*, p. 1300.
32   *Q*, pp. 1591, 1580.
33   *Q*, pp. 1387–9.
34   Cf. *Q*, p. 1235 and the letter of 17 August 1931 to Tatiana where he confessed to having been 'to some degree part of the movement of moral and intellectual reform initiated in Italy by Benedetto Croce', *LC*, n. 464, p. 464.
35   *Q*, p. 1234.
36   This sketch draws on the following of my earlier analyses of Croce's thought: 'Liberalism and historicism: Benedetto Croce and the political role of idealism in modern Italy *c.* 1890–1952', in Athanasias Moulakis (ed.), *The Promise of History: Essays in Political Philosophy*. Berlin/New York: De Gruyter, 1985, pp. 69–109; *Modern Italian Social Theory*, ch. 5; 'Gramsci, Croce and the Italian political tradition', *History of Political*

Thought, XI (1990), pp. 313–37; and 'Between economic and ethical liberalism: Benedetto Croce and the dilemmas of liberal politics', *History of the Human Sciences*, 4 (1991), pp. 175–95.

37   G. W. F. Hegel, *Philosophy of Right*, trans. T. M. Knox, Oxford: Clarendon, 1952, p. 10.

38   E.g. Benedetto Croce, *Saggio sullo Hegel*. Bari: Laterza, 1913, p. 41 and *idem, Indagini sul Hegel e scharimenti filosofici*. Bari: Laterza, 1952, p. 10.

39   B. Croce, 'Intorno all'idealismo attuale', *La Voce*, V. 46 (1913), pp. 1195–7; V. 1, no. 1, (1914), pp. 4–15

40   E.g. 'Storia economico-politica e storia etico-politica', *La critica*, 22 (1924), pp. 334–41.

41   B. Croce, *Teoria e storia della storiografia*. (1917) Bari: Laterza, 1943, p. 87.

42   B. Croce, *La storia come pensiero e come azione*. (1938) Edizione economica, Bari: Laterza, 1978, esp. pp. 33–4.

43   Q, pp. 1211, 1234–5.

44   Q, p. 1216. Cf B. Croce's article 'Contro i sistemi definitivi' (1916), in *idem, Cultura e vita morale: intermezzi polemici*. 3rd ed. Bari: Laterza, 1955, pp. 201–9.

45   B. Croce, *Materialismo storico e economia marxista*. (1899) Edizione economica, Bari: Laterza, 1978, pref. to 1917 edition.

46   Giovanni Gentile, 'Il marxismo di Benedetto Croce', *Resto del Carlino*, 14 May 1918.

47   Q, p. 1271.

48   Q, p. 1224.

49   Q, pp. 1208, 1224, 1225.

50   Pp. 1269–70, 1316–17.

51   Q, p. 1226.

52   Q, p. 1227.

53   See B. Croce, *Conversazioni critiche*. Serie I, Bari: Laterza, 1918, p. 298–300, where he discusses Marx's *Theses on Feuerbach*, and Gramsci's commentary in Q, pp. 1269–74.

54   Q, p. 1238.

55   Q, p. 1241.

56   Q, p. 1134.

57   Q, pp. 1229–30.

58   Q, p. 1241.

59   Q, p. 1293.

60   Q, p. 1307.

61   Q, p. 1231.

62   Q, pp. 886, 1241.

63   Q, p. 1233.

64   For further elaboration of these points, see Gunn, 'Marxism and philosophy' and Ernest Gellner's wonderful critique of post-Wittgensteinian linguistic philosophy, *Words and Things*. Harmondsworth: Penguin, 1968.

65   The two main advocates of this view are C. Reichers, *Antonio Gramsci: Marxismus in Italien*. Frankfurt: Europaische Verlagenstalt, 1970

and A. Del Noce, *Il suicidio della rivoluzione*. Milan: Rusconi, 1978.
66   *Q*, p. 1263.
67   See Franco Sbarberi, *Gramsci: un socialismo armonico*. Milan: Franco Angeli, 1986.
68   *Q*, p. 1234, 1470.
69   *Q*, pp. 755, 783.
70   G. Gentile, *Che cosa è il fascismo?*. Florence: Valecchi, 1925, pp. 36, 50–1. See Bellamy, *Modern Italian Social Theory*, ch. 6 for an overview of Gentile's philosophy.
71   *Q*, pp. 1651–2.
72   *Q*, pp. 1355–6.
73   E.g. Antonio Labriola, *Discorrendo di socialismo e di filosofia* (1898) in *idem*, *La concezione materialistica della storia* ed. Eugenio Garin, Bari: Laterza, 1965, pp. 216–17.
74   The translations appear in Notebook 7, which also contains several of the original drafts of his remarks on Bukharin and Croce. They are reproduced as an appendix to the critical edition of the *Quaderni*, pp. 2355–60.
75   The eighth thesis as translated by Gramsci at *Q*, p. 2357.
76   *Q*, pp. 1343–6.
77   E.g. *Q*, p. 572, where he referred to the *Theses* as demonstrating 'how far Marx had superseded the philosophical position of vulgar materialism'.
78   *Q*, p. 1441.
79   E.g. *Q*, pp. 455, 869, 1422, 1579 and p. 2359 for Gramsci's translation. On pp. 1439–40 Gramsci employed Labriola's translation as cited by Croce, *Materialismo storico*, p. 38.
80   *Q*, pp. 1249, 1492, 1592.
81   *Q*, p. 1569.
82   *Q*, p. 868.
83   *Q*, p. 1593.
84   *Q*, pp. 1440–1.
85   *Q*, p. 1346.
86   *Q*, p. 1441.
87   *Q*, pp. 2139–40.
88   E.g. *Q*, pp. 1057, 1480.
89   *Q*, p. 1583.
90   *Q*, p. 1446.
91   *Q*, p. 1338.
92   *Q*, pp. 747–8.
93   *Q*, pp. 1479–80.
94   *Q*, p. 1244.
95   E.g. Morera, *Gramsci's Historicism*, p. 41.
96   E.g. Bhaskar, *Reclaiming Reality*, p. 140.
97   *Q*, p. 894.
98   *Q*, p. 1492.
99   *Q*, pp. 1419–20.
100   E.g. *Q*, p. 1291.

101   Vico's historicism played a vital part in the Italian idealist tradition, from Bertrando Spaventa to Croce, Gentile and Gramsci, and was given a decidedly Marxist slant by Labriola. See Bellamy, *Modern Italian Social Theory*, pp. 55, 57, 63, 81, 102–3.
102   Q, pp. 1415–16.
103   Q, pp. 1051–2.
104   Q, p. 1320.
105   Q, p. 1331.
106   Q, pp. 1051–2.
107   Q, p. 1338.
108   Q, p. 1057.
109   Q, p. 1250.
110   E.g. Alex Callinicos, *The Revenge of History: Marxism and the East European Revolutions*. Cambridge: Polity, 1991.
111   Q, p. 1338.
112   Q, p. 1337.
113   Q, pp. 1392–3.
114   Q, pp. 1379–85.
115   Q, p. 1434.
116   Q, p. 1250.
117   Q, pp. 1488–9.
118   Q, p. 1402.
119   Q, pp. 1375, 1378, 1423, 1437, 1826–7.
120   Michael Rosen, *Hegel's Dialectic and its Criticism*. Cambridge: Cambridge University Press, 1982, ch. 2.
121   Max Weber, 'Politics as a vocation', in *From Max Weber: Essays in Sociology*. London: Routledge, 1970, p. 122.
122   Q, pp. 1393–4.

Notes to chapter 5

1   Norberto Bobbio, 'Gramsci and the conception of civil society', in his *Which Socialism? Marxism, Socialism and Democracy*, ed. R. Bellamy. Cambridge: Polity, 1986, pp. 139–61.
2   This section draws on R. Bellamy, 'Introduction' to Bobbio, *Which Socialism?*.
3   Bobbio, 'Gramsci', p. 139.
4   For a fuller account of the logic of Hegel's argument, see Richard Bellamy, 'Hegel and liberalism', *History of European Ideas*, 8 (1987), pp. 693–708.
5   Karl Marx, 'Preface to a Contribution to the Critique of Political Economy' in *Early Writings*. Harmondsworth: Penguin, 1975, p. 425.
6   I owe the inspiration for these points to John Hoffman's *The Gramscian Challenge: Coercion and Consent in Marxist Political Theory*. Oxford: Basil Blackwell, 1984, especially chs. 4 and 5, although I elaborate them in a rather different and far less detailed way to him. There is a useful discussion of Marx's understanding of abstraction in Richard Gunn, 'Marxism and philosophy: a critique of critical realism', *Capital and Class*, 37

(1989), pp. 105–8.

7 K. Marx, *Capital I*. London: Lawrence and Wishart, 1970, pp. 84, 168, 176, *idem*, 'On the Jewish Question' in *Early Writings*, p. 234.

8 Marx, 'On the Jewish Question', p. 230.

9 Marx, 'On the Jewish Question', p. 220.

10 K. Marx, 'Critique of Hegel's Philosophy of Right: Introduction' in *Early Writings*, p. 244.

11 Marx, 'Critique of Hegel', pp. 255–6.

12 K. Marx, 'The Civil War in France' in *The First International and After*. Harmondsworth: Penguin, 1975, p. 250.

13 K. Marx and F. Engels, *Manifesto of the Communist Party*, in *The Revolutions of 1848*. Harmondsworth: Penguin, 1973, p. 87.

14 Marx, *On the Jewish Question*, p. 234.

15 For a full analysis see Darrow Schecter, *Gramsci and the Theory of Industrial Democracy*. Aldershot: Avebury/Gower, 1991.

16 *Quaderni del carcere*. 4 vols., Turin: Einaudi, 1977, hereinafter *Q*, pp. 1518–9.

17 *Q*, p. 1519.

18 *Q*, p. 1590.

19 *Q*, pp. 1589, 1591, 328–32.

20 *Q*, p. 1638.

21 *Q*, p. 801.

22 *Q*, p. 1590.

23 *Q*, p. 763.

24 *Q*, pp. 810–11.

25 *Q*, p. 1765.

26 Gramsci, *Lettre dal carcere*. Turin: Einaudi, 1965, hereinafter *LC*, n. 210, 7 sett. 1931, p. 481.

27 E.g. Perry Anderson, 'The antinomies of Antonio Gramsci', *New Left Review*, 100 (1976–7), pp. 40, 49.

28 See for details G. Framcioni, *L'officina gramsciana – Ipotesi sulla struttura dei 'Quaderni del carcere'*. Napoli: 1984, pp. 147–228.

29 E.g. *Q*, p. 1254–5.

30 E.g. Hoffman, *Gramscian Challenge*, ch. 4.

31 A. Gramsci, 'Il consiglio di fabbrica', *Ordine nuovo*, 5 June 1920, *L'Ordine nuovo 1919–1920*. Turin: Einaudi, 1987, hereinafter *ON*, pp. 532–7.

32 For an instructive Marxist criticism from this point of view of those recent Marxists who have sought to develop Gramsci's productivist thesis, see Werner Bonefeld, 'The reformulation of state theory' in Werner Bonefeld and John Holloway (eds.), *Post-Fordism and Social Form*. London: Macmillan, 1991.

33 *Q*, p. 2146.

34 *Q*, pp. 2141, 2145, 2147.

35 *Q*, pp. 641, 658, 1822, 2053.

36 *Q*, pp. 302–3, 2287.

37 *Q*, p. 2010.

38 *Q*, p. 1584.

39 Q, p. 1591.
40 Q, pp. 1049–50, 757.
41 Q, p. 56.
42 Q, p. 937.
43 Q, p. 2287.
44 Q, p. 1638.
45 Q, p. 1053.
46 Q, p. 1049.
47 Q, pp. 1360–61.
48 Q, pp. 1775–6.
49 Q, pp. 1360–61.
50 Q, p. 937.
51 Q, p. 1101.
52 Q, pp. 1312–13.
53 Q, pp. 1077–8.
54 Q, pp. 311–12, 862–3, 1603.
55 See R. Bellamy, 'From ethical to economic liberalism: the sociology of Pareto's politics', *Economy and Society*, 19 (1990), pp. 431–55 for a discussion of this work, especially pp. 446–8.
56 Q, pp. 929–30, 876.
57 Q, pp. 1228, 1281–2, 2140.
58 Q, pp. 110, 2175–8, 1756.
59 Q, p. 1348.
60 Q, p. 800.
61 Q, p. 937.
62 Q, p. 1050.
63 Q, pp. 1570–71 and see pp. 1049–50, 1565–6.
64 Q, p. 764. See p. 693 for a contrast between the 'class-State' and 'regulated society'.
65 Q, pp. 734, 1020.
66 Q, pp. 1330–31.
67 Q, p. 800.
68 Q, pp. 703, 56–7.
69 Q, pp. 1049, 56–7.
70 For a full analysis see Giuliano Marini, 'Elaborazione di temi hegeliani in Gramsci', *Archivio di storia della cultura*, III (1990), pp. 315–38.
71 Much of the following analysis is indebted to the discussion of Franco Sbarberi, *Gramsci: un socialismo armonico*. Franco Angeli: Milano, 1986, Ch. 5.
72 Q, p. 863, and see p. 743 for similar sentiments.
73 Q, 2160–61.
74 Q, p. 1138.
75 Q, pp. 2139, 2146, 2165–6.
76 Q, p. 2166.
77 Q, p. 866.
78 Q, pp. 1615–16.
79 Q, p. 1566.

80   Q, pp. 1566–7.
81   Q, pp. 1578–89, 2286–9.
82   Q, p. 1584.
83   Q, p. 1386.
84   Q, p. 1516.
85   Q, p. 1515; *LC*, n. 210, 7 Sept. 1931, p. 451.
86   Q, p. 1513.
87   Q, pp. 2041, 1516–17.
88   Q, pp. 401, 1857–64, 1221–2, 1293–4, 1304.
89   Q, pp. 1384–5, 1381–2.
90   Q, p. 1558.
91   Q, p. 1560.
92   Q, p. 1561.
93   Q, p. 937.
94   Q, pp. 1733–4.
95   E.g. Q, pp. 866, 882, 1249–50.
96   For details, see Anderson, 'The antinomies of Antonio Gramsci', pp. 15–18.
97   V. Lenin, *What is to be Done?*, in K. Marx, F. Engels, V. Lenin, *On Historical Materialism*. Moscow: Progress Publishers, 1972, pp. 388–92.
98   Q, pp. 328–32.
99   Q, p. 1386.
100 Q, p. 1331.
101 Q, p. 1505.
102 Q, pp. 1691–2.
103 J. Femia, 'Gramsci and the question of totalitarianism', Department of Political Theory and Institutions, The University of Liverpool, Working Paper no. 27, p. 9.
104 Q, p. 1561.
105 Q, p. 800.
106 Q, p. 1053.
107 Q, pp. 1565–6.
108 Q, p. 1566.

Notes to chapter 6

1   There is a fuller analysis of this tradition in Richard Bellamy, *Liberalism and Modern Society*. Cambridge: Polity, 1992, ch. 3 section 1. For this section I have also drawn on *idem*, 'Croce, Gentile and Hegel and the doctine of the ethical state', *Rivista di Studi Crociani*, 20 (1983), pp. 263–81, 21 (1984), pp. 67–73; *idem*, *Modern Italian Social Theory*. Cambridge: Polity, 1987, ch. 1 and *idem*, 'Gramsci, Croce and the Italian political tradition', *History of Political Thought*, 11 (1990), pp. 313–37.
2   Vincenzo Gioberti, *Del rinnovamento civile d'Italia*. Paris and Turin: Bocca, 1851, vol. 2, pp. 203–4. For a consideration of Gioberti's influence on Gramsci, see A. Asor Rosa, *Scrittori e popolo*. Rome: Savelli, 1979.
3   Gioberti, *Del rinnovamento*, 2, pp. 271–3.
4   The Neapolitan neo-Hegelians included writiers such as A. C. De

Meis, F. Fiorentino, Bertrando and Silvio Spaventa and F. De Sanctis. De Sanctis and Silvio Spaventa especially were both influential politicians, Spaventa becoming the official spokesman of the Right following their fall from power. For details of the group, see G. Oldrini, *La cultura filosofica napoletana dell'Ottocento*. Bari: Laterza, 1973.

5 F. de Sanctis, *Storia della letteratura italiana*. (1872–3.) Milan: Feltrinelli, 1964, vol. 2, ch. 15.

6 For a full account of this tradition see S. Onufrio, 'Lo "Stato etico" e gli hegeliani di Napoli', *Nuovi Quaderni Meridionali*, 7 (1969), pp. 76–90, 171–88, 271–87, 436–80, 8 (1970), pp. 64–78, 196–214.

7 Silvio Spaventa, 'Discorso parlamentare del 24 giugno 1876', in *idem*, *Discorsi parlamentari*. Rome: 1913, p. 413.

8 B. Spaventa, *Principii di etica*. (1869.) Naples: Pierro, 1904, pp. 140–41.

9 Spaventa, *Principii*, p. 142.

10 B. Spaventa, 'False accuse contro l'hegelismo' (1851), *La Critica*, 18 (1920), p. 248.

11 Spaventa, *Principii*, pp. 158–9.

12 For an analysis of the dominance of this view within Italian public law, see P. Costa, *Lo stato imaginario: metafore e paradigmi nella cultura giuridica fra ottocento e novecento*. Milan: Giuffre, 1986.

13 E.g. Denis Mack Smith, *Italy: A Modern History*. 2nd ed. Ann Arbor: University of Michigan Press, 1969, p. 104; Roberto Romanelli, *L'Italia liberale (1861–1900)*. Bologna: Il Mulino, 1979, pp. 22–7.

14 For a defence of a liberal reading, see Richard Bellamy, 'Hegel and liberalism', *History of European Ideas*, 8 (1987), pp. 693–708. See too the contrasts drawn between the liberal and Fascist views of Hegelian political philosophy held by Croce and Gentile respectively in *idem*, 'Croce, Gentile and Hegel'.

15 E.g. Roberto Ardigo, *La morale dei positivisti*. (1879.) Padua: Angelo Draghi, 1900.

16 See Daniel Pick, 'The faces of anarchy: Lombroso and the politics of criminal science in post-unification Italy', *History Workshop Journal*, 21 (1986), pp. 60–86.

17 The following remarks follow Romanelli, *L'Italia liberale*; and R. Vivarelli, *Il fallimento del liberalismo: studi sulle origini del fascismo*. Bologna: Il Mulino, 1981, ch. 1. For a discussion of the place of the 'Southern Question' in Italian history, see Massimo Salvadori, *Il mito del buongoverno: la questione meridionale da Cavour a Gramsci*. Turin: Einaudi, 1960.

18 Franceso De Sanctis, 'L'uomo di Guicciardini' (1896) in *idem*, *Saggi critici*. 3 vols., Bari: Laterza, 1979, III, pp. 25, 22.

19 Benito Mussolini, 'Forza e consenso', *Gerarchia*, II, 3 March 1923. For an explicit link with Machiavelli see *idem*, 'Preludio a Machiavelli', *Gerarchia*, II, 4 April 1923.

20 Giovanni Gentile, 'Il fascismo e la Sicilia', speech at Palermo, 31 March 1924, reprinted in *idem*, *Che cosa è il fascismo?*. FLorence: Valecchi, 1925, p. 50–51.

21   For a detailed study of these debts to Spaventa and of his theory of the State more generally, see Franco Sbarberi, 'Gentile politico: un mistico dell'onnipotenza dello stato', in S. R. Ghibaudi and F. Barcia (eds.), *Studi politici in onore di Luigi Firpo*. 3 vols, Milan: Franco Angeli, 1990, III, pp. 831–50. The following draws on this article together with Bellamy, *Modern Italian Social Theory*, ch. 6 (on Gentile).

22   As Sbarberi rightly insists, and as we noted in ch. 1, Gentile had expressed these views some time before the advent of Fascism – notably during the First World War. See e.g. G. Gentile, *Guerra e fede*. Naples: Riccardi, 1919, pp. 27, 79–83, 105–9.

23   G. Gentile, *I fondamenti della filosofia del diritto*. (1916.) 3rd ed., Florence: Sansoni, 1937, pp. 74–5.

24   Gentile, '*Che cosa è il fascismo?*, p. 50 and see pp. 36–7.

25   Gentile, *Che cosa è il fascismo?*, p. 50.

26   G. Gentile, *Dottrina politica del fascismo*. Padova: Cedam, 1937, p. 21; idem, *Genesi e dottrina della società*, Firenze: Sansoni, 1946, pp. 61–6, 114.

27   G. Gentile, *Origini e dottrina del fascismo*. 3rd ed. Rome: Libreria del Littorio, 1934, pp. 36–7.

28   Although they had privately broken off relations in 1924 (see Croce's last letter to Gentile of 24 October 1924 in B. Croce, *Lettere a Giovanni Gentile (1896–1924)*. Ed. A. Croce. Milan: Mondadori, 1981, p. 670), the break only really became public in 1925 when Croce was persuaded by Amendola to write a 'Protest' against Gentile's 'Manifesto of Fascist intellectuals' on behalf of the liberal opposition. For Croce's account of this affair, see his *Terze pagine sparse*. 2 vols. Bari: Laterza, 1955, II, pp. 265–6. Croce was particularly stung into action by Gentile's claim that his continued adherence to liberalism was an affectation and that 'the entire philosophical education and the constant and most profound inspiration of Croce's thought make him a hard-line fascist without a black shirt' (Gentile, *Che cosa è il fascismo?*, p. 160).

29   B. Croce, *Materialismo storico ed economia marxista*. Edizione economica, Bari:, Laterza, 1978, p. 98 n. 1 and preface to 1917 edition, p. xiii.

30   G. Gentile, 'Il Marxismo di Benedetto Croce', *Resto del Carlino*, 14 May 1918, republished in idem, *Saggi critici*. Second series, Florence: Vallecchi, 1927, p. 41.

31   B. Croce, 'Liberalismo e fascismo – intervista', *Giornale d'Italia*, 23: 256, 27 October 1923.

32   B. Croce, 'La situazione politica – intervista', *Giornale d'Italia*, 25: 164, 9 July 1924.

33   B. Croce, review of N. Machiavelli, *Il principe*, ed. F. Chabod, *La critica*, 22 (1924), pp. 334–41.

34   B. Croce, 'Lo Stato e l'etica' (1924), reproduced in idem, *Etica e politica*. Edizione economica, Bari: Laterza, pp. 187–8.

35   B. Croce, 'Il senso politico' (1924), in *Etica e politica*, p. 178.

36   B. Croce, 'La concezione liberale come concezione della vita' (1927) in *Etica e politica*, p. 253.

37   B. Croce, 'Liberismo e liberalismo' (1928), in *Etica e politica*, pp. 263–7.

38   B. Croce, *Storia d'Italia dal 1871 al 1915*. Bari: Laterza, 1977, p. 205.

39   What follows summarises the more detailed examination of Mosca's views in Richard Bellamy, *Modern Italian Social Theory*. Polity: Cambridge, 1987, ch. 3.

40   *Q*, p. 912.

41   Valuable examinations of Gramsci's interpretation of the *Risorgimento*, on which I have drawn, are provided by Giuseppe Galasso, 'Gramsci e il problema della storia Italiana', in AA VV, *Gramsci e la cultura contemporanea*, 2 vols. Rome: Riuniti, 1969, II, pp. 305–54; Paul Ginsburg, 'Gramsci and the era of bourgeois revolution in Italy', in John Davis (ed.), *Gramsci and Italy's Passive Revolution*. London: Croom Helm, 1979; and Walter Adamson, *Hegemony and Revolution: A Study of Antonio Gramsci's Political and Cultural Theory*. Berkeley and Los Angeles: University of California Press, 1980, ch. 6.

42   *Q*, p. 2010.

43   *Q*, pp. 1822–5.

44   *Q*, p. 2013.

45   *Q*, p. 2046.

46   *Q*, pp. 2012–13, 2048–54.

47   *Q*, pp. 2024, 2011, 2035–46, 1767–8.

48   *Q*, pp. 1775, 2011. Vincenzo Cuoco (1770–1823) could be roughly described as the Italian Burke. The phrase comes from his *Saggio storico sulla rivoluzione del 1799*. 2nd ed. Milan: Gian Battista San Zogno, 1806.

49   *Q*, p. 1325.

50   *Q*, p. 2028. Gramsci's remark here is aimed at Croce's view of Jacobinism in 'Il senso politico', p. 181. In his pre-prison writings Gramsci had also held this negative view.

51   *Q*, p. 2029.

52   *Q*, p. 2053.

53   *Q*, pp. 747, 1822–3.

54   *Q*, p. 2011.

55   *Q*, p. 1056.

56   *Q*, p. 2054.

57   *Q*, pp. 962–3.

58   *Q*, pp. 1602–3.

59   *Q*, pp. 386–7, 1602–3.

60   *Q*, p. 311. See too *Q*, pp. 1602–3.

61   *Q*, pp. 912–13.

62   *Q*, p. 1603. Gramsci had been able to read Weber's *Parlament und Regierung im neugeordneten Deutschland* (1918) which Croce had translated into Italian by Laterza as early as 1919. At *Q*, p. 231 he correctly associates charisma with Weber and his three-fold typology of legitimation.

63   For Caesarism see *Q*, pp.1619–22, 1680–81. Gramsci's debts were to Michels, *Political Parties* and Marx, *The Eighteenth Brumaire*. The comparison between Mussolini and Caesar was common, although in Fas-

cist discourse with a rather different emphasis. Gramsci explores the link at *Q*, p. 1924.

64 *Q*, pp. 1089, 1227–8.
65 *Q*, pp. 1556, 1578.
66 Letter to Tatiana, 7 Sept. 1931, *LC*, n. 210, p. 482.
67 *Q*, p. 1560.
68 *Q*, pp. 956, 1565, 1607.
69 *Q*, p. 1235.
70 *Q*, pp. 1224, 1238.
71 *Q*, pp. 1087, 1223, 1302.
72 *Q*, p. 1590.
73 *Q*, p. 691.
74 *Q*, pp. 755, 1245, 1770–71.
75 *Q*, pp. 764, 1020, 1028–9, 1771.
76 *Q*, p. 2058.
77 *Q*, pp. 2010–11.
78 For a critique from this point of view, see Perry Anderson, 'Antinomies of Antonio Gramsci', *New Left Review*, 100 (1976–7), pp. 5–80.
79 Guido De Ruggiero, 'Il problema dell'autorità', *Il Paese*, 8 Dec. 1921, reprinted in *Scritti politici 1916–26*. ed. R. De Felice. Bologna: Cappelli, 1963, pp. 421–2. For an account of De Ruggiero's politics, see R. Bellamy, 'Idealism and liberalism in an Italian "new liberal" theorist: Guido De Ruggiero's *History of European Liberalism*', *Historical Journal*, 30 (1987), pp. 191–200.
80 *Q*, p. 1522.
81 See M. Clark and D. Hine, 'The Italian Communist Party: between Leninism and social democracy', in *The Changing Face of Western Communism*. Ed. D. Childs, London: Croom Helm, 1980, pp. 112–46.
82 *Q*, p. 1708.
83 *Q*, p. 1626.
84 *Q*, p. 1020.
85 *Q*, p. 1771.
86 For further quotes expressing this view, see *Q*, pp. 340, 1028–9.
87 *Q*, pp. 1706–7.
88 Karl Marx, 'The Civil War in France', in *The First International and After*. Harmondsworth: Penguin, 1975, p. 210.
89 Marx, 'Critique of the Gotha Programme' in *First International and After*, pp. 346–7.
90 Marx, 'Civil War in France', p. 210.
91 Marx, 'Conspectus of Bakunin's "Statism and Anarchy"' in *First International and After*, p. 336.
92 See Christopher Pierson, *Marxist Theory and Democratic Politics*. Cambridge: Polity, 1986 for a review of the recent literature on this topic.
93 I owe the following reflections to D. Zolo, *Complessità e democrazia*. Turin: Giappichelli editore, 1987, ch. 5.

Bibliography

Abrate, Mario. *La lotta sindacale nella industrializzazione in Italia*. Milan: Franco Angeli, 1967.

Adamson, Walter. *Hegemony and Revolution: A Study of Antonio Gramsci's Political and Cultural Theory*. Berkeley: University of California Press, 1980.

Agazzi, Emilio. *Il giovane Croce e il marxismo*. Turin: Einaudi, 1962.

Agazzi, Emilio. 'Filosofia della prassi e filosofia dello spirito' in Caracciola, Alberto (ed.). *La Città futura*. Turin: Einaudi, 1959.

Alcara, Rosa. *La formazione e i primi anni del PCI nella storiografia marxista*. Milan: Jaca Book, 1970.

Amendola, Giorgio. *Storia del PCI, 1921–1943*. Rome: Editori Riuniti, 1978.

Anderson, Perry. 'The Antinomies of Antonio Gramsci', *New Left Review*, 100, 1976–7.

Ardigo, Roberto. *La morale dei positivisti* (1879). Padua: Angelo Draghi, 1900.

Arfe, Gaetano. *Storia del socialismo italiano, 1892–1926*. Turin: Einaudi, 1965.

Asor Rosa, Alberto. *Scrittori e popolo*. Rome: Savelli, 1979.

Badaloni, Nicola. 'Filosofia della praxis' in *Gramsci: le sue idee nel nostro tempo*. Rome: Editrice l'Unità, 1987.

Baehr, Peter. 'Critical realism, cautionary realism', *Sociological Review*, 38, 1990.

Beetham, David. *Marxists in the Face of Fascism*. Manchester: Manchester University Press, 1983.

Bellamy, Richard. *Liberalism and Modern Society: An Historical Argument*. Cambridge: Polity Press, 1992.

Bellamy, Richard. 'Between economic and ethical liberalism: Benedetto Croce and the dilemmas of liberal politics', *History of the Human Sciences*, 4, 1991.

Bellamy, Richard. 'From ethical to economic liberalism: the sociology of Pareto's politics', *Economy and Society*, 19, 1990.

Bellamy, Richard. 'Gramsci, Croce and the Italian political tradition', *His-

tory of Political Thought, XI, 1990.

Bellamy, Richard. 'Hegel and liberalism', *History of European Ideas*, 8, 1987.

Bellamy, Richard. 'Idealism and liberalism in an Italian "new liberal" theorist: Guido De Ruggero's *History of European Liberalism*, *Historical Journal*, 30, 1987.

Bellamy, Richard. *Modern Italian Social Theory: Ideology and Politics from Pareto to the Present*. Cambridge: Polity Press, 1987.

Bellamy, Richard. 'Introduction' to Bobbio, Norberto, *Which Socialism?* Cambridge: Polity Press, 1987.

Bellamy, Richard. 'Liberalism and historicism: Benedetto Croce and the political role of idealism in modern Italy *c.* 1890–1952' in Moulakis, A. (ed.). *The Promise of History: Essays in Political Philosophy*. Berlin/New York: De Gruyter, 1985.

Bellamy, Richard. 'Croce, Gentile and Hegel and the doctrine of the ethical state', *Rivista di Studi Crociani*, 20, 1983.

Bergami, Giancarlo. *Il giovane Gramsci e il Marxismo*. Milan: Feltrinelli, 1977.

Berti, Giuseppe. *I primi anni di vita del PCI*. Milan: Feltrinelli, 1967.

Bhaskar, Roy. *Reclaiming Reality: A Critical Introduction to Contemporary Philosophy*. London: Verso, 1989.

Bobbio, Norberto. 'Gramsci and the conception of civil society' in *Which Socialism? Marxism, Socialism and Democracy*. Cambridge: Polity Press, 1987.

Bobbio, Norberto. *Politica e cultura*. Turin: Einaudi, 1955.

Bonefeld, Werner. 'The reformulation of state theory' in Bonefeld, Werner, and Holloway, John (eds.). *Post-Fordism and Social Form*. London: Macmillan, 1991.

Bordiga, Amadeo. 'Per la costituzione dei consigli operai in Italia', *Il Soviet*, 3, 1920.

Braunthal, Julius. *History of the International, Volume II: 1914–1943*. Bristol: Nelson and Sons, 1967.

Buci-Glucksmann, Christine. *Gramsci and the State*. London: Lawrence and Wishart, 1980.

Callinicos, Alex. *The Revenge of History: Marxism and the East European Revolutions*. Cambridge: Polity Press, 1991.

Cammett, John. *Antonio Gramsci and the Origins of Italian Communism*. Stanford: Stanford University Press, 1967.

Cappa, Alberto. *Due rivoluzione mancate: dati sviluppo e scioglimento della crisi politica italiana*. Foligno: F. Campitelli Editore, 1923.

Caracciola, Alberto. *Stato e società civile: problemi dell'unificazione italiana*. Turin: Einaudi, 1960.

Carsten, F. L. *The Rise of Fascism*. London: B. T. Batsford, 1967.

Cavallari, Giovanna. *Classe dirigente e minoranze rivoluzionarie*. Camerino: Jovene Editori, 1983.

Chabod, Federico. *L'Italia contemporanea (1919–1948)*. Turin: Einaudi, 1961.

Chabod, Federico. *Storia della politica estera italiano del 1870 al 1896*,

Volume I. Bari: Laterza, 1965.

Ciuffoletti, Zefiro. 'La fondazione del Partito Socialista Italiano e l'azione di Filippo Turati' in Arfe, Gaetano (ed.). *Lezione del PSI, 1892–1975*. Florence: Cooperativa Editrice Universitaria, 1976.

Clark, Martin, and Hine, David. 'The Italian Communist Party: Between Leninism and Social Democracy' in *The Changing Face of Western Communism*. London: Croom Helm, 1980.

Clark, Martin. *Antonio Gramsci and the Revolution that Failed*. New Haven: Yale University Press, 1977.

Clark, Martin. 'Factory Councils and the Italian labour movement, 1916–1921', Ph.D. thesis in the Department of History, University of London, 1966.

Clementi, Andreina De. *Amadeo Bordiga*. Turin: Einaudi, 1971.

Cortesi, Luigi. 'Introduzione' to Tasca, *I primi dieci anni del PCI*. Bari: Laterza, 1971.

Cortesi, Luigi. *Le origini del PCI*. Bari: Laterza, 1972.

Costa, P. *Lo Stato immaginario: metafore e paradigmi nella cultura giuridica fra ottocento e novecento*. Milan: Giuffre, 1986.

Croce, Benedetto. *Lettere a Giovanni Gentile (1896–1924)*. Milan: Mondadori, 1981.

Croce, Benedetto. *Materialismo storico e economia marxista* (1899). Bari: Laterza, 1978.

Croce, Benedetto. *La storia come pensiero e come azione* (1938). Bari: Laterza, 1978.

Croce, Benedetto. *Storia d'Italia dal 1871 al 1915*. Bari: Laterza, 1977.

Croce, Benedetto. *Terze pagine sparse* (2 Vols.). Bari: Laterza, 1955.

Croce, Benedetto. *Indagini sul Hegel e schiarimenti filosofici*. Bari: Laterza, 1952.

Croce, Benedetto. *Teoria e storia della storiografia* (1917). Bari: Laterza, 1943.

Croce, Benedetto. *Cultura e vita morale*. Bari: Laterza, 1926.

Croce, Benedetto. *Etica e politica*. Bari: Laterza, 1924.

Croce, Benedetto. Review of Machiavelli's *Il Principe*, ed. Chabod, Federico, *La Critica*, 22, 1924.

Croce, Benedetto. 'Storia economico-politica e storia etico-politica', *La Critica*, 22, 1924.

Croce, Benedetto. 'La situazione politica – intervista', *Giornale d'Italia*, 9 July 1924.

Croce, Benedetto. 'Liberalismo e fascismo – intervista', *Giornale d'Italia*, 27 October 1923.

Croce, Benedetto. *Conversazioni critiche, seria I*. Bari: Laterza, 1918.

Croce, Benedetto. 'Intorno all'idealismo attuale', *La Voce*, 46, 1913.

Croce, Benedetto. *Saggio sul Hegel*. Bari: Laterza, 1913.

Davidson, Alaistair. 'Gramsci and Lenin 1917–1921', *Socialist Register*, 1974.

De Felice, Franco. *Serrati, Bordiga, Gramsci e il problema della rivoluzione in Italia*. Bari: De Donato, 1971.

De Felice, Renzo. *Interpretations of Fascism*. Cambridge: Harvard Univer-

sity Press, 1977.
De Felice, Renzo. *Mussolini il fascista: (I) la conquista del potere, 1921–1925*. Turin: Einaudi, 1966.
De Grand, Alexander. *The Italian Left in the Twentieth Century*. Bloomington and Indianapolis: Indiana University Press, 1989.
De Ruggiero, Guido. *Scritti politici, 1916–1926*. Bologna: Cappelli, 1963.
De Sanctis, S. Francesco. *Saggi critici*. Bari: Laterza, 1979.
De Sanctis, S. Francesco. *Storia della letteratura italiana, 1872–1873* (2 Vols). Milan: Feltrinelli, 1964.
Degras, Jane (ed.). *The Communist International 1919–1943: Documents*. Oxford: Oxford University Press, 1956.
della Volpe, Gaetano. *Rousseau e Marx*. Rome: Editore Riuniti, 1957.
Detti, Tommasso. *Serrati e la formazione del Partito Comunista Italiano: storia della frazione terzinternazionalista, 1921–24*. Rome: Editori Riuniti, 1972.
Dorso, Guido. *La rivoluzione meridionale*. Turin: Einaudi (1925), 1972 edition.
Femia, Joseph. 'Gramsci and the question of totalitarianism', Working Paper Number 27, Department of Political Theory and Institutions, University of Liverpool.
Femia, Joseph. *Gramsci's Political Thought: Hegemony, Consciousness and the Revolutionary Process*. Oxford: Clarendon Press, 1981.
Ferrara, Marcella and Maurizio. *Conversando con Togliatti*. Rome: Edizioni di Cultura Sociale, 1954.
Fiori, Giuseppe. *Gramsci, Togliatti, Stalin*. Bari: Laterza, 1991.
Fiori, Giuseppe. *Antonio Gramsci: Life of a Revolutionary*. London: New Left Books, 1970.
Fiori, Giuseppe. *Vita di Antonio Gramsci*. Bari: Laterza, 1966.
Framcioni, Giuseppe. *L'officina gramsciana – ipotesi sulla struttura dei 'Quaderni del carcere'*. Naples, 1984.
Galasso, Giuseppe. *Passato e presente del meridionalismo. Volume I: Genesi e sviluppi*. Naples: Guida Editori, 1978.
Galasso, Giuseppe. 'Gramsci e il problema della storia italiana' in *Gramsci e la cultura contemporanea* (2 Vols). Rome: Editori Riuniti, 1969.
Galli, Giorgio. *Storia del Partito Comunista Italiano*. Milan: Schwarz Editore, 1958.
Garin, Eugenio. *Intellecttuali italiani del XX secolo*. Rome: Riuniti Editore, 1974.
Garin, Eugenio (ed.). *La concezione materialista della storia*. Bari: Laterza, 1965.
Garin, Eugenio. *Cronache di filosofia italiana, 1900–1943*. Bari: Laterza, 1955.
Gellner, Ernest. *Words and Things*. Harmondsworth: Penguin, 1968.
Gentile, Emilio. *Il mito dello stato nuovo: dell' antigiolittismo al fascismo*. Bari: Laterza 1982.
Gentile, Emilio. *La Voce e l'età giolittiana*. Milan: Pan editore, 1972.
Gentile, Giovanni. *Genesi e dottrina della società*. Florence: Sansoni, 1946.
Gentile, Giovanni. *Dottrina politica del fascismo*. Padua: Cedam, 1937.

Gentile, Giovanni. *Origini e dottrina del fascismo* (3rd ed). Rome: Libreria del littorio, 1934.

Gentile, Giovanni. *Che cosa è il fascismo?* Florence: Valecchi, 1925.

Gentile, Giovanni. *Guerra e fede.* Naples: Riccardi, 1919.

Gentile, Giovanni. 'Il marxismo di Benedetto Croce', *Resto del Carlino*, 14 May, 1918.

Gentile, Giovanni. *I fondamenti della filosofia del diritto.* Florence: Sansoni, 1916.

Gentile, Giovanni. *Teoria generale dello spirito come atto puro.* Florence: Sansoni, 1916.

Germino, Dante. *Antonio Gramsci: Architect of a New Politics.* Baton Rouge: Louisiana State University Press, 1990.

Ghibaudi, S. R., and Barcia, F. (eds.). *Studi Politici in onore di Luigi Firpo* (3 Vols). Milan: Franco Angeli, 1990.

Ginzburg, Paul. 'Gramsci and the era of bourgeois revolution in Italy' in Davis, John (ed.). *Gramsci and Italy's Passive Revolution.* London: Croom Helm, 1979.

Gioberti, Vincenzo. *Del rinnovamento civile d'Italia* (Volume 2). Paris and Turin: Bocca, 1851.

Gobetti, Piero. 'Processo al trasformismo', *La Rivoluzione Liberale*, III, 1924, now in Gobetti, Piero, *Scritti politici.* Turin: Einaudi, 1960.

Gorzka, Gabriele. *A. Bogdanov und der russische Proletkult: Theorie und Praxis ein Sozialistischen Kulturrevolution.* Frankfurt: Campus Verlag, 1980.

Gramsci, Antonio. *L'Ordine nuovo 1919–1920.* Turin: Einaudi, 1987.

Gramsci, Antonio. *La Città futura.* Turin: Einuadi, 1982.

Gramsci, Antonio. *Quaderni del carcere* (4 Vols), edited by Valentino Gerratana. Turin: Einaudi, 1977.

Gramsci, Antonio. *Scritti giovanili, 1914–1918.* Turin: Einaudi, 1975.

Gramsci, Antonio. *La Costruzione del Partito communista italiano, 1923–1926.* Turin: Einaudi, 1971.

Gramsci, Antonio. *Scritti 1915–21*, edited by Sergio Capriolo. Vicenza: 'Il Corpo', 1968.

Gramsci, Antonio. *Socialismo e fascismo: L'Ordine nuovo 1921–1922.* Turin: Einaudi, 1967.

Gramsci, Antonio. *Lettere dal carcere.* Turin: Einaudi, 1965.

Guarnieri, Maurizio. *I Consigli di fabbrica.* Città di Castello: Il Solco, 1946.

Gunn, Richard. 'Marxism and philosophy: a critique of critical realism', *Capital and Class*, 37, 1989.

Hegel, G. W. F. *The Philosophy of Right* (Knox translation). Oxford: Clarendon Press, 1952.

Hirst, Paul. 'The state, civil society, and the collapse of Soviet communism', *Economy and Society*, 20, 1991.

Hoffman, John. *The Gramscian Challenge: Coercion and Consent in Marxist Political Theory.* Oxford: Basil Blackwell, 1984.

Hulse, James W. *The Forming of the Communist International.* Stanford: Stanford University Press, 1964.

Joll, James. *Gramsci.* Glasgow: William Collins Sons and Co., 1977.

Labriola, Antonio. 'Discorrendo di socialismo e di filosofia' (1898) in *La concezione materialista della storia*.

Labriola, Arturo. 'Sindacati e socialismo', *Il Divenire Sociale*, I, 1906.

Labriola, Arturo. *Sindacalismo e riformismo*. Florence: G. Nerbini Editore, 1905.

Labriola, Arturo. *Storia di dieci anni 1899–1909*. Milan: Casa Editrice 'Il Viandante', 1910.

Labriola, Arturo. 'L'onesta polemica contro Giorgio Plekhanoff e per il sindacalismo', *Pagine Libere*, II, 1908.

Lenin, V. I. *Collected Works*. Moscow: Progress Publishers, 1975.

Leone, Enrico. 'L'azione elettorale e il socialismo', *Il Divenire Sociale*, II, 1906.

Levrero, Antonio. *La formazione del PCI*. Rome: Editori Riuniti, 1971.

Lewerenz, Elfriede. 'Zur Bestimmung des imperialistischen Wesens des Fascismus durch die Kommunistische Internationale', Eichholtz, Dietrich and Gassweiler, Kurt (eds.), *Fascismus Forschung: Positionen, Probleme, Polemik*. Koln: Pahl Rugenstein Verlag, 1980.

Lumley, Bob. 'Gramsci's writings on the State and hegemony, 1916–35 – a critical analysis'. Birmingham: Centre for Contemporary Cultural Studies, Birmingham University, Stencilled Occasional Papers, General Series, SP no. 51.

Magri, Francesco. *La crisi industriale e il controllo Operaia*. Milan: Editrice Unitas, 1922.

Maione, Giuseppe. *Il biennio rosso: autonomia e spontaneita operaia nel 1919–1920*. Bologna: Il Mulino, 1977.

Marini, Guliano. 'Elaborazione di temi hegeliani in Gramsci', *Archivio di storia della cultura*, III, 1990.

Martinelli, Renzo. 'Il PCI al Congresso di Lione: un documento sconosciuto della Centrale', *Critica Marxista*, 1, 1991.

Marx, Karl. *Early Writings*. Harmondsworth: Penguin, 1975.

Marx, Karl. *The First International and After*. Harmondsworth: Penguin, 1975.

Marx, Karl. *The Revolutionaries of 1848*. Harmondsworth: Penguin, 1975.

Marx, Karl. *Capital, Volume I*. London: Lawrence and Wishart, 1970.

Marx, Karl, and Engels, Friedrich. *Selected Works in One Volume*. London: Lawrence and Wishart, 1968.

Merli, Stefano, (ed). *Fronte antifascista e politica di classe: socialisti e comunisti in Italia, 1923–1939*. Bari: De Donato, 1975.

Morera, Esteve. *Gramsci's Historicism: a Realist Interpretation*. London: Routledge, 1990.

Musso, Stefano. 'Operai e cultura del lavoro nell'Ordine Nuovo' in Franco Sbarberi (ed.), *Teoria politica e societa industriale*. Turin: Bollati Boringhieri, 1988.

Mussolini, Benito. 'Preludio a Machiavelli', *Gerarchia*, II, 4 April 1923.

Mussolini, Benito. 'Forza e consenso', *Gerarchia*, II, 3 March 1923.

Nairn, Tom, 'Antonu su Gobbu' in Sassoon, Anne Showstack, (ed.), *Approaches to Gramsci*. London: Writers' and Readers' Cooperative, 1982.

Natoli, Aldo. 'Gramsci in carcere: il Partito, il Comintern', *Belfagor*, XLII, 1988.

Oldrini, Guido. *La cultura filosofica napoletana dell'ottocento*. Bari: Laterza, 1973.

Onufrio, S. 'Lo "Stato etico" e gli hegeliani di Napoli', *Nuovi Quaderni Meridionali*, 7, 1964.

Orano, Paolo. 'Perchè il sindacalismo non è populare in Italia?', *Il Divenire Sociale*, II, 1907.

Panunzio, Sergio. *La persistenza del diritto*. Pescara: Casa Editrice Abbruzzese, 1910.

Panunzio, Sergio. 'Socialismo, liberismo, anarchismo', *Il Divenire Sociale*, II 1906.

Pick, D. 'The faces of anarchy: Lombroso and the politics of criminal science in post-unification Italy', *History Workshop Journal*, 21, 1986.

Pierson, Christopher. *Marxist Theory and Democratic Politics*. Cambridge: Polity Press, 1986.

Prezzolini, Giuseppe. *La teoria sindacalista*. Naples: Francesco Perrella Editore, 1909.

Riosa, Alceo. *Il sindacalismo rivoluzionario in Italia*. Bari: De Donato 1976.

Roberts, David. *The Syndicalist Tradition and Italian Fascism*. Manchester: Manchester University Press, 1979.

Romanelli, R. *L'Italia liberale (1861–1900)*. Bologna: Il Mulino, 1979.

Romano, S. F. *Storia della questione meridionale*. Palermo: Edizioni Pantea, 1945.

Rosen, Michael. *Hegel's Dialectic and its Criticism*. Cambridge: Cambridge University Press, 1982.

Rutigliano, Enzo. 'Gramsci and capitalist rationalization', *Telos*, 31, 1977.

Salvadori, Massimo. *Gramsci e il problema storica della democrazia*. Turin: Einaudi, 1977.

Salvadori, Massimo. *Il mito del buongoverno: Il Questione meridionale da Cavour a Gramsci*. Turin: Einaudi, 1960.

Salvemini, Gaetano, and Roselli, Bruno. *L'Italia sotto il Fascismo*. New York: Martello Editrice, 1927.

Salvemini, Gaetano. *Scritti sulla Questione meridionale, 1896–1952*. Turin: Einaudi, 1958.

Santarelli, Enzo. 'Introduzione' to Santarelli, Enzo (ed.). *Sul Fascismo*. Rome: Editori Riuniti, 1973.

Santarelli, Enzo. *La revisione del marxismo in Italia*. Milan: Feltrinelli Economica, 1977.

Sassoon, Anne Showstack, 'Gramsci's life' in Anne Showstack Sassoon (ed.), *Approaches to Gramsci*. London: Writers' and Readers' Cooperative, 1982.

Sbarberi, Franco (ed.). *Teoria politica e societa industriale*. Turin: Bollati Boringhieri, 1988.

Sbarberi, Franco. *Gramsci: un socialismo armonico*. Milan: Franco Angeli, 1986.

Schecter, Darrow. *Gramsci and the Theory of Industrial Democracy*. Aldershot: Avebury, 1991.

Schecter, Darrow. 'Gramsci, Gentile and the theory of the ethical state in Italy', *History of Political Thought*, 11, 1990.

Schecter, Darrow. 'Two views of the revolution: Gramsci and Sorel, 1916–1920', *History of European Ideas*, 12, 1990.

Selucky, Radoslav. *Marxism, Socialism and Freedom*. London: Macmillan Press Ltd., 1979.

Sirianni, Carmen. *Workers' Control and Socialist Democracy: The Soviet Experience*. London: Verso, 1982.

Sirianni, Carmen J. 'Workers' control in the era of World War I', *Theory and Society*, 9, 1980.

Smith, Dennis Mack. *Italy: A Modern History* (2nd ed). Ann Arbor: University of Michigan Press, 1969.

Soave, Emlio. 'L'ocupazione delle fabbriche e i problemi del partito e della rivoluzione in Italia', *Rivista Storica del Socialismo*, 8, 1965.

Soldani, Franco. *La struttura del dominio nel sindacalismo rivoluzionario e nel giovane Gramsci*. Milan: Unicapo, 1985.

Spaventa, Bertrando. 'False accuse contro l'hegelismo' (1851), *La Critica*, 18, 1920.

Spaventa, Silvio. *Discorsi parlamentari*. Rome: Tipografia della Camera, 1913.

Spaventa, Silvio. *Principii di etica* (1869). Naples: Pierro, 1904.

Spriano, Paolo. *Antonio Gramsci and the Party: The Prison Years*. London: Lawrence and Wishart, 1977.

Spriano, Paolo. *Gramsci e Gobetti*. Turin: Einaudi, 1977.

Spriano, Paolo. *Storia di Torino operaia e socialista da De Amicis a Gramsci*. Turin: Einaudi, 1972

Spriano, Paolo. *L'Ordine nuovo e i consigli di fabbrica*. Turin: Einaudi, 1971.

Spriano, Paolo. *Storia del Partito Communista Italiano I: da Bordiga a Gramsci*. Turin: Einaudi, 1967.

Spriano, Paolo. 'Gobetti e i comunisti', *Rinascita*, 7, 1966.

Spriano, Paolo. *L'occupazione delle fabbriche*. Turin: Einaudi, 1964.

Spriano, Paolo. 'Il dibattito tra Il Soviet e L'Ordine nuovo', in *Rinascita*, 1, 1961.

Spriano, Paolo. *Torino operaia nella grande guerra*. Turin: 1960.

Tasca, Angelo. *I primi dieci anni del PCI*. Bari: Laterza, 1971.

Tasca, Angelo. *Nascita e avvento del Fascismo: l'Italia dal 1918 al 1922*. Florence: La Nuova Italia, 1950.

Tasca, Angelo. 'Gradualismo e rivoluzionarismo nei consigli di fabbrica', *L'Ordine nuovo*, 2, 1920.

Terracini, Umberto. 'Come reagirono i comunisti al colpo di stato di Mussolini', *Rinascita*, 29, 1972.

Togliatti, Palmiro. *La formazione del gruppo dirigente del Partito Comunista Italiano*. Rome: Editori Riuniti, 1962.

Valiani, Leo. *Gli sviluppi ideologici del socialismo in Italia*. Rome: Editore Opere Nuove, 1956.

Vivarelli, Roberto. *Il fallimento del liberalismo: studi sulle origini del fascismo*. Bologna: Il Mulino, 1981.

Weber, Max. 'Politics as a Vocation' in *From Max Weber: Essays in Sociology*. London: Routledge, 1970.

Williams, Gwynn A. *Proletarian Order*. London: Pluto Press, 1975.

Woolf, S. J. 'Italy' in Woolf, S. J. (ed.). *Fascism in Europe*. London: Methuen, 1968.

Zamus, Guido. 'Gramsci a Vienna nel 1924', *Rinascita*, 47, 1964.

Zolo, Danilo. *Complessità e democrazia*. Turin: Giappichelli Editore, 1987.

Index